GW00382600

UAE

YEARBOOK
1996

Published by Trident Press Ltd
Text copyright © 1996: Trident Press Ltd
Additional text copyright © 1996: Contributing authors
Pictures copyright © 1996: Mediatec LLC. & Ministry of Information & Culture, UAE
Additional pictures copyright © 1996: individual photographers

Editors: Ibrahim Al Abed, Dr Peter J. Vine, Paula Vine

Principal commissioned photographers (see picture credit list):
    Adam Woolfitt, Hanne and Jens Eriksen, Charles Crowell
Photographic collections: historical photographs reproduced with kind permission of
    the British Petroleum Company, Mohammed Badr, Nour Ali Rashid, and the
    UAE government who retain respective copyrights. The publishers also wish to
    thank Al Ittihad, Khaleej Times and Gulf News for contributed photographs.
Photographic laboratory services: Omar Saeed
Research: Fiona Macmillan, Fakhri Wadha
Additional material: D.T. Potts, Abdullah Jabali, P.Hellyer, Shafiq Asadi
English edition typesetting: Johan Hofsteenge
Arabic edition typing: Omar Abeedo
Arabic translators: Makawi Khalifa, Abbas Al Zubair

Published with the cooperation of the Higher Committee for the UAE Silver Jubilee
and the Ministry of Information and Culture, United Arab Emirates.

In addition to the above, the editors and publishers wish to acknowledge the cooperation and assistance of Emirates News Agency, the Central Bank, all federal and
regional government departments, museums, commercial companies, other organizations and individuals that have contributed directly, or indirectly, to the creation of this
Yearbook.

Yearbook information is, by definition, subject to change. The current volume aims to
be up to date at the time of going to press. Whilst every care has been taken to achieve
accuracy and consistency, the publishers cannot accept any liability for consequences
arising from the use of information contained in this book. Enquiries may be addressed
to: Ministry of Information and Culture, PO Box 17, Abu Dhabi, United Arab Emirates.
Tel: (971 2) 453000; Fax: (971 2) 450458. E-mail: mininfex@emirates.net.ae

Trident Press Ltd., 2-5 Old Bond Street, London W1X3TB
British Library Cataloguing in Publication Data
A CIP catalogue record for this book is available from the British Library.
ISBN: 1-900724-01-4

CONTENTS

Clockwise from left: *The town of Abu Dhabi, with the ruler's palace in the foreground, in 1966.*
A corner of the ruler's palace in Abu Dhabi, taken in 1954.
Grinding coffee at Asab in Liwa, March 1962.
Drawing water in Abu Dhabi from the supply of fresh water that was piped from near Al-Ain. May 1966.
Caravan leaving Asab oasis for Shah village, 1962.
A scene in Dubai Harbour, 1960.

FOREWORD

Opposite page:
*The Abu Dhabi
shoreline in 1954.*

T HIS IS A VERY SPECIAL YEAR, both for the country as a whole and for its President, Sheikh Zayed bin Sultan Al Nahyan. In August he celebrated 30 years as Ruler of Abu Dhabi whilst on 2 December the United Arab Emirates commemorates its Silver Jubilee and 25 years of Zayed as its President. Both occasions will stimulate national and international media to publish at considerable length about the great influence that this desert leader, national President and international statesman has had upon development of the United Arab Emirates and of the whole region. It will not be the first time that journalists, writers and political analysts turn their attention to Zayed and neither will it be the last. Much that has already been written has a tendency towards the sycophantic style of journalism that mistakes adulation for appraisal and steers a wide course from any suggestion of serious critique. But Zayed is a man who prefers to be judged by the results of his actions and by his deeds rather than by words. Despite a truly meteoric rise from hard pressed tribal leader to Head of State in one of the world's wealthiest countries, Sheikh Zayed has kept his feet firmly planted on the ground. He remains by nature a humble, spiritual, family man who is blessed with the qualities of common sense, good judgement, moral strength, practicality, realism and commitment to work that have guided him throughout his own life's mission. The results of his work are evident throughout the UAE and much further afield.

*Sheikh Zayed bin
Sultan Al Nahyan
together with
Sheikh Rashid bin
Saeed Al
Maktoum in 1972.*

'Adma Enterprise' being towed from Das Island to site of Umm Shaif 1 well in 1958

As the pages of this Yearbook more than amply illustrate, it is impossible not to be impressed by the physical evidence of progress in the United Arab Emirates. When one realizes that virtually everything that one sees has been built or established in one brief quarter century, it is clear that a strong guiding hand has been on the national helm and that considerable credit must go to the country's president. But whilst Zayed has genuinely earned the gratitude of his people and the admiration of the international community, he is the first to admit to his fallibility and to the limits to what one man can achieve. It is probably true to say that he regards himself as a facilitator for his people, helping to ensure that the country's wealth is wisely invested for the improvement of all.

Sheikh Zayed reading Al-Ittihad newspaper in 1972

Whilst it is also true that he has worked tirelessly and continuously, devoting virtually his entire life to his country, he readily acknowledges the efforts of his colleagues, both in Abu Dhabi itself and in each of the seven emirates that make up the Federation of the UAE. But had it not been for Sheikh Zayed's vision and strong leadership there is little doubt that the seven emirates would have remained separated. History will record the great benefits that federation has brought to the Emirates as well as to the whole region. In Zayed's view it was the only path that could secure stability, strength and prosperity for its people and in this he has been well vindicated. His vision was the

driving force in establishment of the Federation and popular national support, together with international recognition for the great benefits of unification, have since then created the shield that protects and nourishes its continued growth.

Zayed himself has often alluded to the transitory nature of monetary wealth. The real wealth of a nation, he says, is in its people. The UAE is particularly blessed, not only in the strength of character of its men and women, but especially in that of its leaders. The UAE President is a man who is driven by a deep and genuine love for his fellow countrymen and he has literally devoted all his efforts and resources to promoting their welfare and progress.

As mentioned above, Sheikh Zayed is a man of action who prefers solid work to lengthy speeches. He prefers to be judged by the tangible results of his efforts. This book provides ample evidence that his principled leadership has brought major dividends for an entire nation, and indeed for the world community. It is however only a small glimpse into a story much larger than one slim volume can recount. Let it be seen as one tiny piece in a much greater tapestry so deftly and skilfully woven by H.H. Sheikh Zayed bin Sultan Al Nahyan.

Khalfan bin Mohammed Al Roumi
Minister of Information and Culture

Sheikh Zayed leading dancers at the end of the Ramadan ceremonies, Buraimi, March 1962.

PROFILE OF A PRESIDENT
H.H. Sheikh Zayed bin Sultan Al Nahyan

A LITTLE OVER 30 YEARS AGO, with the beginning of oil exports from Abu Dhabi, first from the offshore Umm Shaif field, and then from onshore at Bab, the states that now form the United Arab Emirates began a process of change that has led to the developed and modern society of today. For the first time since the collapse of the pearling industry in the 1930s, there was a steady flow of revenue into the state's coffers, a flow, moreover, which steadily increased as further oil fields came on stream. With increasing revenues, so too were there rising expectations among the people who

Right:
H.H. Sheikh Zayed bin Sultan Al Nahyan.

Left:
Sheikh Zayed inaugurating Abu Dhabi Radio Station on 25 February 1969.

sought the benefits that oil production promised. To ensure those expectations were met, the Al Nahyan family, the Sheikhs of Abu Dhabi for over 250 years, met and decided that a new leader was required to steer the ship of state into the uncharted waters of wealth and development. Their choice was a foregone conclusion - the man who for the previous 20 years had made such a success of the task of Ruler's Representative in Abu Dhabi's Eastern Region, His Highness Sheikh Zayed bin Sultan Al Nahyan. On 6 August 1966, 30 years ago, the Emirate of Abu Dhabi entered the modern era, with Sheikh Zayed's accession as Ruler. For 25 years, since 2 December

Zayed the horseman.

1971, he has also been the President of the federation of seven states known as the United Arab Emirates (UAE) of which he was a key architect.

Sheikh Zayed is the grandson of Sheikh Zayed bin Khalifa Al Nahyan, Ruler from 1855-1909, the longest reign in the Emirate's history. His father, Sheikh Sultan, was Ruler between 1922 and 1926, and then, after a brief reign by an uncle, Sheikh Zayed's brother, Sheikh Shakhbut, came to the throne at the beginning of 1928. At the time, Abu Dhabi, like the six other Trucial States on the southern shores of the Arabian Gulf that today make up the United Arab Emirates, was in treaty relations with Britain which had first established its presence in the region as early as 1820, signing a series of agreements on maritime truce with local rulers that gave the area its name.

Abu Dhabi was poor and undeveloped, with an economy based upon fishing and pearl-diving along the coast, and on simple agriculture in scattered oases inland, like Liwa and Al-Ain. When the world market for Gulf pearls collapsed in the 1930s, the already poor emirate suffered a catastrophic blow. Sheikh Zayed's family, like their people, fell upon hard times. As the young Zayed was growing up, there was not a single school anywhere in the Trucial States. Like his fellows, he received only a basic instruction in the principles of Islam from the local preacher, although a thirst for knowledge took him out into the desert with bedouin tribesmen to absorb all he could about the way of life of the people. He recalls with pleasure all that his expeditions taught him about desert life, including falconry, which has remained a life-long passion, and about the companionship it created among the people.

In 1972, meeting citizens.

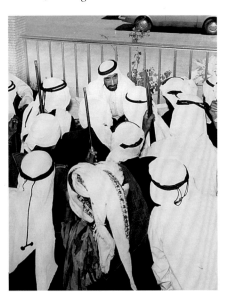

In his book, *Falconry: Our Arab Heritage*, published in 1977, he noted that a falconry expedition *brings together a group of men, never more than 60 and never less than ten . . . each of them is animated by the prospect of an agreeable and refreshing change, away from the clamour of the city and*

the monotony of daily life. The companionship of a hunting party, he adds, *permits each and every member in the expedition to speak freely and express his ideas and viewpoints without inhibition or restraint, and allows the one responsible to acquaint himself with the wishes of his people, to know their problems and perceive their views accurately, and thus to be in a position to help and improve their situation.*

These early years taught Sheikh Zayed much about his country and his people. In the early 1930s, when the first oil company teams arrived to carry out a preliminary surface geological survey, it was Sheikh Zayed who was given the task of guiding them around the desert, giving him his first exposure to the industry that was later to have such a great effect upon his country. He performed well, and in 1946, he was the obvious choice to fill a vacancy as Ruler's Representative in the oasis of Al-Ain, then a cluster of small villages, though today a thriving city with a population of around 200,000.

Zayed the falconer.

An early European visitor to Al-Ain, shortly after Sheikh Zayed took up his post, was Edward Henderson, an oil company representative. In his memoirs, he recounted the impression the young Zayed made upon him: *He was then around thirty years old*, Henderson recalls. *He was handsome, with humorous and intelligent eyes, of presence and bearing, simply dressed and clearly a man of action and resolution . . . Although he was young, and had only been formally in charge of the Abu Dhabi sector of the oasis and its surrounding deserts for some two years, he was experienced in the politics of the region, and was already by far the most prominent personality in the area. He had a sure touch with the bedouin.*

Another visitor, the explorer Sir Wilfred Thesiger, whose book *Arabian Sands* remains a classic of travel writing, wrote that he was like the head of a big family: *He was always available to listen to the problems of people, and he tried the problems of those who came to him for judgement so that they would leave quietly, content with his judgements which were distinguished by their astute insights, wisdom and fairness.*

The job of Ruler's Representative not only involved the task of administering Al-Ain itself, but also the whole region nearby, giving Zayed an opportunity to learn the techniques of government, and also, during the Buraimi dispute in the late 1940s and early 1950s, to gain experience of politics on a broader plane.

During that affair, he dealt closely with the Trucial Oman Scouts, a British-officered peacekeeping force that had units based in Al-Ain. One of the TOS officers, Anthony Shepherd, later recalled: *I used to visit him weekly in his fort, and he would always describe the local political situation to me in an excellent manner. I always came to him with great respect and I left him with even greater respect. He was one of the few great men I have met, and if we did not always agree, the reason for our disagreement was my ignorance.*

A key task was that of beginning the development of Al-Ain itself, where he ensured that the subterranean water channels, or *falajes*, were maintained, and a new one built, helping to stimulate agriculture in the area. In a foretaste of today's massive afforestation programme, Sheikh Zayed also began the planting of ornamental trees that now, grown to maturity, have made Al-Ain one of the greenest cities in Arabia.

In 1953, accompanying his brother, Sheikh Zayed paid his first visit to Britain and France, recalling years later how he had been impressed by the schools and the hospitals. In the future, he decided, his own people must have the benefit of similar facilities. He recalled later: *There were a lot of dreams. I was dreaming about our land catching up with the modern world, but I was not able to do anything because I didn't have the wherewithal in my hands to achieve these dreams. I was sure, however, that one day they would become true.*

Yet, even lacking sufficient resources, during the 20 years he was in Al-Ain, Sheikh Zayed succeeded in moving ahead with development of the area faster than anyone, except perhaps himself, would have expected. One British Political Agent, Sir Hugh Boustead, recorded his astonishment that *everything he managed to accomplish in Al-Ain and the surrounding areas were all for the benefit of the people.*

When revenues from oil exports offered the opportunity to develop the emirate as a whole, Sheikh Zayed was the obvious choice to tackle the challenges ahead. He was a man in a hurry. With revenues growing, he was determined to use them in the service of the people, and a massive modernisation programme was initiated, involving construction of roads, schools, houses and hospitals.

Upon acceding to power in 1966, he called openly for the seven emirates comprising the Trucial Sates to come closer together: *Federation is the way to power, the way to strength, the way to well-being, a high reputation . . . Lesser entities have no standing in the world today, and so it has ever been in history.* As always, Sheikh Zayed followed up his

words with concrete action, donating substantial funds to the Trucial States Development Council which had been established a decade or so before to promote development projects. By 1968, Abu Dhabi was the Fund's largest donor.

When in 1968 Britain announced its intention of leaving the Gulf by the end of 1971, he was ready to act. Together with the late Ruler of the Emirate of Dubai, Sheikh Rashid bin Saeed Al Maktoum, later UAE Vice President and Prime Minister, he took the lead in calling for a federation among the emirates and in July 1971 it was agreed to form the United Arab Emirates. Initially, the seven Trucial States were joined by Qatar and Bahrain, who eventually chose to seek their own separate paths. Holding out the hand of co-operation to Ras al-Khaimah, which initially declined to join, but did so in early 1972, and to Qatar and Bahrain, Sheikh Zayed commented: *I am not imposing unity on anyone. That is tyranny. All of us have our opinions and these opinions can*

Sheikh Zayed inspires youth.

change. Sometimes we put all opinions together and then extract from them a single common point of view. This is our democracy. Sheikh Zayed was elected the first President of the Federation, a post to which he has been successively re-elected at five yearly intervals, while Sheikh Rashid Al Maktoum was elected Vice President, a post he held until his death in 1990. The UAE formally came into existence on 2 December 1971, and in a statement issued that day by the first meeting of the new state's Supreme Council of Rulers it was declared: *The United Arab Emirates has been established as an independent state, possessing sovereignty. It is part of the greater Arab nation. Its aim is to maintain its independence, its sovereignty, its security and its stability in defence against any attack on its entity or on the entity of any of its member emirates. It also seeks to protect the freedoms and rights of its people and to achieve trustworthy co-operation between the emirates for the common good. Among its aims, in addition to the purposes above described, is to work for the sake of the progress of the country in all fields, for the sake of providing a better life for its citizens, to give assistance and support to Arab causes and interests, and to support the Charter of the United Nations and international morals.*

When the flag of the UAE was raised on 2 December 1971, the individual emirates moved into a new period of their history, facing the future as one. Twenty-five years have now passed since that first National Day, and the UAE has been utterly trans-formed. Whereas in 1971, the population was around 180,000, it is now nearly 2.4 million. Where there were less than 30,000 students, there are now nearly 500,000 in schools that cover the smallest mountain and desert settlement as well as the cities, in addition to 15,000 students undergoing higher education, most of them at the Emirates University in Al-Ain and a chain of six Higher Colleges of Technology. The 'real wealth of a nation,' as Sheikh Zayed terms the new generation, now has access to opportunities that their fathers, and Sheikh Zayed himself, lacked.

These chances extend to both sexes. *Women have the right to work everywhere,* Sheikh Zayed believes. Islam, he adds, *gives women their rightful status, and encourages them to work in all sectors as long as they are afforded the appropriate respect. The basic role of women is the upbringing of children, but, over and above that, we have to support a woman who chooses to perform other functions.*

What women have accomplished in the Emirates in only a short space of time makes me both happy and content, he says. *We sowed our seeds yesterday, and today the fruit has already begun to appear. We praise God for the role that women play in our society, and it is clear that this role is beneficial both for present and future generations.* In commerce and banking, in

Sheikh Zayed is a keen camel owner.

education and health, UAE's women are now playing an increasingly important role in the society in which they are, after all, equal partners. In a move without parallel anywhere else in the Gulf states, Sheikh Zayed, with the active encouragement of the First Lady, Her Highness Sheikha Fatima bint Mubarak, approved volunteer military training for women during the Kuwait crisis. A number now form the nucleus of the country's first women's military unit.

Elsewhere, Sheikh Zayed and Sheikha Fatima, through the UAE Women's Federation, headed by the First Lady, have sought to promote adult literacy among women, health education and the preservation and stimulation of traditional crafts, all designed to help women play their due role in the development of the state.

Development has touched all aspects of life in the Emirates, from roads to schools, from social services to housing. One key area has been in agriculture and afforestation, with over 100,000 hectares brought under the plough, and with nearly 100 million trees planted to hold back the desert sands. Since his days in Al-Ain, Sheikh Zayed has dreamed of making a green and pleasant land in his desert country. That dream is now coming true.

In a broader reflection of his own interest in the environment, Sheikh Zayed has long displayed a concern to ensure that the country's wildlife is protected and preserved. As far back as the 1960s, he ordered the establishment of a zoo in Al-Ain that is now the largest in the whole of the Middle East. A decade later, recognizing the threat that uncontrolled hunting posed to the survival of the country's wildlife, he promoted federal legislation that effectively outlawed hunting throughout the country, following this up with the establishment of a Higher Environmental

Sheikh Zayed in Liwa in 1972.

Zayed has always had a strong interest in freshwater resources.

Council which, now transformed into the Federal Environmental Agency, is charged with ensuring that man's construction does not have a damaging effect upon the land; and also with preserving the country's flora and fauna.

At a personal level, on his island reserve of Sir Bani Yas, Sheikh Zayed has created a protected area free of predators, so that endangered species like the Arabian oryx and the sand gazelle may breed freely. Sheikh Zayed believes that care for the environment is important, not simply because it is held in trust for future generations, but also because an understanding of it is an essential part of comprehending the heritage and history of the people of the UAE. Only through recognition of the structure of the local environment and its fragility was it possible for man to survive in the harsh climate of the Emirates, but, by doing so, the ancestors of today's UAE citizens were able to create a society that did not simply survive; it also flourished over thousands of years, establishing trading links that stretched as far away as China.

The preservation of the national heritage, Sheikh Zayed believes, is important in helping today's generation to prepare for tomorrow, and within that context he has displayed an active interest in the country's past, supporting the establishment of research institutes and ordering the creation of the Abu Dhabi Islands Archaeological Survey which is charged with investigating the evidence of past civilizations. *The country's young people must enquire about our history, and go back to study it again and again,* he stresses, *whether it be our recent history, or that of the far distant past, until they understand what has taken place in this country, and how past generations were able to cope with life here. They should do this because he who does not know his past will certainly not understand the present. If man knows the past, he will, too, understand the present, and will from that understand what lies ahead in the future.*

The whole process of development has benefited substantially from the energy and devoted leadership offered by Sheikh Zayed, now involved for 50 years in the governance of his people. He is, with due cause, satisfied with the results of the federal experiment: *Our experiment in federation, in the first instance, rose from a desire to increase the ties that bind us, as well as from the conviction of all that they were part of one family, and that they must gather together under one leadership. We had never* (previously) *had an experiment in federation, but our proximity to each other and the ties of blood relationships between us are factors which led us to believe that we must establish a federation that should compensate for the disunity and fragmentation that earlier prevailed. Our security, from the first, was important, and the federation has been a success.*

We now feel that our hopes have been realized, and that the federation has become a recognized entity with an excellent reputation both internally and abroad, and that it now occupies a significant and worthy place in the world . . . That which has been accomplished has exceeded all our expectations, and that, with the help of God, and with a sincere will, confirms that there is nothing that cannot be achieved in the service of the people if determination is firm and intentions sincere. . . . With the help of God, we have arrived at a stage where our feet are firmly planted on the way to building a nation, and we have achieved goals that once appeared to be far away.

Much of what has been achieved can be ascribed to Sheikh Zayed's own style of government, which has always been one of direct involvement, rather than of giving orders from afar. Back in the 1940s and 1950s, when he was Ruler's Representative in Al-Ain, one of the most important tasks he undertook was the cleaning out of the *falaj* irrigation system, so as to improve the amount of water available for the date groves and gardens of the oasis, thus helping to stimulate the local agricultural economy. When the cleaning and digging was under way, he was frequently to be seen lending a hand, down in the channels with the labourers.

The same process of active participation has been a characteristic of his style of government ever since he became Ruler of Abu Dhabi and then President of

Sheikh Zayed reviews the corniche development in Abu Dhabi.

the United Arab Emirates. As the process of development got under way, he embarked upon a regular programme of visits to construction sites, often appearing unannounced and unaccompanied to see for himself how work was progressing. Urged by other senior officials to leave the task of following up on projects to others, he rejected the suggestion, always preferring a hands-on approach: *I am the number one responsible*

Sheikh Zayed is essentially a man of the people. A natural leader who is strongly influenced by bedouin traditions, he gained an early reputation for hard work and wise judgement. He continues to attend gatherings such as that shown here in 1980.

official in the state. How can my conscience be clear if I do not look around and follow up the progress of work on development projects? How can I know whether or not there is serious progress in the work, if it is being neglected? I prefer to know that projects are being carried out in the best possible way.

Over the years, a number of senior Government officials have come to rue Sheikh Zayed's practice of personal inspection of projects, finding that they are called to account unexpectedly when he visits a project for which they are responsible, and finds evidence of shoddy construction or of inefficient management. If the officials may on occasion have been discomfited, sometimes losing their jobs on the spot, those for whom the projects are intended, the country's people, are well aware that there is super-vision from the highest level within the state of the projects being built to serve them.

The traditional form of government among the people of the United Arab Emirates has, since time immemorial, been one where the sheikh of a tribe has led his people on the basis of consultation and consensus. In the modern society that the United Arab Emirates has now become, Sheikh Zayed has been at pains both to ensure that the channels of communication remain open, and that he and his fellow members of the Supreme Council continue to rule in the same manner. Speaking at a recent meeting of the Supreme Council of the Federation, he told his colleagues: *The most important of our duties as Rulers is to raise the standard of living of the people. I bear the prime responsibility for looking after the country and its citizens. To carry out one's duty is a responsibility given by God, and to follow up on work is the responsi-bility of everyone, both the old and the young. In such a way, we can do all that is within our power because the people always focus their attention on the leadership, and what that leadership is doing on their behalf . . . Many things may remain concealed from a man, and there are many things that I may not know even though I am the first among the state's officials.* Sheikh Zayed added: *You must tell me if there are any shortcomings. You are my aides in performing my duty, and I cannot blame anyone other than you as Rulers and as my partners who are responsible to me in dealing with shortcomings. I will accept every comment with an open mind and a capacious heart.*

It is easy, he continued, *for a man to look after his family and his relatives, but to bear the responsibility for looking after a whole people is a difficult matter. Since God has preferred man over all his other creatures, it is incumbent upon us to work in the service of man, in an effort to make him content. If God has favoured some of us over others, and has blessed us with wealth, then we should remember that this wealth is not our property, but has been given by God with the intention that it should be used in the service of those who worship him.*

While showing clearly through his own actions that he is prepared to take an active lead in the building of a better society for his people, Sheikh Zayed has also made it plain that he expects others, too, to take on some of the responsibilities. At the same time, however, he has recognized that, in order for this to happen, it is essential that the citizens of the UAE are equipped to deal with the task they have been set, and that this can be done only through provision of the appropriate access to education.

We were confident from the beginning that it is the individual human being who is the basis of all civilized life, for it is on him that progress depends, he has noted. *Within this context, we must foster the right individual, by being generous in the allocation of effort and financial resources, to create an educated human being who will be the basic support upon whom the state will depend in its march towards progress.*

The real wealth of the country, he notes, lies not in its financial resources, but in its people. *Wealth is not money. Wealth lies in men. That is where true power lies, the power that we value. They are the shield behind which we seek protection. This is what has convinced us to direct all our resources to building the individual and to using the wealth with which God has provided us in the service of the nation, so that it may grow and prosper, and so that* (the new generation) *will be able able to take upon their shoulders the responsibilities, at the appropriate time, when their roles will be of a help to us and to our brothers.* In the process, he has encouraged his people to strive for development, meeting them in cities and villages throughout the land to ensure that he keeps his finger firmly on the pulse of public opinion.

Sheikh Zayed reviews a model of Zayed Sports City, prior to its construction.

Consultation and mediation are the stuff of bedouin life, and Sheikh Zayed has been a skilled practitioner of both since early manhood. Now the skills honed in Al-Ain are being put to good use far beyond the borders of the UAE. Deeply committed to the long-term objective of Arab unity, Sheikh Zayed has spared no effort to build co-operation between his fellow Arabs. He was a prime mover in the establishment in 1981 of the Arab Gulf Cooperation Council, which groups the UAE, Kuwait, Saudi Arabia, Bahrain, Qatar and Oman, which he saw, not without reason, as a logical outgrowth of the successful experiment in cooperation represented by the UAE itself. Commitment to the AGCC, and to the principles of international law and brotherhood enshrined in the Charter of the United Nations saw Sheikh Zayed and the UAE first offer support to fellow AGCC member Kuwait after its invasion by Iraq in 1990, and then commit UAE troops to UNISOM II, the force created to restore peace and order to strife-ridden Somalia.

Not just an Arab nationalist, but also a devout Muslim, Sheikh Zayed has ensured that the UAE adopts a policy of support for the poor and down-trodden. During the peak of the fighting in Bosnia, for example, when that country's Muslim community was suffering under the genocidal attacks launched by the Serbs, Sheikh Zayed made an impassioned appeal for the international community to act. *The continuing Serbian aggression against Bosnia is an aggression against the human conscience and against human rights*, he said. *It is a mark of disgrace upon the forehead of humanity . . . He who fails to put a stop to aggression is himself a partner in the injustice and the aggression.*

The tragedy being perpetrated against the rights of the Bosnian people, and all similar tragedies, Sheikh Zayed stated, *are first and foremost the responsibilities of the great powers, who always brag about their concern for human rights and justice. These countries are capable of moving with force to stop this injustice and put an end to this tragedy.*

Power must always be used on the side of the weak and it must support the injured party so as to uproot injustice, Sheikh Zayed believes: *Power must not be used for amusement, oppression and tyranny. Rather it must stand for right and justice, and act as a deterrent against iniquity.*

Peoples throughout the developing world have benefited from a steady flow of development assistance. Well over $5 billion has been provided in aid to over 40 countries on three continents, while in a further expression of his commitment to help the needy, Sheikh Zayed has created a special humanitarian fund that is offering assistance overseas. Among its earliest donations were several million dollars to help in the restoration of Muslim and Christian holy places in the city of Jerusalem.

Sheikh Zayed has long supported the cause of the Palestinian people, visiting Palestinian fighters on the front line in the Jordan valley as early as 1969. The UAE, reflecting his views, supports the Palestinian struggle for a just and lasting peace based upon United Nations Security Council resolutions and on the principle of 'land for peace'. At the same time, preservation of the special status of the Holy City of Jerusalem is also a cause close to his heart. In comments in late 1995 on the occasion of a special conference on Jerusalem held in Abu Dhabi, he stressed: *We have supported the Palestinian people, and we will continue to*

Sheikh Zayed presents a prize at a recent equestrian event

support them until they fulfil their ambition of achieving an independent state, as all of their brothers in the Arab nation have done.

. . .All help that is required by the city of Jerusalem shall be offered to it, for it is the most deserving of support and assistance. Underlying that commitment is the President's recognition that the very essence of the city, its Arab nature and its status as a holy place for both Muslims and Christians, is under threat.

Studying a model of the new mosque to be built in Abu Dhabi.

Naturally, however, his main pre-occupation, as Sheikh, as Ruler and as President, has always been with his own people. One such concern has been the impact of the wealth now available in UAE society upon traditional values, and, in particular, the way in which those who are less wealthy are spending far beyond their means. He has been particularly critical of the growing habit of extravagant weddings and of the reluctance of some young people to contribute in a positive way towards society. The phenomenon of expensive weddings, he notes, make it increasingly difficult for local young men to marry fellow citizens. If they did, he added, they would be burdened by debt, with the result that many now preferred to marry young women from abroad, leaving young UAE ladies unmarried, and affecting the country's culture and heritage. *Extremely high dowries, extravagance at wedding parties and everything else which burdens young people with debt when they are on the threshold of their lives as a family are matters for which there can be no justification*, he said. *Such are in contradiction with the principles of Islamic Sharia law, and, furthermore, they are in contradiction with the customs of our ancestors.*

To counteract this trend, Sheikh Zayed ordered the creation of a special Marriage Fund with a capital of Dh80 million to offer grants of up to Dh70,000 to young men wishing to marry, and also urged the country's tribes to take action to discourage expensive parties and large dowries. The response was immediate, both from tribal elders throughout the UAE, and from young nationals, who flocked to apply for help from the

Marriage Fund. Unique in Arabia, the Fund seems set to make a major contribution to the preservation of local culture. Nearly 5000 young couples have now benefited from it.

At the same time, Sheikh Zayed has urged young people to be realistic, and to live within their means: *Why should our young men buy cars that are inappropriate to their level of income?* he asks. *Why should a family have a large number of housemaids, cooks, drivers and so on? Why does a housewife prefer to go to expensive tailors when she can have a sewing machine in her house?*

He urges parents to take more care to ensure that their children are properly raised, noting that a number of young people have been sent to rehabilitation centres after falling into bad ways. *But more than 80 per cent of those who have passed through this government programme of correction and rehabilitation have returned to normal life, and are now taking up their national obligations with a sense of responsibility*, he notes. Regardless of an individual's wealth, or that of his family, it is important that young people should work, thereby contributing to society, Sheikh Zayed believes: *Work is of great importance, and of great value in building both individuals and societies, both of which are dependent on the strong arms of a country's young people. The size of a salary is not a measure of the worth of an individual. What is important is an individual's sense of dignity and self respect.*

It is my duty as the leader of the young people of this country . . . to encourage them to work and to exert themselves in order to raise their own standards and to be of service to the country. They must be encouraged to exert all possible efforts in order to take up responsibilities and to share in the building of the country . . . The individual who is healthy and of a sound mind and body but who does not work commits a crime against himself, and against society. He who is not prepared to work will find problems in his path, and this will lead to disaster.

Sheikh Zayed is a keen horticulturist.

Sheikh Zayed is also keen to promote a proper understanding of Islam amongst his people. In so doing he stands uncompromisingly against the extremist tendencies now affecting the Muslim world. Extremism, as shown for example, by the killing of foreigners, has no place in Islam, Sheikh Zayed believes. Instead, he stresses: *Islam is a civilizing religion that gives mankind dignity . . .* (and) *is not basically inconsistent with*

Sheikh Zayed at a family wedding in the spring of 1996.

progress. He notes that: *Islamic principles call for building progress, prosperity and raising the standard of living of society. We in our country are bound by those principles. We do not deviate by one iota from them, and nor do we abandon our heritage, customs of traditions.*

All men are equal, and social justice cannot play its (proper) *role without this concept,* he adds. *It is Islamic social justice which has asked every Muslim to respect others. To treat every person, no matter what his creed or race, as a special soul is a mark of Islam. It is just that point, embodied in the humanitarian tenets of Islam, that makes us so proud of it.* With such a clear view of the essential tolerance of Islam, Sheikh Zayed has spelt out very plainly his rejection of those who would follow an extremist path. Addressing a group of newly arrived ambassadors in late 1995, he commented: *In these times, we see around us violent men who claim to talk on behalf of Islam. Islam is far removed from their pronouncements. If such people really wish for recognition from Muslims and the world, they should themselves first heed the words of God and His Prophet. Regrettably, however, these people have nothing whatsoever that connects them to Islam. They are apostates and criminals. We see them slaughtering children and the innocent. They kill people, spill their blood and destroy their property, and then claim to be Muslims. We would like you to know Islam in its true meaning,* Sheikh Zayed told the ambassadors, *a Muslim is he who does not inflict evil upon others. Islam is the religion of tolerance and forgiveness, of advice and not of war, of dialogue and understanding.*

Sheikh Zayed went on to call for a better understanding between people of the world's faiths: *A Muslim should be familiar with the true teachings of Christianity, and a Christian with the true teachings of Islam. Sincere people from both sides should enter into dialogue, and should not leave the floor to the extremists who are there amongst both Christians and Muslims. A true dialogue between religions is the real deterrent and a strong defence against fundamentalism and extremism.*

The faith and tolerance implicit in Sheikh Zayed's stand against extremism is well summed up in a statement explaining the essential basis of his own belief. *My religion is based neither on hope nor on fear,* he says, *I worship my God because I love him.* In 30 years as a Ruler, and 25 years as a President, Sheikh Zayed has shown statesmanship, vision, wisdom and understanding that has not only served him and his country well abroad, but has also deservedly won him the loyalty and affection of his people.

POLITICAL SYSTEM

The POLITICAL SYSTEM of the United Arab Emirates is a unique combination of the traditional and the modern, offering an interesting study of the way in which it is possible for a country to move forward with the mechanics of a modern administrative structure while, at the same time, ensuring that the best of the traditions of the past are maintained, adapted and preserved.

The above historic picture was taken on 2 December 1971, after first hoisting the flag of the United Arab Emirates.

The state was created in 1971, a federation between seven emirates, formerly known as the Trucial States, which, for the previous 150 years, had been in treaty relations with the British. The name itself was derived from a Perpetual Treaty of Maritime Truce, signed by the Rulers and the British in the 1850s, which was designed to guarantee peace at sea, particularly during the pearling season.

Apart from a similar series of agreements with neighbouring Gulf states, the agreements between the emirates and the British were unique, with no immediate parallels anywhere else in the world. Evolving during the course of the nineteenth century, the agreements involved the rulers of the emirates permitting Britain to undertake responsibility for their foreign affairs and external defence while, in turn, the British undertook not to intervene in the internal affairs of the emirates or in land-based relations between them.

TRUCIAL STATES

During the period of British direct involvement in the region, and protected from external threat, the traditional structures of governance that were in place at the beginning of the nineteenth century were gradually modified according to the changing conditions, and in accordance with the wishes of the rulers and people.

To some extent, indeed, the relationship of Britain with the emirates, apart from matters of foreign affairs and defence, can best be described as one of benign neglect. Until the mid-1950s, virtually no attention was paid by the British to the economic development of the country, and even then, it was the rulers themselves who took the initiative in creating a modern infrastructure.

Following the British announcement, in early 1968, that they would be terminating their agreements with the Trucial States by the end of 1971, the rulers of the seven emirates, Abu Dhabi, Dubai, Sharjah, Ras al-Khaimah, Fujairah, Umm al-Qaiwain and Ajman, met to discuss their future. Recognizing that more united than divided them, they agreed to establish a federal state, in order to venture together upon a new and challenging future.

FEDERAL CONSTITUTION

At the time, the country's population was a mere 180,000, in an area of 83,600 square kilometres. There were, however, substantial differences between the individual emirates, in terms of size, population, economic resources and degree of development.

The larger emirates of Abu Dhabi and Dubai were already oil exporters, and the process of economic development was well under way. At the other end of the scale, Ajman, the smallest emirate, had an area of only 260 square kilometres, whilst the east coast emirate of Fujairah, with only a few tens of thousands of inhabitants, was not even connected by a proper road through the mountains to the rest of the country.

In a spirit of consensus and collaboration, the rulers agreed that each of them would be a member of a Supreme Council of Rulers, which became the top policy-making body in the new state. They agreed also that they would elect a president and a vice-president from amongst their number, to serve for a five year term of office. The Ruler of Abu Dhabi, Sheikh Zayed bin Sultan Al Nahyan, was elected as the first President, a post to which he has been re-elected at successive five yearly intervals, while the Ruler of Dubai, Sheikh Rashid bin Saeed Al Maktoum, was elected as first Vice President, a post he continued to hold until his death in 1990, at which point his eldest son and heir, Sheikh Maktoum bin Rashid Al Maktoum, was elected to succeed him.

First meeting of the Federal Supreme Council after Ras al-Khaimah joined, in February 1972.

Each of the components of the Federation, officially entitled *Dawlat al-Imarat al-Arabiyya al-Muttahida* (States of the United Arab Emirates), had its own existing institutions of government, and to provide for the effective governing of the new state, the Rulers agreed to draw up a federal constitution which specified the powers to be allocated to the federal institutions, all others remaining the prerogative of the individual emirates.

Assigned to the federal authorities, under Articles 120 and 121 of the Constitution, were responsibility for foreign affairs, security and defence, nationality and immigration issues, education, public health, currency, postal, telephone and other communications services, air traffic control and licensing of aircraft, and a number of other topics specifically prescribed, including labour relations, banking, delimitation of territorial waters and extradition of criminals.

In parallel, the Constitution also stated in Article 116 that: 'the Emirates shall exercise all powers not assigned to the Federation by this Constitution'. This was reaffirmed in Article 122, which stated that: 'the Emirates shall have jurisdiction in all matters not assigned to the exclusive jurisdiction of the Federation, in accordance with the provision of the preceding two Articles'.

A meeting of the Supreme Council which took place on 20 March 1989.

ORGANS OF GOVERNMENT

The Federation's system of government is composed of a Supreme Council, a Cabinet, or Council of Ministers, a parliamentary body, the Federal National Council, and an independent judiciary, at the peak of which is the Federal Supreme Court.

THE SUPREME COUNCIL

The Supreme Council, the highest authority in the UAE, comprises the Rulers of the seven emirates and is chaired by H.H. Sheikh Zayed bin Sultan Al Nahyan.

Current Members:

- H.H. President Sheikh Zayed bin Sultan Al Nahyan, Ruler of Abu Dhabi
- H.H. Vice President and Prime Minister Sheikh Maktoum bin Rashid Al Maktoum, Ruler of Dubai
- H.H. Dr Sheikh Sultan bin Mohammed Al Qassimi, Ruler of Sharjah
- H.H. Sheikh Saqr bin Mohammed Al Qassimi, Ruler of Ras al-Khaimah
- H.H. Sheikh Rashid bin Ahmed Al Mu'alla, Ruler of Umm al-Qaiwain
- H.H. Sheikh Humaid bin Rashid Al Nuaimi, Ruler of Ajman
- H.H. Sheikh Hamad bin Mohammed Al Sharqi, Ruler of Fujairah

Crown Princes and Deputies of the Rulers:

- H.H. Sheikh Khalifa bin Zayed Al Nahyan, Crown Prince and Deputy Supreme Commander of the UAE Armed Forces, Chairman of the Executive Council of the Emirate of Abu Dhabi
- H. E. Sheikh Hamdan bin Rashid Al Maktoum, Deputy Ruler of Dubai, Minister of Finance and Industry
- Lt. General H.E. Sheikh Mohammed bin Rashid Al Maktoum, Crown Prince of Dubai and Minister of Defence
- H.E. Sheikh Ahmed bin Sultan Al Qassimi, Deputy Ruler of Sharjah
- H.E. Sheikh Khalid bin Saqr Al Qassimi, Crown Prince and Deputy Ruler of Ras al-Khaimah
- H.E. Sheikh Saud bin Rashid Al Mu'alla, Crown Prince of Umm al-Qaiwain
- H.E. Sheikh Ammar bin Humaid Al Nuaimi, Crown Prince of Ajman
- H.E. Sheikh Hamad bin Saif Al Sharqi, Deputy Ruler of Fujairah

The Supreme Council of the Federation is vested with legislative as well as executive powers. It ratifies laws and decrees of the Federation, plans general policy, approves the nomination of the Prime Minister and accepts his resignation. It also exempts him from his post upon the recommendation of the President. The Supreme Council elects the President and his Deputy for five year terms, both may be re-elected.

At their historic meeting on 20 May 1996 the Federal Supreme Council approved a draft amendment to the country's provisional constitution, making it the permanent constitution of the UAE. The draft amendment names Abu Dhabi as the capital of the state. The Supreme Council also decided to extend the term of office of the special constitutional review committee, headed by Dubai Deputy Ruler and Federal Finance Minister, Sheikh Hamdan bin Rashid Al Maktoum, for a further year. In addition, the Supreme Council decided to establish a special committee charged with the task of following up the requirements of UAE nationals and securing for them all means of a comfortable life.

Sheikh Zayed, opening the Supreme Council meeting, affirmed his absolute support for the federal march, and deep interest in providing a prosperous life for the UAE's citizens. He said: *One of our most important tasks as rulers is to work together as one to improve the standard of living of our people . . . I hold primary responsibility for the welfare of the country and citizens, and for fulfilling the national duties . . . the follow-up process is the*

Supreme Council, 20 May 1996 when the UAE Constitution was made permanent.

responsibility of all citizens - youth and adults, to perform all possible tasks in the best possible way. People always depend on leaders and the efforts they exert for their well being. A man could be unaware of many things and I, as the first official of this country could be unaware of such things.

Sheikh Zayed urged the Supreme Council members to make him aware of any short-comings, saying: *It is incumbent on you to help me in fulfilling my duties and I will not blame anyone except you in your capacity as rulers and my partners in responsibility for any short-coming. I will accept everything with an open heart . . . each of us has to think of the general interest and not of personal interest as we are all responsible for the welfare of the whole nation and not for a small family . . . it is easy for one person to run the affairs of a single family or his relatives, but to carry the responsibilities of a whole country is a difficult task. God has favoured man over all other creatures and given him the ability to exploit the wealth of the land and sea; therefore, we have to work for the service and happiness of mankind..*

Sheikh Zayed urged the Rulers to work for the interest of the country and for satisfying the needs of all citizens. He reiterated his eagerness to provide jobs for national graduates to enable them to take part in the building of the country.

Council of Ministers in 1974

COUNCIL OF MINISTERS

The Council of Ministers includes the usual complement of ministerial portfolios, and is headed by the Prime Minister. The Prime Minister, currently the Vice President, although this has not always been the case, then selects the Ministers, who may be drawn from any of the Federation's component emirates, although, naturally, the more populous emirates have generally provided more members of each Cabinet.

The Council of Ministers is the executive authority of the Federation, and is responsible for dealing with all domestic and foreign affairs. The list of the powers of the Council covers ten points, underlining its legislative capacity. Federal laws are drafted by the Council and then submitted to the National Assembly before presenting to the President. The Council of Ministers also drafts decrees and various decisions. The Prime Minister and fellow members of the Council are responsible for their work under the supreme control of the President of the Federation and the Supreme Council.

First Council of Ministers

Hamdan bin Rashid Al Maktoum
Deputy Prime Minister and
Minister of Finance, Economy and
Industry

Mubarak bin Mohammed Al Nahyan
Minister of the Interior

Mohammed bin Rashid Al Maktoum
Minister of Defence

Ahmed Khalifa Al Suweidi
Minister of Foreign Affairs

Sultan bin Ahmed Al Mu'alla
Minister of Health

Mohammed bin Sultan Al Qassimi
Minister of Public Works

Sultan bin Mohammed Al Qassimi
Minister of Education

Abdulaziz bin Rashid Al Nuaimi
Minister of Communications

Hamad bin Mohammed Al Sharqi
Minister of Agriculture and Fisheries

Ahmed bin Sultan bin Sulaim
Minister State for Finance and
Industry

Ahmed bin Hamid
Minister of Information

Mohammed Saeed Al Mulla
Minister of State for Federation and
Gulf Affairs and
Acting Minister of Electricity

Mohammed Khalifa Al Kindi
Minister of State for Planning and
Acting Minister of Housing

Mohammed Habroush Al Suweidi
Minister of State and Acting Minister
of State for Supreme Council Affairs

Otaiba bin Abdulla Al Otaiba
Minister of State for Council of
Ministers Affairs

Abdulla Omran Taryam
Minister of Justice

Rashid bin Humaid
Minister of Youth and Sports

Thani bin Essa bin Harib
Minister of Labour and Social Affairs

Hamad bin Saif Al Sharqi
Minister of State

Second Council of Ministers

On 30 April 1979, the Supreme Council designated the late Vice President Sheikh Rashid bin Saeed Al Maktoum, Ruler of Dubai, to form the new Council of Ministers. Sheikh Rashid praised the decision and pledged to continue the march of the Federation with help from God and support of his brothers in the Supreme Council. He formed his Cabinet on 1 July 1979, and declared the objectives of his Government and its responsibilities towards the people of the UAE.

The Present Council of Ministers

On 20 November 1990, H.H. President Sheikh Zayed bin Sultan Al Nahyan issued a decree forming the new Council of Ministers of the UAE. The present Council is constituted as follows:

H.H. Vice President, Sheikh Maktoum bin Rashid Al Maktoum
Ruler of Dubai: Prime Minister

Sheikh Sultan bin Zayed Al Nahyan
Deputy Prime Minister

Sheikh Hamdan bin Rashid Al Maktoum,
Deputy Ruler of Dubai
Minister of Finance and Industry

Lt. General Sheikh Mohammed bin Rashid Al Maktoum, Crown Prince of Dubai and Minister of Defence

Mohammed Saeed Al Badi
Minister of the Interior

Rashid Abdulla Al Nuaimi
Minister of Foreign Affairs

Mohammed Saeed Al Mulla
Minister of Communications

Humaid bin Ahmed Al Mu'alla
Minister of Planning

Mohammed bin Ahmed Al Khazraji
Minister of Islamic Affairs and Awqaf

Humaid bin Nasser Al Owais
Minister of Electricity and Water

Saeed Ghobash
Minister of Economy and Commerce

Saeed Al Raqbani
Minister of Agriculture and Fish Resources

Seif Al Jarwan
Minister of Labour and Social Affairs

Saeed Al Ghaith
Minister of State for Cabinet Affairs

Khalfan bin Mohammed Al Roumi
Minister of Information and Culture

Hamad Abdulrahman Al Madfa
Minister of Education and Acting Minister of Health

Ahmed Humaid Al Tayer
Minister of State for Financial Affairs and Industry

Sheikh Hamdan bin Zayed Al Nahyan
Minister of State for Foreign Affairs

Mohammed bin Saqr bin Mohammed Al Qassimi
Minister of State for Supreme Council Affairs

Sheikh Nahyan bin Mubarak Al Nahyan
Minister of Higher Education

Dr Abdulla bin Omran Taryam
Minister of Justice

Rakad bin Salim bin Rakad
Minister of Public Works and Housing and Acting Minister of Petroleum and Mineral Resources

Sheikh Faisal bin Khalid bin Mohammed Al Qassimi
Minister of Youth and Sports

Members of the Federal National Council with Sheikh Zayed.

H.H. Sheikh Zayed received Vice President and Prime Minister H.H. Sheikh Maktoum bin Rashid Al Maktoum following the swearing in of the new Council of Ministers. The President told the members of the Cabinet: *A man responsible for a family of only five persons would always be pre-occupied with such a family. You, however, are responsible for the whole country, its people, land and territorial waters. Therefore, you have to live up to your responsibilities.*

Addressing Sheikh Maktoum, Sheikh Zayed said: *You have, from the start, truly and successfully worked with sincerity, standing by the side of your late father Sheikh Rashid bin Saeed Al Maktoum. Before your new post, you were Deputy Prime Minister and Crown Prince of Dubai. But today, you have become the Ruler of Dubai and Prime Minister of the UAE. We empowered you to select members of the Cabinet who would help in realizing the needs of this country in the various fields. And you have done well, selecting men in whom you have vested trust and confidence. Like you, I have great hopes in the members of the new Cabinet.*

FEDERAL NATIONAL COUNCIL

From the day of its formation on 2 December 1971, the UAE adhered to a democratic system of government. Thus, in Article 68, the Constitution provided for the setting-up of a Federal National Council. The Council held its first session two months after the birth of the state, and within the past 25 years it has played a major role in co-operating with the Government in achieving the hopes and ambitions of the nation in development and progress.

H.H. Sheikh Zayed outlined the role and responsibilities of the Council in its first session held on 13 February 1972, based on the traditional principle of *shura*, or consultation. The President addressed the Council members saying that the people of the UAE were looking to the Council to achieve their hopes and dreams and build a good future for coming generations. He said that the Council is able to play an important role in achieving the goal of building a prosperous and dignified society.

The Council has legislative powers stipulated in the Constitution which help the Government in the proper performance of its constitutional duties. Since its formation, the Council has discussed and ratified 294 draft laws, and also debated 182 subjects concerned with the country and its nationals, in addition to general policies of federal Ministries. The members of the Council presented more than 100 questions to the concerned ministers about national affairs and policies of the ministries dealing with them.

The Federal National Council gave unanimous approval for the proposed amendments to the country's constitution which was adopted by the Supreme Council at its last meeting. The amendments found warm support from the deputies in a historical session held on 18 June 1996. The amendments include deletion of the term 'provisional' from the existing constitution adopted in 1971, and the confirmation of Abu Dhabi as the country's capital.

As for external matters, the Council plays a prominent role as a member of both International and Pan-Arab Parliamentary organizations. In all meeting of these forums, the Council explains the foreign policies of the UAE and its viewpoint on regional and international issues. The Council participated in many regional parliamentary meetings, such as the Arab-European and African dialogues, and exchanged visits with similar councils in Arab and friendly states.

The Federal National Council has 40 members drawn from the emirates on the basis of their population, with eight for each of Abu Dhabi and Dubai, six each for Sharjah and Ras al-Khaimah, and four each for Fujairah, Umm al-Qaiwain and Ajman. The Council is presided over by a Speaker, or either of two Deputy Speakers elected from amongst their number. It has an executive committee formed by the Speaker with the membership of the Council Under Secretary, Secretary, and three other elected members.

The Council has eight sub-committees empowered with the study of draft laws referred to it from the cabinet, they also handle complaints and appeals. These committees deal with: Defence and Interior, Financial and Economic Affairs, Judicial and Legislative Affairs, Health, Labour, Social Affairs, Education, Youth, Information and Culture, Foreign Affairs, Planning, Oil, Mineral Resources, Agriculture, Fisheries Affairs, Islamic and Endowment and Public Places.

THE FEDERAL JUDICIARY

The Constitution of the UAE asserts that justice is the basis of rule, and that judges are independent in their judgement in accordance with the law of the country. The Federal Judicial system consists of the Federal Supreme Court and Federal Courts of First Instance.

The Supreme Court is composed of a Chairman and other judges, numbering not more than five, appointed by decree issued by the President of the Federation with the approval of the Supreme Council.

The Constitution stipulates that the Chairman and members of the Supreme Court should not be dismissed and their terms of office should not be limited or changed except in case of death, resignation, end of contracts, reaching the age of retirement, inability to perform their duties due to health reasons. Termination can arise under certain circumstances, in cases of infringement of the law and on the assumption of another post.

The Supreme Court has jurisdiction in interpreting the rules of the Constitution and in discussion of the constitutional law and federal legislation in general, disputes between the federal members (emirates), and very serious crimes that endanger the Federation. The Federal Supreme Court holds its sessions at the capital of the Federation only and its rulings are final.

Abu Dhabi city, federal capital of the UAE.

Federal Courts of First Instance deal with civil, commercial, criminal and personal status disputes. All rulings of these courts are not final.

LOCAL GOVERNMENT

Parallel to, and, on occasion, interlocking with, the federal institutions, each of the seven emirates also has its own local government. Although all have expanded significantly as a result of the country's growth in the last quarter of a century, these differ in size and complexity from emirate to emirate, depending on a variety of factors such as population, area, and degree of development.

The capital city of the Emirate of Dubai.

Thus the largest and most populous emirate, Abu Dhabi, has its own central governing organ, the Executive Council, chaired by the Crown Prince, Sheikh Khalifa bin Zayed Al Nahyan, and is divided into two regions, the Eastern and Western, both headed by an official with the title of Ruler's Representative. There is also a Ruler's Representative on the important oil terminal island of Das.

The main cities, Abu Dhabi and Al-Ain, the latter also the capital of the Eastern Region, are administered by Municipalities, each of which has a nominated Municipal Council, while the National Consultative Council, chaired by a Speaker, and with 60 members drawn from among the emirate's main tribes and families, undertakes a role similar to that of the FNC on a country-wide level, questioning officials and examining and endorsing local legislation. It is also a source of vocal suggestion for the introduction or revision of federal legislation.

Administration in the emirate is implemented by a number of local departments, covering topics such as public works, water and electricity, finance, customs, and management. Some have a responsibility for the whole of the emirate, although in certain spheres, such as water and electricity, there are also departments covering only the Eastern Region.

A similar pattern of municipalities and departments can be found in each of the other emirates, while Sharjah, with its three enclaves on the country's east coast, has also adopted the practice of devolving some authority on a local basis, with branches in both Kalba and Khor Fakkan of the Sharjah Emiri Diwan (Court), headed by deputy chairmen.

In smaller or remoter settlements, the Ruler and government of each emirate may choose a local representative, an emir or wali, to act as a conduit through which the concerns of inhabitants may be directed to government. In most cases, these are the leading local tribal figures, whose influence and authority derives both from their fellow tribesmen and from the confidence placed in them by the Ruler, an example of the way in which local leaders within the traditional system have become involved with, and lend legitimacy to, the new structures of government.

RELATIONSHIP BETWEEN FEDERAL AND LOCAL GOVERNMENTS

The powers of the various federal institutions and their relationship with the separate institutions in each emirate, laid down in the constitution, have evolved and changed since the establishment of the state. Under the terms of the Constitution, Rulers may, if they wish, relinquish certain areas of authority prescribed as being the responsibility of individual emirates to the federal government. One significant such decision being that to unify the Armed Forces in the mid-1970s. The 1971 Constitution also permitted each emirate to retain or to take up membership in the Organization of Petroleum Exporting Countries and the Organization of Arab Petroleum Exporting Countries, although none have done so; the only emirate to be a member in 1971, Abu Dhabi, having chosen to relinquish its memberships in favour of the Federation.

The capital city of the Emirate of Sharjah.

39

Over the course of the 25 years since the Federation was established, the United Arab Emirates has grown dramatically as a result of a sustained development programme, which has not only seen the completion of a modern infrastructure that reaches into the remotest mountain villages, but has also seen population rise more than ten fold.

With such a pace of growth, the organs of government, both federal and local, have also developed impressively, and their influence now affect almost all aspects of life, for both UAE citizens and expatriates. As with other relatively young states, new institutions that were created for the first time, have derived their legitimacy and status from the extent of their activities and achievements, and from acknowledgement and appreciation of their role by the people.

The relationship between the new systems of government, federal and local, has itself evolved in a constructive manner. As the smaller emirates have benefited from development in terms of, for example, education, so they have been able to find the personnel to extend the variety of services provided by their own local governments, which had once been handled on their behalf by federal institutions, such as tourism. At the same time, in other areas, such as the judiciary, there has been an evolving trend towards a further voluntary relinquishment of local authority to the federal institutions. These new systems of government have not, however, replaced the traditional forms, which coexist and evolve alongside them.

Sheikh Zayed with Sheikh Maktoum and Sheikh Khalifa.

TRADITIONAL GOVERNMENT

Traditionally, the ruler of an emirate, the sheikh, was the leader of the most powerful, though not necessarily the most populous, tribe, while each individual tribe, and often its various sub-sections, also generally had a chief or sheikh. Such rulers and chiefs maintained their authority only insofar as they were able to retain the loyalty and support of their people, in essence a form of direct democracy, though without the paraphernalia of western forms of suffrage. Part of that democracy was the unwritten but strong principle that the people should have free access to their sheikh, and that he should hold a frequent and open *majlis,* or council, in which his fellow tribesmen could voice their opinions.

Such a direct democracy, of course, may be ideally suited to small and relatively uncomplicated societies, but becomes steadily more difficult to maintain as populations grow, while the increasing sophistication of the elements of government, through the various federal ministries and local departments and municipalities, means that on a day to day basis, many of the inhabitants of the Emirates now find it more appropriate to deal directly with these institutions on most matters, rather than to seek to meet directly with their Ruler or sheikh.

One fascinating aspect of life in the Emirates today, and one that is essential to an understanding of its political system, is the way in which the institution of the *majlis* has continued to maintain its relevance. In larger emirates, not only the Ruler, but also a number of other senior members of his family, continue to hold open *majlises,* in which participants may raise a wide range of topics, from a request for a piece of land, or for a scholarship for a son or daughter to go abroad, to more weighty subjects such as the impact of large-scale foreign immigration upon society or complaints about perceived flaws in the practices of various ministries and departments.

In smaller emirates, the *majlis* of the Ruler himself, or of the Crown-Prince or Deputy Ruler, remain the main focus. In Fujairah, for example, the Ruler holds an open *majlis* at least once a week, as well as daily during the Muslim holy fasting month of Ramadan, which may be attended by both citizens and expatriates. To these *majlises* come traditionally-minded tribesmen who may have waited several months for the opportunity to discuss with their ruler directly, rather than choose to pursue their requests or complaints through a modern governmental structure.

In modern society, of course, as President Sheikh Zayed himself has commented, it is naturally easier for a ruler to go to meet his people than for them to come to meet him. Sheikh Zayed frequently travels within the UAE, providing opportunities for him to meet with citizens away from the formal surroundings of an office or palace. During his regular inspection tours of projects, he also takes pains to ensure that citizens living nearby are guaranteed easy access to him.

Over the years since the United Arab Emirates was formed, the attitude of its people towards the modern and the traditional forms of government have, naturally, evolved. The ministries, departments and municipalities are now well established, and deal with a broad range of activities. As their functions have expanded, so they have taken over responsibility for a number of tasks with which, traditionally, a ruler would have dealt on a personal basis. Moreover, for the younger generation, who have grown up under the umbrella of such institutions, there is now a growing tendency to pay less attention to the old forms of governance, even though they may frequently attend *majlises*, particularly of the younger sheikhs. Among the older generation, however, traditional ways have retained their popularity, even if, on occasion, approaches may be made through the government machinery.

Just as the modern institutions have developed in response to public need and demand, however, so the traditional forms of tribal administration have adapted. With many relatively routine matters now being dealt with by the modern institutions, so the traditional ones, like the *majlis*, have been able to focus on more complex issues rather than on the routine matters with which they were once heavily involved.

In the *majlises*, for example, it is possible to hear detailed, and often heated, discussions between sheikhs and other citizens on questions such as the policy that should

The Emirate of Umm al-Qaiwain and its environs.

The capital city of Ras al-Khaimah Emirate.

be adopted towards the evolution of the machinery of government, or the nature of relations with neighbouring countries. On matters more directly affecting the individual,

The Emirate city of Ajman.

such as the topic of unemployment among young UAE graduates, debates often tend to begin in the *majlises*, where discussion can be fast and furious, before a consensus approach is evolved that is subsequently reflected in changes in government policy.

Through such means, the traditional methods of government in the United Arab Emirates have been able to retain both their relevance and vitality, and they continue to play an important, although often unpublicized, role in the evolution of the state today.

A BALANCED APPROACH

In many relatively new countries, government leaders have chosen to adopt uncritically forms of political administration that have been developed in, and for, other countries with different social and economic conditions. As a corollary, they have neglected, and have often formally abolished, the traditional forms of government which once prevailed. The result, as has become sadly clear over the course of the last 20 or 30 years, has been that often governments have become divorced from their people, with a consequent failure to obtain or to retain popular legitimacy.

In the United Arab Emirates, however, a different approach has been adopted: that of creating modern forms of administration, but, at the same time, of preserving traditional institutions, with the vitality and legitimacy they draw from history.

When the rulers of the emirates met 25 years ago to agree on the forms of government for their new federal state, they chose deliberately not simply to copy from others. They chose, instead, to work towards a society that would offer the best of modern administration, while at the same time retaining the traditional forms of government, that, with their inherent commitment to consensus, discussion and direct democracy, offered the best features of the past.

The capital city of the Emirate of Fujairah.

With the benefit of a quarter of century of hindsight, it is evident that they made the correct choice, for, despite the massive economic growth and the social dislocation caused by an explosion in the population, the state has enjoyed an enviable stability. During the course of the last few decades, moreover, there have been numerous attempts to create federal states, both in the Arab world and elsewhere, but the UAE is the only one in the Arab world to have stood the test of time.

Perhaps one reason for the success of the federal experiment in the United Arab Emirates has been the fact that its leaders and people have avoided the temptation to copy from elsewhere, or to adopt a rigid political ideology that owes its origins to other countries and other societies, preferring instead to hold fast to the essential principles on which local society has been governed for centuries.

Whatever the cause, however, the result has been the evolution of a society where modern and traditional forms of government are not only both relevant but are also both evolving harmoniously alongside each other, in pursuit of the greater goal of a stable, prosperous, confident and democratic society.

FOREIGN POLICY

S INCE THE ESTABLISHMENT of the Federation on 2 December 1971, the United Arab Emirates has remained true to the original foundations of its foreign policy. The policies themselves are pillars which embody the country's stands vis-à-vis Arab and Islamic development, and underpin its excellent relations with all the peace and justice loving nations in the world.

In the Gulf, the United Arab Emirates represents the first successful experiment in unification in the Arab world. It is also a founding member of the Arab Gulf Cooperation Council (AGCC), in the birth of which it played a special role. The AGCC, which was established on 25 May 1981, reflected the natural development of the strong fraternal ties which have long existed between the peoples and states of the Arab Gulf. These close relations are based upon, and continue to be supported by, a shared heritage and common aspirations among the member states. His Highness Sheikh Zayed underlined these common bonds in a speech in which he said: *We in the Arab Gulf are one family: we work together hand in hand; we stand united, shoulder to shoulder; and we walk along the same path together, the path of unity, a unity which is a part of the greater Arab unity.*

H.H. Sheikh Zayed at the Gulf Summit on 18 December, 1989.

The UAE also seeks to coordinate its policies, together with its regional and international relations, in line with national interests which are linked to Arab and Islamic development. Sheikh Zayed succinctly commented on the philosophy and goals of the AGCC thus: *This Council does not represent a shift in policy or ideas. It is not a new regional or independent group. The opposite is true. It is only new protective armour for the body of the greater Arab nation.* Further stressing the AGCC's supportive role for Arab states and their associated institutions, he added: *We are looking to this Council in its capacity as a part of the continuing Arab efforts to strengthen the Arab position and to increase the effectiveness of the Arab League.*

THE THREE UAE ISLANDS

The United Arab Emirates has pursued a quiet and wise diplomatic path in dealing with the continuing occupation by Iran of the three islands belonging to the Emirates. They are the Greater Tunb, the Lesser Tunb and Abu Musa, which were occupied by Iran on 29 November 1971. In the declaration issued by the Supreme Council of the Federation on 2 December 1971, it was stated as follows: *The Federation condemns the principle of the use of force and it regrets that Iran has recently occupied part of the Arab nation and it therefore deems it necessary to honour legal rights and to discuss possible repercussions which might ensue because of disputes between nations. Such discussions should be conducted in ways which are internationally recognized.*

From that date onwards, for 25 years, the United Arab Emirates has worked to end the Iranian occupation of the islands, calling for a peaceful settlement within the framework of mutual understanding and a dialogue for strengthening security and stability in the region. However, on 24 August 1992 Iran clearly violated the Memorandum of Understanding on Abu Musa which aimed at strengthening cooperation, when it refused landing permission to a passenger ship. Aboard the ship were more than 100 teachers, their families, UAE nationals employed on the island and residents of the island. Because of the Iranian action, it became impossible for them to reach their job sites or their dwellings on Abu Musa, which is part of the United Arab Emirates.

On 1 September 1992, a Ministry of Foreign Affairs spokesman branded the Iranian officials' actions on the island of Abu Musa as not in accordance with the relations between the United Arab Emirates and the Islamic Republic of Iran. On the contrary they reflected negatively on the cooperation between the two countries at a time when the UAE wished to establish good neighbourly relations and cooperation. Throughout the dispute, and right up to the present time, the United Arab Emirates has continued to hope that the historic friendly relations between the two countries can be maintained.

Rashid Abdulla, the Minister of Foreign Affairs, raised this subject in his speech before the United Nations on 30 September 1992 when he said: *The Iranian authorities have undertaken a number of illegal measures and arrangements with regard to the island of Abu Musa. These measures violate the Memorandum of Understanding of 1971. My country has expressed its rejection of these measures as being a clear violation of the sovereignty and territorial integrity of the Emirates as well as the principle of good neighbourliness. They also contradict the original provisions and spirit of the Memorandum of Understanding which demand justice and equivalency of treatment; taking into consideration that this Memo was signed under duress which according to international law makes it null and void.*

The latest Iranian measures are aimed at assuming control of the island of Abu Musa and tacitly annexing it to Iran, just as the Iranian Government did in 1971 when it militarily occupied the two islands of the Lesser and Greater Tunbs which belong to the United Arab Emirates. Because of the nature of these measures, tension is bound to increase in the area and security and stability will be endangered, since these actions are incompatible with the principle of coexistence, good neighbourliness and the traditional relations which exist between the two countries.

Because of the keen concern of the United Arab Emirates to settle regional disputes through dialogue and understanding, bilateral meetings were held between the two countries in the city of Abu Dhabi on 27-28 September 1992, with the aim of arriving at a peaceful negotiated settlement. However, the Iranian side refused to discuss the military occupation of the three islands. It also refused to reach an agreement on referring the matter to the International Court of Justice. During this meeting, the United Arab Emirates made the following proposals to the Islamic Republic of Iran:

- Iran should bring to an end its military occupation of the Lesser and Greater Tunbs.
- Iran should confirm its commitment to the Memorandum of Understanding of 1971 with regard to the island of Abu Musa.
- Iran should refrain from interference under any circumstances whatsoever in the exercise by the United Arab Emirates of its entire sovereign power over that part of the island of Abu Musa designated to it under the terms of the Memorandum of Understanding.
- Iran should cancel all arrangements and undertakings which adversely affect UAE nationals, non-UAE residents and the state's institutions on the island of Abu Musa.
- Both sides should work together to create a suitable framework for settling the question of the sovereignty of the island of Abu Musa within a fixed period of time.

A statement issued by the UAE delegation at the end of the meeting stated: *As a result of the Iranian side's refusal to debate the question of the ending of the Iranian occupation of the two Tunbs, or to agree to refer the question to the International Court of Justice, it was not feasible to debate other questions and subjects during this meeting.*

With respect to the sovereignty of the Lesser and Greater Tunbs, the United Arab Emirates wishes to draw attention to the fact that the two islands have long been, and continue to be, a part of the United Arab Emirates. The Iranian military occupation of the two islands in November 1971 does not change the firm legal position of the two islands in international law, whereby occupation through the use of force is never rewarded by sovereignty over the occupied territory for the occupying country, no matter how long that occupation continues.

The United Arab Emirates takes the view that the Iranian side must bear the responsibility for the lack of any progress in the discussions. As a result of Iran's refusal to cooperate, the United Arab Emirates has no recourse but to use all peaceful ways and means at its disposal to affirm its sovereignty over the three islands.

In a fresh initiative on the twenty-second National Day in December 1993, Sheikh Zayed called on Iran to begin a direct dialogue to end its occupation of the three islands. He said: *We think it is necessary for us to commit ourselves through dialogue to a peaceful end to this occupation and a return of the three islands to the sovereignty of the United Arab Emirates, in accordance with international laws and usages, the principles of good neighbourliness and mutual respect among countries.*

Sheikh Zayed repeated these words on the twenty-third National Day on 2 December 1994, calling for Iran either to be bound by the principle of constructive and objective dialogue, or to resort to international arbitration. He said: *Based on its religious principles, the United Arab Emirates has tirelessly pursued a firm policy of brotherhood and mutual forgiveness with its neighbours. Accordingly, we have repeated our call to our brothers in the Islamic Republic of Iran either to seek a legal judgment on the principle of constructive objective dialogue, or to resort to international arbitration to solve the problem of our occupied islands, the Lesser and Greater Tunbs and Abu Musa.*

Sheikh Zayed with H.M.Sultan Qaboos of Oman.

The United Arab Emirates responded positively to the Qatar initiative, which suggested a meeting of experts with Iran, to be held in Doha on 18 November 1995. The Emirates, keen to see the negotiations succeed, proposed the following four point agenda:

- An end to the military occupation of the Lesser and Greater Tunb islands.
- A commitment to the Memorandum of Understanding of 1971 with regard to the island of Abu Musa and a cancellation of the arrangements and undertakings which violate its stipulations.
- A settlement of the question of the sovereignty of the island of Abu Musa.
- An agreement to refer the dispute of the islands of the Lesser and Greater Tunbs and Abu Musa to the International Court of Justice should it become impossible to arrive at a negotiated settlement within a fixed period of time.

On 21 November 1995, the delegation of the United Arab Emirates issued a press statement on the results of the negotiations. It confirmed that the meeting of experts from the UAE and Iran had failed to reach an agreement on the preparation of an agenda for negotiations between the two countries to solve the dispute existing between them over the three islands, the Lesser and Greater Tunbs and Abu Musa.

Khalifa Shahin Al Mirri, the head of the UAE delegation, said that the Iranian position represented a rebuff of the good offices extended by the state of Qatar, since it was an obvious violation of the clear stipulations laid out in the letter of invitation issued by Sheikh Hamad bin Jassim bin Jabir Al Thani, the Qatar Minister of Foreign Affairs. The Qatar letter had stipulated that the meeting would be held for the limited purpose of arriving at an agreement on an agenda for bilateral negotiations, the aim of which was to solve the existing dispute between the two countries.

Mr Al Mirri concluded by saying that: *The UAE feels that the refusal of the Iranian delegation to fix the requested agenda undermined the authority of the meeting and the goal for which it had been convened.* He said that the UAE confirmed its desire to continue good neighbourly relations with the Islamic Republic of Iran and to maintain historic bilateral ties: *However, the UAE takes the view that good relations are not attainable unless (i) there is a peaceful atmosphere, (ii) the circumstances are more tranquil and (iii) suitable working methods have been established between the two countries. It also takes the view that the above are only attainable through respect for the international principles of law, which demand that the sovereignty of nations and their territorial integrity be honoured, that disputes be settled by peaceful means including recourse, where necessary, to the International Court of Justice and that the threat or use of force to achieve territorial gains or changes be prohibited.*

As a result of the response of Iran to all diplomatic attempts made by the United Arab Emirates to end the Iranian occupation of the three islands, the UAE began an initiative calling for the referral of the dispute to the International Court of Justice. Among the organizations announcing their support for this move were the Arab Gulf Cooperation Council (AGCC), the AGCC Ministerial Council, the Arab League, the Ministers of Foreign Affairs of the Damascus Declaration states and many other countries worldwide.

In his speech before the General Assembly of the United Nations on 4 October 1995, the UAE Minister of Foreign Affairs stated: *The United Arab Emirates reaffirms its stand calling for the holding of direct, unconditional, bilateral negotiations with Iran to end its military occupation of the three islands which has lasted since 1971. These islands are an indivisible part of the regional sovereignty of the UAE. In the event that this call is declined, then the UAE would like to renew its initiative, announced at the last session, calling for the dispute to be referred to the International Court of Justice, the international body empowered to settle disputes, to which many nations in the past have resorted, among them Iran, to resolve similar disputes.* The UAE minister further stated that this peaceful course of action has received the support of its fellow states in the AGCC and other friendly and peace-loving countries. He went on to say that not only had *Iran rejected these initiatives, but it had imposed further illegal measures to consolidate the occupation. These measures are incompatible with the principle of peaceful coexistence and good neighbourly relations and they are in contradiction of the provisions of the Charter of the Islamic Conference, the Charter of the United Nations and the principles of international law.*

One of the most recent attempts by Iran to consolidate its occupation of the three islands was its installation, in April 1996, of a power plant on the island of Greater

Tunb. The UAE considers this action to be an infraction of the principles of international law and a violation of the sovereignty of the UAE over Greater Tunb and not to accord with any of the rights of the occupation authority.

The UAE Minister of Foreign Affairs, also stated in his speech before the United Nations on 30 September 1992 that: *All the historical and geographical facts and documents confirm that the sovereignty of the three islands has historically lain with the UAE. It continues to do so. The Iranian military occupation of these islands cannot change their legal status which is fixed by international law, and the occupation which occurred through the use of force will never give the occupying power sovereignty over the occupied territory no matter how long the occupation lasts.*

Sheikh Zayed with President Mubarak of Egypt in 1988.

The Iranian occupation of these islands, and the events and measures which followed, are in contradiction to the principles of the Charter and its purposes. They are also incompatible with the principles of international law itself, most especially those laws concerning the independence and sovereignty of nations; the unity of their territories; good neighbourliness; non-interference in the internal affairs of a nation; the repudiation of threats or use of force; and the resolution of disputes by peaceful means.

In its concluding statement of 2 June 1996, after its meeting in Riyadh, the Ministerial Council of the AGCC confirmed its resolute and firm position of support for the United Arab Emirates, and for any peaceful measures and means which it may adopt to restore its sovereignty over the three islands of the Lesser and Greater Tunbs and Abu Musa. It also renewed its call to Iran to accept the referral of the dispute to the International Court of Justice. After reviewing the latest changes in relations between the AGCC states and Iran, as well as the continuing question of the occupation of the UAE islands, the Council confirmed that it took notice of the fact that the Iranian Government is continuing to consolidate its occupation of the islands. It also noted that Iran's policy of maintaining its illegal position by force shows a determination to continue its unjustified provocative actions, violates the sovereignty of the United Arab Emirates, and is inimical to its rights. These acts also put the security and stability of the region in danger and are incompatible with the principles of international law.

Sheikh Hamdan bin Zayed Al Nahyan, the Minister of State for Foreign Affairs, confirmed that the file on the Iranian occupation of the three islands has been with the Security Council since the occupation began, just as the UAE was being established, on 2 December 1971. In an interview with the Egyptian newspaper, *Al-Ahram*, on 4 June 1996, he made the following remarks: *The Security Council looked into the matter in December 1971 at the request of the Arab group and the files on the dispute remain in its possession.* He expressed his desire for good relations between the UAE and Iran, saying that: *We on our part have confirmed our serious desire to see our relations with the Islamic Republic of Iran governed by clarity, good neighbourliness and Islamic brotherhood, exemplified by a policy of non-interference in each other's internal affairs. We would also like to see a suitable climate for economic development and prosperity for the peoples of the region created by a spirit of mutual understanding. Furthermore, we see the security and stability necessary for development and construction as requiring an atmosphere of agreement and conformity. Therefore, we are determined to follow all peaceful means in seeking a solution to the existing dispute over the three islands and to restore our sovereignty over them according to the precepts of international law, including the presentation of this dispute to the International Court of Justice. We ask the Islamic Republic of Iran to respond clearly and effectively to this endeavour in a way which is in keeping with our open call for the strengthening of its relations with the Arab countries.*

Sheikh Hamdan stressed that the actions taken by the Iranian Government on the three occupied islands will not earn them any rights. These actions include the establishment of an airport on the island of Abu Musa; an invitation to set up tourism facilities; an announcement of its intention to establish a new port on the island and the setting-up of an electricity plant on Greater Tunb; besides the other documented infringements since the Iranian occupation of these islands. The aim of these transgressions is to consolidate the fact of occupation and to maintain their illegal position by force *at a time when they know that no rights over the occupied islands can accrue to them by this method. Their actions only serve to complicate the dispute and to cast doubt on the credibility of any possible future moves towards negotiation on the part of the Iranian government.*

In the final communiqué, issued on 14 July 1996 at the end of their two-day meeting in Muscat, Oman, Foreign Ministers of the Damascus Declaration states, in their strongest statement to date, reiterated the UAE's right of sovereignty over its occupied islands. The Ministers expressed full support for all measures and peaceful means taken by the UAE to regain the three islands. The text of the communiqué stated: *The Ministers have reviewed with great concern the issue of the Iranian occupation of the UAE's three islands of Abu Musa, Greater Tunb and Lesser Tunb and the efforts that the UAE is exerting to restore its sovereignty over its three islands, by peaceful means in accordance with international codes, rules and procedures to solve disputes between states peacefully and in accordance with the principles and rules of international law, including referral of the issue to the International Court of Justice.*

The Ministers recalled the continuous, serious and honest calls and initiatives to the Islamic Republic of Iran from the United Arab Emirates, the Arab Gulf Cooperation Council, AGCC, the Damascus Declaration, the Arab League Ministerial Council and the Arab Summit in Cairo. The Ministers renewed their affirmation of the sovereignty of the UAE over its three islands of Abu Musa and the Greater and Lesser Tunbs and their support and absolute backing to all peaceful means, methods and measures that the UAE takes to restore its sovereignty over these islands. The Ministers reiterated their call to the Iranian Government to end its occupation of the three islands and desist from exercising de facto policy by force and effecting the implementation of any unilateral measures in the three islands and to follow peaceful means to solve the dispute over these islands in accordance with the principles, rules and regulations of international law and to accept the referral of the issue to the International Court of Justice.

While the Ministers affirm that the security and stability of the UAE, and the protection and preservation of its independence and territorial integrity and its support, is considered an integral part of the security of the Arab Gulf countries and Arab national security, they affirm the necessity of the Iranian Republic of Iran sticking to principles of good neighbourliness, respect of the independence, sovereignty and territorial integrity of the countries of the region and the non-interference in their internal affairs and of resorting to peaceful means to find the solution of disputes between these countries and the obligations which ensue from these obligations.

AGCC

Bahrain

The UAE has adopted a clear and forthright stand towards the terrorism which Bahrain is undergoing. H.H. Sheikh Zayed has stressed that the United Arab Emirates continues to stand by Bahrain's side at all times and in all circumstances. In a telephone call on 4 June 1996 to H.H. Sheikh Isa bin Salman Al Khalifa, the Amir of Bahrain, he condemned the interference in the internal affairs of the State of Bahrain and the disturbances created by mercenary elements. In his talks with the Amir of Bahrain, he said that: *The situation which is facing you is also facing us and the actions of the mercenaries will not affect you because your people will rally around your leadership and your brothers will also support you.*

Sheikh Zayed visiting UAE troops who helped to liberate Kuwait.

Saudi Arabia

The UAE strongly condemned the terrorist explosion which occurred in June in the Saudi City of Al-Khobar, denouncing the heinous crime as a terrorist act alien to Islamic principles of tolerance: *The UAE affirms its close solidarity with, and full support for, the brotherly Kingdom of Saudi Arabia in order to confront this phenomenon, which is alien to our society,* an official source stated. *The UAE reiterates that these evil acts will not harm the gains and achievements attained by the Arab Gulf Cooperation Council states during the past decades and calls upon all AGCC states, the brotherly Arab countries and the inter-national community to join in efforts to uproot all forms of the terrorism phenomenon, whatever their motives and excuses.* H.H. President Sheikh Zayed bin Sultan Al Nahyan, in his cable of condolence to King Fahd bin Abdul Aziz of Saudi Arabia, also condemned the

criminal act which, he said, was committed against innocent people. *The criminal attack which occurred in Saudi Arabia targeted all of us because what affects the Saudi Government and people affects the UAE Government and people too*, Sheikh Zayed said. He also emphasized the UAE's full solidarity with the Saudi Government and people.

ARAB AND ISLAMIC SOLIDARITY

The achievement of Arab Islamic solidarity is one of the major features of the permanent foreign policy of the United Arab Emirates, because it believes that rejection of division and differences is the only way to power and solidarity.

Sheikh Zayed, elaborating on this principle, said that: *The success of the greater Arab nation in making itself known to the world and in supporting our solidarity does not depend on the Arab nation alone. Our solidarity also requires that the entire Islamic community works for the good of the Arab nation as the Arab nation works for the good of the Islamic community. There should be no barriers between the two because the ways of the two are as one Muslim way and the Holy Qur'an is, and always will be, our common constitution.*

The UAE has exerted its fullest efforts to achieve Arab Islamic solidarity. Sheikh Zayed has played a prominent role in settling a number of differences in the Arab arena since the beginning of the 1970s and his good offices have been successful in restoring calm to relations between a number of capitals of the Arab nation. The UAE

President also played a prominent role in restoring Egypt to the Arab ranks after his initiative brought the matter to the attention of the emergency Arab Summit Conference in Amman in November 1987.

Proceeding from this certitude and with his strong belief in the power of enduring ties to overcome the negative effects of the Iraqi invasion of Kuwait in August 1990, Sheikh Zayed, on 16 October 1995, called for complete Arab reconciliation, saying: *the time for Arab reconciliation has come.* He referred to the countless historical precedents of war and subsequent reconciliation, pointing to the examples of Russia, Europe and America, which confronted each other in wars and then joined forces in a spirit of cooperation. *Why can't we, the Arabs, be like them? Why can we not attempt to erase this page from the past and cooperate with each other again?*

The efforts of Sheikh Zayed to promote goodwill have earned the favour and great appreciation of the Arab peoples and countries, as well as the Arab League which, in December 1992, bestowed on him the sash of the *Man of Growth and Development*.

The Minister of State for Foreign Affairs, Sheikh Hamdan bin Zayed Al Nahyan, confirmed in an interview held on 4 June 1996 with the Egyptian newspaper, *Al-Ahram*, that: *the guiding initiatives which have been made by the UAE for the last two decades in an attempt to establish a joint and indissoluble Arab stance represent, in effect, an attempt to put into practice the resolutions of the Arab League by translating the policy of Arab self-dependence into tangible results. The foreign policy of the Emirates depends on certain fixed principles: the establishment of dialogue and bridges and the pursuit of a balanced, impartial and credible diplomacy which shares in the Arab movement, while remaining outside of conflicts in order to participate more easily in containing and then solving them.*

Sheikh Hamdan continued by saying: *The initiatives of Sheikh Zayed, put forward to help solve the problems and ambiguities of the Arab nation which arose in Lebanon, in the Arab Maghrib, in the Gulf and other places, were based on these principles.*

Palestinan leader Yasser Arafat with Sh. Zayed in 1981

THE PALESTINIAN CAUSE AND JERUSALEM

In line with its firmly held and consistent position, the United Arab Emirates supports the Palestinian cause and the struggle of the Palestinian people to restore their national rights and to establish an independent state. The Emirates welcomed the convening of the Madrid Peace Conference, while supporting the negotiations between the two concerned parties within the scope of that conference based on legal international foundations as represented in the resolutions of the United Nations, especially the two resolutions No. 242 of 1967 and No. 338 of 1973, and the principle of land for peace.

Within this framework, the UAE confirmed its support for the right of the Palestinian people to self determination and the restoration of their legal rights. Sheikh Zayed also confirmed the support of the UAE for the PLO-Israel agreement, and he personally hoped that this might represent a true step towards achieving long sought Palestinian objectives and interests.

Sheikh Zayed with dignitaries at Jerusalem Week in Abu Dhabi in 1995.

The UAE Minister of Foreign Affairs, in his speech before the United Nations in October 1995, confirmed that: *the implementation of these agreements by the Israeli Government is considered an important basic step on the way towards enabling the Palestinian people to exercise their right to self determination and to establishing their independent state on their national soil, in line with all other peoples of the world.*

The UAE takes the view that the achievement of a lasting, comprehensive and just peace in the Middle East demands the achievement of tangible progress on the Syrian and Lebanese fronts. This is a matter which demands greater international effort, particularly from the sponsors of the peace conference, in order to make the Israeli Government implement its pledges and obligations within the framework of the principle of *land for peace* and Security Council resolutions Nos. 242, 338 and 425. These resolutions demand a complete and unconditional Israeli withdrawal from *all the Palestinian Arab occupied territories, including the City of Jerusalem, the Syrian Golan Heights and the South of Lebanon.* The UAE has given unlimited support to the Palestinian Cause and it was in the vanguard of nations which upheld the cause of Jerusalem and supported the tenacity of the Holy City in resisting Israeli plans to judaize it and confiscate its territory. It also strongly criticized the decision of the United States Congress to transfer the US Embassy to Jerusalem.

In receiving the delegations participating in the *O! Jerusalem* Festival which was mounted by the UAE on 31 October 1995, Sheikh Zayed told them: *We supported the Palestinian people and we will continue to support them until they achieve their ambition of establishing an independent state as all their brothers within the Arab nation have done.*

Sheikh Zayed also expressed his readiness to extend whatever aid is required to assist the Palestinians in the building of their nation, confirming that: *All required help will be extended to the City of Jerusalem, which is the most deserving of support and aid.*

Sheikh Abdullah bin Zayed Al Nahyan, Undersecretary at the Ministry of Information and Culture, speaking at the inauguration of the Festival *O! Jerusalem*, announced plans, initiated by Sheikh Zayed, for establishment of a number of new housing projects in the City of Jerusalem, together with a number of renovation projects in the city. He also reported that Sheikh Zayed had ordered the Zayed Philanthropic Foundation and UAE Red Crescent Society to meet the medical, educational and social requirements of the residents in occupied Jerusalem and to provide whatever aid may be required by the relevant institutions in these areas to make it easier for the Holy City to hold out bravely against the continuing attempts to judaize it.

Having a deep concern for the religious, civic and humanitarian situation, particularly as it pertains to the City of Jerusalem, the UAE was immediately and highly critical of the resolution of the United States Congress on 24 October 1995 to transfer the US Embassy from Tel Aviv to Jerusalem at the end of May 1999. It considers the resolution to be a great blow, because it demonstrates a complete partiality for the Israeli position. To a large extent it also confirms the United States of America's doubtful credibility as a great power and as one of the sponsors of the peace process in the Middle East, and threatens to break up the pillars of support for peace in the region.

Sheikh Hamdan bin Zayed Al Nahyan, the Minister of State for Foreign Affairs, said that this resolution was an obvious challenge to the feelings of the entire Islamic community: *The City of Jerusalem holds a special religious, cultural and humanitarian position and, most especially, it is a place of significance for all Semitic religions. Therefore, its destiny must not be determined by one side alone.*

He expressed the hope that the American administration would continue to play its neutral role as an honourable and effective partner in the peace process, and that it would continue to participate in the search for a permanent, comprehensive and fair solution to the Arab/Israeli conflict.

Upon taking up the presidency of the Arab League in March 1996, the UAE at once sought the issuance of a Security Council resolution condemning the Israeli Government for its confiscation of 52 hectares of land in east Jerusalem on which to establish settlements. In May 1996, the UAE demanded the convening of an emergency session of the Security Council to approve the draft resolution tabled by the non-aligned nations in the Security Council calling for the cancellation of the confiscation. On 18 May 1996, when the United States of America vetoed the draft resolution, the UAE expressed its regret and astonishment at the negative position of the United States.

BOSNIA-HERCEGOVINA

Sheikh Zayed with President Izebegovich of Bosnia, 1995.

From the time it first exploded, the problem of Bosnia-Hercegovina has won the attention of Sheikh Zayed, the President of the Federation, and the people of the Emirates. The United Arab Emirates was at the forefront of the countries which adopted clear and principled positions in aid and support of the people of Bosnia against Serbian crimes and aggression. It also criticized the negative positions of the great powers and the United Nations in dealing with this problem.

As the Serbian ethnic cleansing, killings and rapes of the people of Bosnia escalated, the UAE President, on 19 July 1995, demanded that: *The Arab Islamic countries adopt a decisive, unified stand vis-à-vis (i) the great powers which remain on the sidelines observing the massacre of the innocents, (ii) the Serbian aggressors and (iii) the United Nations, an organization which is supposed to represent the conscience of the entire world, which has stood idly by, powerless, as if it were a deaf god made of stone and thereby rendered unfeeling and insensitive to the suffering of the Bosnian people.*

Sheikh Zayed called for: *the immediate lifting of the arms embargo on the people of Bosnia and Hercegovina to enable them to defend themselves and to resist the indefensible racist attacks to which they have been subjected for years.*

The United Arab Emirates was among the first countries to give aid to the people of Bosnia, by sending a number of shipments of relief aid, such as food and medicines, and by accepting scores of wounded for treatment in its hospitals. It also commissioned the setting-up of dozens of families in furnished apartments, the provision of work opportunities for the adults and full educational facilities for the children.

To help to implement this policy, the United Arab Emirates organized *Bosnia Day* on 28 July 1995 with the aim of collecting funds for the benefit of the Muslims of Bosnia and Hercegovina, while simultaneously publicizing the political dimension of this crisis.

On *Bosnia Day* during a television broadcast, Sheikh Zayed called on the country's nationals and those Arabs and Muslims who are resident in the country to give aid and assistance to the people of Bosnia. He said: *I have confidence that all the peoples of the Emirates and those of the Arab and Islamic countries who are resident in the country, and everyone on the side of right, justice and humanity, will do their duty and respond to this call for donations in cash and kind by giving all they can to relieve the suffering of the people of Bosnia, to help establish their rights and to protect them from injustice.*

Sheikh Zayed again called on the great powers to assume their historic responsibilities and not just to stand by as observers. He said: *the tragedy which is being perpetrated against the rights of the Bosnian people is, like all similar crises, primarily the responsibility of the great powers who set such store by justice and the protection of human rights.*

Sheikh Zayed condemned the negative positions taken by the great powers in regard to what is happening in Bosnia as being open to suspicion. He said that silence in the face of aggression and even more silence at the degradation of mankind conceals unclear objectives. He continued by saying: *If the great powers, which possess volumes of aid, fail to act, then it falls to the rest of the states of the world to defend those who are being wronged and to oppose the wrongdoer in all possible ways, because humanity cannot countenance oppression.*

Donations during *Bosnia Day* amounted to 158 million dirhams in addition to donations in kind such as trinkets, gems and gold jewellery.

The role of the United Arab Emirates has not been restricted to international gatherings. It has done more than that by bravely and uniquely criticizing the Russian Federation for its stand in support of the Serb aggressors. Sheikh Hamdan bin Zayed Al Nahyan, the Minister of State for Foreign Affairs, called in the Russian Ambassador to the UAE on 1 August 1995 and expressed United Arab Emirates' condemnation of the completely one-sided support of the Russian Federation for the Serbs and their continuous crimes against the people of Bosnia-Hercegovina.

In his speech before the United Nations in October 1995, Rashid Abdulla, the Minister of Foreign Affairs, referred to the matter of Bosnia and Hercegovina which was witnessing a new turn in its affairs. Peace negotiations had recently taken place and a preliminary agreement on basic principles for a comprehensive settlement based on the international legal resolutions had been reached.

The Minister renewed the support of the United Arab Emirates for all efforts being exerted by the international community, and especially the contact units of the Islamic Conference, the European Union and the Government of the United States of America to solve the dispute peacefully in a way which will guarantee respect for the regional sovereignty of the state of Bosnia-Hercegovina. At the same time, he stressed the importance of lifting the arms embargo against Bosnia and Hercegovina in accordance with Article 51 of the United Nations Charter as a means of preventing, with no further repetition, the aggression, massacres and ethnic cleansing operations which the Serbian forces have deliberately committed against Bosnian civilians and especially the Bosnian Muslims.

In line with the United Arab Emirates' general policy of support for Islamic causes and its particular commitment to aiding the Government and people of Bosnia-Hercegovina, Sheikh Zayed, on 3 June 1996, ordered that 15 million dollars and some military equipment and ammunition be given to Bosnia and Hercegovina as part of the UAE's commitment to the re-arming of the Bosnian army.

THE EMIRATES AND THE ARAB LEAGUE

Since it joined the organization on 6 December 1971, the United Arab Emirates has been an effective advocate of joint Arab action through the Arab League and Sheikh Zayed has played a prominent role in Arab summit conferences. In these conferences he has consistently championed the principles of Arab unification through mutual assistance, cooperation and the solution of internal differences, and the advancement of the Arab presence internationally. He has always encouraged positive attitudes and approaches to conflict resolution, as well as rapid humanitarian responses to disasters and crises.

ARAB AFFAIRS

When the Lebanese crisis erupted in 1975, the United Arab Emirates confirmed its great desire for peace in Lebanon, and for the preservation of its territories, its sovereignty and its Arab character. Within this framework, Sheikh Zayed took many initiatives which ended in dialogue between the warring factions and agreement on the restoration of stability to Lebanon. At the end of the civil war, the United Arab Emirates confirmed its readiness to participate in the re-building of Lebanon. Sheikh Zayed confirmed the complete support of the United Arab Emirates for Lebanon in its efforts to establish security and stability for the Lebanese people. The UAE also stood by Lebanon against the repeated Israeli aggressions on its territories and citizens.

On 12 April 1996, the UAE condemned the continuing Israeli aggressions against Lebanon, confirmed its support for its brothers in Lebanon, and demanded a cessation of Israeli violations; calling for action to implement Security Council Resolution No. 425 in relation to ending the Israeli occupation of Lebanese territory in the south.

When civil war broke out in Yemen in May 1994, Sheikh Zayed worked tirelessly for peace between the warring factions, and to protect Yemen and the accomplishments of its people. He called repeatedly on the leaders in Yemen to stop the bloodletting and to seek a compromise based on rational dialogue as being in the best interests of Yemen and its people.

From the outbreak of the civil war in Somalia, the Emirates was one of the first nations to respond to the call for action by the leaders of the Arab countries to save Somalia from its ordeal. When the Arab initiative had failed to stop the bloodletting,

Sheikh Zayed was one of the first leaders to call for speedy international intervention. The Emirates participated in the United Nations' operation, *Restore Hope*, to re-establish stability in Somalia. It also dispatched huge shipments of humanitarian, medical and educational aid to Somalia.

The Emirates actively participates in the organizations, federations and institutions of the Arab League. It holds membership in all pan-Arab organizations.

THE EMIRATES AND THE UNITED NATIONS

H.H.Sheikh Zayed conferring an award on President Nelson Mandela in 1995.

The Emirates took the initiative, after its own establishment, of becoming a member of the United Nations on 9 December 1971. It became a non-permanent member of the Security Council for the years 1986-7 and participated actively during these two years in the preparation and issuing of a number of important international resolutions. The armed forces of the UAE took part in a number of UN peace keeping operations, and engaged in the war to liberate Kuwait as part of the international coalition forces. As mentioned above, it also formed part of the international operation *Restore Hope* in Somalia.

As a mark of the deep interest which the United Arab Emirates has in the international organization's role in Arab affairs, Sheikh Zayed deputed Sheikh Sultan bin Zayed Al Nahyan to represent him at the UN celebration of its fiftieth anniversary. The celebrations were held in New York during the period 22-24 October 1995.

In his speech on 24 October 1995, Sheikh Sultan confirmed that the peoples of the states of the Arab region are looking to the United Nations to take a greater role in dealing with the problems deriving from the many conflicts and wars which have plagued the Middle East region during the past decades. The region's inhabitants want the United Nations to find solutions in order that their hopes and aspirations for the achievement of peace, justice, development and stability can be realized. He said: *Our participation in these celebrations very clearly reflects the fact that we are convinced of the historic role which the United Nations has played in establishing a new era of international relations and strengthening security and peace, especially in our Arab area.*

His Excellency Rashid Abdulla, the Minister of Foreign Affairs, also confirmed in his speech before the United Nations in October 1995 that: *The United Arab Emirates supports the international trend which is asking for the re-evaluation, reform and development of the ancillary organizations of the United Nations. The United Arab Emirates particularly supports the demand for increased membership in the Security Council because it is felt that membership should be determined on the basis of a fair geographical distribution which will enable the international organization to confront immense challenges, whether they involve international security and peace or the strengthening of economic and social development.*

The Minister also stressed the importance of cooperation between the United Nations and regional organizations. Such cooperation, he emphasized, will be enhanced if there is a wider framework for coordination and consultation, which is aimed at finding joint peaceful solutions to existing disputes, solutions which are based on international legal foundations and through which security, stability and growth can be strengthened.

In keeping with the policy of the United Arab Emirates on disarmament and the prevention of the spread of nuclear weapons, the UAE requested the international community to adopt more decisive positions in these matters. The Emirates have always stressed that the goal of maintaining international peace and security is a collective international responsibility which requires the political will, a new approach and the adoption of an open policy without double standards. It also stressed that a new way must be found for giving real form and body to declared disarmament intentions, including declared intentions to destroy weapons of mass destruction.

Rashid Abdulla in his speech before the General Assembly declared that: *The Government of the United Arab Emirates, which is convinced of the importance of the achievement of collective security, and noting that on 25 September 1995 it completed all the legal measures for establishing membership in the Treaty on the Non-Proliferation of Atomic Weapons, confirms that it is the Emirates' policy to support the establishment of zones which are free from all weapons of mass destruction, especially in the Middle East region. However, this can never be achieved so long as Israel refuses to cooperate with the supervisory organization. Israel also refuses to rely on international guarantees and it does not adhere to the Treaty for the Non-Proliferation of Atomic Weapons both of which actions, if effected, would give credibility to this treaty.*

H.H. President Sheikh Zayed bin Sultan Al Nahyan approved the UAE's accession to the Nuclear Non-Proliferation Treaty in July 1996.

The United Arab Emirates pays great attention to the new world order but, as the UAE Minister of Foreign Affairs pointed out in his UN speech, anomalies remain. In spite of the positive gains brought about by changes during recent years in the socio-economic situation, on national, regional and international levels, the developing countries are still suffering from the effects of hunger, poverty, the increasing danger of the burden of debts and the decline of prices of basic commodities. In addition, the unjust measures which are undertaken by developed nations to impose and maintain their economic and commercial policies only help to widen the economic and social gap between themselves and the developing countries. The Minister of Foreign Affairs charged the international community with the responsibility for the resumption of the dialogue between the North and South in such a way as to serve in equal measure the common interests of the advanced countries and the developing countries.

DIPLOMATIC RELATIONS

Owing to the foresight of Sheikh Zayed in extending bridges of friendship and cooperation with all nations of the world, the United Arab Emirates maintains diplomatic relations with 137 of the 184 nations of the world. The nation maintains 39 embassies abroad as well as five consulates general and two permanent missions located in New York and Geneva. There are 62 nations which maintain embassies in the UAE and the number of non-resident embassies rose from 30 to 37 in 1995, following the accreditation of three non-resident ambassadors to the country from Cameroon, the Ivory Coast and Singapore. In Dubai there are 31 consulates now that the Consulate of Palestine is open.

FOREIGN AID

The country's foreign aid policy springs from its deep-rooted Arab characteristics and from its commitment to high Islamic principles and values. Believing in the importance of humanitarian relations between peoples and nations, the UAE grants loans to, and has undertaken joint investment and development projects with, like-minded and friendly countries. It has also given aid and succour in emergency humanitarian cases and has participated in alleviating the suffering of brotherly and friendly nations afflicted by natural disaster and misfortunes.

The Abu Dhabi Fund for Development was established in 1975 on the directions of Sheikh Zayed. Since that time it has given Dh10.448 billion in loans, aid and grants for 169 development projects in many fields. In Morocco, some 50 vital projects were established under Sheikh Zayed's instructions. They include infrastructure projects as well as projects for housing, agriculture, health, education and electricity, in addition to the provision of basic services for distant regions. In Yemen, the UAE has participated in financing a number of media, educational, housing and tourism projects, in addition to rebuilding the historic Marib Dam and the highway which connects Sana'a and Marib. The latter was privately funded by Sheikh Zayed.

The United Arab Emirates has participated in more than 71 projects in Egypt, which include vital agricultural, housing, infrastructural and services projects. In Pakistan, the United Arab Emirates has executed dozens of basic projects in health and educational services as well as projects involving housing, scientific research and the care of orphans.

H.H.Sheikh Zayed visits the site of the new Marib Dam in Yemen which was built with the UAE's financial help.

Abu Dhabi Fund for Economic Development   Units are in Dhs 000s

Total Loans	6,355,103
Grants	466,635
Contributions	457,509
Loans from the Abu Dhabi Government managed by the Fund	2,913,669
Grants from the Abu Dhabi Government managed by the Fund	2,598,749

Geographic Spread of Loans from the ADFED

Arabian Countries	5,072,687	79.82%
Asian Countries	512,952	8.08%
African Countries	471,464	7.41%
Other countries	298,000	4.69%

Source: ADFED Report 1996.

H.H. Sheikh Zayed on the Great Wall during a visit to China in 1990.

In September 1995, teaching commenced in the Centre for Arab and Islamic Studies in Beijing. This centre was set up at the private expense of Sheikh Zayed, and Sheikh Khalifa bin Zayed Al Nahyan, the Heir Apparent of Abu Dhabi and Deputy Supreme Commander of the Armed Forces. The centre consists of five storeys with 50 rooms and halls for study and lectures.

The Zayed Philanthropic Foundation, which was founded on 5 August 1993, is considered to be one of the most prominent and modern benevolent foundations in the Arab nation and the Islamic world. In the short period since its establishment, it has funded a number of scientific research projects as well as those of a humanitarian nature.

The United Arab Emirates extends this policy of altruism and cooperative aid unstintingly to like-minded nations. It is administered by a number of the state's charitable institutions, at the head of which are the UAE Red Crescent Society and the Abu Dhabi Welfare Society. These organizations play distinguished roles in giving urgent welfare assistance in cases of tragedies and disasters which strike friendly or fellow nations. Their humanitarian activities include the role they play in caring for orphans who are the victims of civil wars.

These two organizations provided welfare assistance to the victims of the floods and earthquakes which in the last few years have struck Algeria, Egypt, Morocco, Pakistan, Bangladesh, Iran and other countries. In addition to their prominent role in assisting the Bosnian victims of Serbian attacks, they also provided urgent aid to the victims of Israeli aggression in the south of Lebanon, as well as aid to people in Palestine and Iraq, the latter in conjunction with the IRCS.

In fact, the UAE Red Crescent Society has been ranked first among the Arab societies and seventh in the world in providing help to the needy and victims of natural calamities and wars, according to the quarterly report of the International Red Crescent and Red Cross Societies. The quarterly report of the International Federation for 1996 showed that the UAE, represented by its Red Crescent Society, ranked among the top ten donors in the world. It said that the UAE ranked first among donors in the Arab world and seventh in the world after the US, Germany, Sweden, Norway, Britain and Holland for donations made during the past three months. The RCS expenditure on relief and aid programmes carried out in 1995 totalled Dh 160 million.

THE ECONOMY

Tracking of the Gross Domestic Product (GDP), taken as a barometer of the economic climate in the UAE, indicates that growth is being sustained despite a degree of turbulence in the global picture. In fact, over the period 1994-1995 the UAE showed a growth rate of a healthy 6.6 per cent. This was attributable to continued development of the non-oil sector as well as to a rise in the average oil price from US$15.6 in 1994 to US$16.7 in 1995. The oil price rise brought the oil sector's contribution to the total GDP up to 34.2 per cent in 1995, from 33.4 per cent in 1994, thus bucking the trend of recent years for a gradual decline of the oil sector's proportional role in the overall GDP.

Contribution to GDP

SECTOR	1994*	1995**
		(in Millions AED)
Agriculture, Live Animals & Fishing	3328	3550
Mining Industries		
A. Crude Oil	45154	49200
B. Other	421	450
Manufacturing Industries	11753	12500
Water & Electricity	2889	3210
Construction & Building	12830	13300
Wholesale & Retail Trade		
Restaurants & Hotels	16806	17800
Transportation, Storage & Communication	8297	8500
Financing, Insurance & Real Estate		
A. Financing & Insurance	6873	7150
B. Real Estate	10770	11700
Other Services	1475	1640
(Minus) Imputed Bank Service Charges	2450	2550
Producers of Government Services	15914	16320
Household	1008	1200
Gross Domestic Product	**135068**	**143970**
Total Non-oil Sectors	**89914**	**94770**

Source: Ministry of Planning and Central Bank Report 1995. * Estimates ** Preliminary Figures

Economic Indicators (Dh. bn.)

	1994	1993	1992
G.D.P.	135.1	132.1	131.7
National Income	110.0	107.8	108.3
National Savings	19.4	21.6	25.3
Final Consumption	87.5	83.2	80.7
Final Government Consumption	24.2	23.4	22.8
Final Private Consumption	63.3	59.8	57.9
Gross Fixed Capital Form.	37.3	36.4	29.8
Emp. Compensation	36.2	34.5	31.9
Per Capita National Income (Dh 000's)	49.3	51.7	53.9
Per Capita Final Consu. Exp. (Dh 000's)	39.3	40.0	40.1
General Average of Wages (Dh000's)	34.7	34.8	34.7
General Average of Lab. Prod. (Dh000's)	86.2	86.5	84.5

Source: Central Statistics Dept., Ministry of Planning 1996.

GENERAL ANALYSIS OF PERFORMANCE IN 1995

Preliminary analysis of the UAE's GDP for 1995, made in the annual economic report of the Ministry of Planning, published in March 1996, was just under Dh144 billion as against Dh135 billion in 1994. The rise in GDP is attributed to the high US dollar rate, an improvement in oil prices and the intensified economic activity in the country.

Banking and monetary indicators also showed encouraging performance in 1995 as total liquidity went up 11 per cent, from Dh89.3 billion in 1994 to Dh99 billion in 1995. Stock markets also made progress as the indicators at the Abu Dhabi Commercial Bank rose to 234 points, or 11.6 per cent rise over results of 1994.

The average price of OPEC's basket of seven crudes stood at around $16.8 in 1995, compared with $15.5 in 1994. The UAE earned nearly a billion dollars more in oil revenue during 1995 than in 1994, as a result of the increase in crude prices. Earnings surged by nearly 8.3 per cent to $12.77 billion from around $11.79 billion in 1994, boosting the country's GDP by 2.3 per cent to $37.08 billion from $36.26 billion.

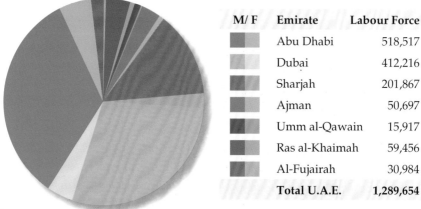

M/ F	Emirate	Labour Force
	Abu Dhabi	518,517
	Dubai	412,216
	Sharjah	201,867
	Ajman	50,697
	Umm al-Qawain	15,917
	Ras al-Khaimah	59,456
	Al-Fujairah	30,984
	Total U.A.E.	**1,289,654**

The GDP was expected to grow at a rate of 5.6 per cent in 1996 over 1995. GDP of the non-oil sectors was also expected to rise, especially the manufacturing, water, electricity, internal trade, tourism, banking, insurance and construction sectors.

Workers by Economic Sectors (000's)	1994	1993	1992
Agriculture, Livestock & Fishing	65.6	64.0	59.6
Mining & Quarrying	12.1	11.7	11.0
Manufacturing	92.5	87.6	81.2
Electricity & Water	22.3	21.8	21.1
Construction	149.7	140.1	133.4
Trade, Restaurants & Hotels	168.8	159.5	110.9
Transport, Storage & Communications	85.5	82.3	78.1
Financing, Insurance & Real Estate	43.5	41.0	20.1
Services	272.9	251.6	284.0
Total	912.9	251.6	284.0

Source: Central Statistics Dept., Ministry of Planning 1996.

EMIRATES INDUSTRIAL BANK REPORT

According to the Emirates Industrial Bank Report of January 1996 the UAE's GDP grew by 6.5 per cent in 1995, reaching Dh143.5 billion, compared with Dh134.8 billion in 1994. The oil sector contribution to the GDP increased 7 per cent to Dh48.3 billion from Dh45.0 billion in 1994, due to an 8 per cent increase in the international oil price in 1995. The oil sector's share in the GDP rose to 33.7 per cent in 1995 from 33.4 per cent a year earlier while the non-oil sector's share slightly declined to 66.3 per cent from 66.6 per cent in 1994. Despite its slight fall in proportion to the overall GDP, the actual non-oil sector showed a real growth of approximately 6.0 per cent in the year. Thus, its contribution to the GDP increased to Dh95.2 billion compared with Dh89.8 billion a year earlier. The bank said the GDP's growth in 1995 shows the non-oil sector is likely to expand further this year. Meanwhile the report stated that the banking sector grew 6 per cent, adding Dh7.2 billion, or 5 per cent, of the overall 1995 GDP.

GDP (figures are in billions AED)	1995 (Provisional)	1994
Oil	143.5	143.8
Non-Oil	48.3	45.0
Manufacturing	11.8	11.2
Construction	14.0	13.2
Trade	16.0	14.9
Finance	7.5	6.8
FOREIGN TRADE		
Exports (inc. Oil & Gas)	96.0	92.9
Imports	73.0	72.2
Re-exports	15.0	13.3

Source: Emirates Industrial Bank Annual Report 1995

The Emirates Industrial Bank Annual Report points out that construction, finance and trade were the most buoyant sectors in the non-oil economy, out-performing manufacturing. Concerns that the construction boom might diminish in 1995 proved unfounded. Apart from continuing high levels of activity in infrastructure both in Abu Dhabi and Dubai, new commercial and residential projects continued to be implemented in the two emirates. Construction activity, in turn, stimulated growth in finance and real estate and to a lesser extent in manufacturing. Since 1990 construction and finance have grown by nearly 35 per cent and trade by over 30 per cent. Manufacturing has performed more modestly growing by around 15 per cent.

FEDERAL GOVERNMENT'S PUBLIC FINANCES

Revenues to the Federal Government increased significantly, by 12 per cent, in 1995, compared with 1994 and most of this increase was made up from collections by federal agencies of new customs duties (e.g. 50 per cent on tobacco products) plus increases in some service charges. The overall picture of revenues and expenditures by the Federal Government is indicated by the following table.

Items (in Million AED)	1994	1995*
Oil Revenues		
1.1 Emirates Contributions	16,437	16,857.1
1.2 Other Revenues	12,731	12,708.2
Public Expenditure	15,889.1	17,800.2
2.1 Current Expenditure	15,154.2	17,257.2
2.2 Development Expenditure	734.3	543.0
2.3 Equity Participation and Capital Payments	1.4	-
Surplus (+) or Deficit (-)	+547.1	(-)943.1

* Adjusted Figures Source: Ministry of Finance and Industry.

As the above table indicates public expenditure increased to Dh17.8 billion in fiscal 1995, compared to Dh15.9 billion in 1994. The percentage increase in expenditure, i.e. 12 per cent, is thus the same as the percentage increase in revenues. The increase itself was due to settlement of certain government dues. A breakdown of the expenditure was presented in the 1995 Central Bank Report as follows:

- Current Expenditure rose by Dh2.1 billion (13.9 per cent) in 1995, to reach Dh 17.3 billion, against Dh15.2 billion in 1994, forming 96.9 per cent of total public expenditure at the end of 1995.
- Development Expenditure dropped by Dh191 million in the fiscal year 1995, reaching Dh 543 million in 1995, against Dh 743.3 million in 1994.
- Equity Participation and Capital Payments: No equity payments or capital payments were recorded during 1995. This item reached Dh1.4 million at the end of 1994. The deficit in the Federal Government's budget reached Dh 943 million in 1995, against a surplus of Dh 547 million in 1994.

FEDERAL BUDGET 1996

The UAE Cabinet approved, on 8 April 1996, a Dh18.254 billion federal budget for 1996, leaving an anticipated deficit of Dh858 million compared to a projected deficit of Dh1.046 billion built into the 1995 budget. The 1996 budget envisaged expenditure of Dh18.254 billion, compared to Dh17.949 billion in the 1995 budget. The budget allotted Dh17.547 million for the Federal National Council, Dh580 million for the Emirates University, Dh190 million for the recently-established Radio and Television Authority, Dh255 million for the Higher Colleges of Technology, Dh16 million for the General Committee for Information, Dh8.019 million for the Administrative Development Institute and Dh6.15 million for the Federal Environmental Agency, FEA.

INFLATION

The inflation rate during 1995 was around 4.5 to 5 per cent.

BALANCE OF PAYMENTS AND FOREIGN TRADE

Preliminary estimates in the 1995 Central Bank Report of the UAE balance of payments indicate that an overall surplus of Dh2.8 billion was achieved for 1995, an increase of 17.8 per cent compared to 1994. The current account surplus meanwhile rose by 23.5 per cent and this

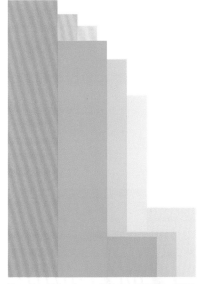

Foreign Trade	1994	1993	1992
Exports	97984	93050	88940
Imports	83606	77069	64328
Trade Balance	14318	15982	24612

Source: Central Statistics Dept., Ministry of Planning 1996.

was achieved in the face of a decline in the trade balance from Dh17.2 billion in 1994 to Dh16.9 billion in 1995. The trade balance was affected by an increase in imports through Jebel Ali Free Zone, amounting to Dh8.4 billion in 1995 compared to Dh5.3 billion in 1994, bringing the total value of UAE imports in 1995 to Dh86.2 billion, against 83.3 billion in 1994. Interestingly, 45 per cent of imports to the UAE in 1995 came from Asia, 39 per cent from Europe and 10 per cent from American countries.

The value of oil exports showed a 6.7 per cent increase in 1995, rising from Dh41.8 billion to Dh44.6 billion. This was brought about as a result of an increase in the average oil price during 1995, which showed an increase of 7.3 per cent with an average price per barrel of US$16.74. In addition, the gas sector continued to develop, with revenues from gas exports rising from Dh5.1 billion in 1994 to Dh5.5 billion in 1995.

Sector	Average Annual Growth (1972-1994)
Crude oil	21.5%
Agriculture	16.5%
General industries	23.6%
Construction and building	17%
Restaurants and hotels	17.4%
Real estate	18.8%
Other services	20%
Government services	20%
Non-oil GDP	18%

Source: Ministry of Planning, November 1995

CAPITAL INVESTMENT IN UAE INDUSTRIES

The overall capital invested in industries in the UAE reached Dh13.7 billion at the end of 1995, an increase of 30 per cent compared to 1991 when investments were Dh10.5 billion, according to statistics released by the Industrial Development Department of the Ministry of Finance and Industry. Annual growth rate was about 1.9 per cent in 1992 while it was 11 per cent in 1993, 3 per cent in 1994 and 11.7 per cent in 1995.

The capital invested in Abu Dhabi in 1991 was Dh482.5 million, reaching Dh1.6 billion during 1995, a growth rate of 227 per cent. The annual growth rate recorded in Abu Dhabi was about 10 per cent in 1995. Capital invested in Dubai reached Dh6.357 billion in 1991, compared with Dh7.7 billion in 1995, a growth rate of 21 per cent. Annual growth rate recorded in Dubai was 11.5 per cent in 1995. Dubai topped the list in overall capital investments in 1995 with 56.2 per cent. In Sharjah, capital investments in 1991 reached Dh1.155 billion, compared with Dh1.543 billion in 1995, with an overall growth rate of 33.1 per cent and annual growth rate of 18.6 per cent in 1995. In Ajman, invested capital in 1991 reached Dh448 million, increasing to Dh618 million in 1995, with an overall growth rate of 38 per cent and an annual growth rate of 29 per cent in 1995. In Ras al-Khaimah, invested capital in 1991 reached Dh1.304 billion, rising to Dh1.359 billion in 1995, an increase of 13 per cent. The annual growth percentage was 7.5 per cent last year. Capital invested in Umm al-Qaiwain rose from Dh331.8 million in 1991 to Dh351.7 million last year, with a growth rate of 6 per cent. Capital invested in Fujairah in 1991 reached Dh508 million compared with Dh526 million in 1995, with an annual growth rate of 3.6 per cent.

FINANCIAL SECTOR

COMMERCIAL BANKS IN THE UAE

THE AGGREGATED BALANCE SHEET of commercial banks reached Dh180.89 billion by the end of 1995 as against Dh171.60 billion at the end of 1994. Net foreign assets of commercial banks stood at Dh35.98 billion at the end of 1995, an 11.2 per cent increase over the previous year. Meanwhile, bank credit extended by commercial banks operating in the UAE increased by Dh8.26 billion or 8.8 per cent, reaching Dh102.01 billion, primarily as a result of increased credit facilities provided to UAE residents. Most of the borrowed funds were allocated to industrial and trading enterprises. Loans extended to the Government formed 15.3 per cent of the total.

If the domestic credit profile can be used as a measure of the overall economy then the figures suggest overall growth and a rather brisk economic climate. Credit to the trade sector increased by 9.8 per cent (Dh30.40 billion at end 1995); credit to the mining and industry sector rose by 16.6 per cent; to the construction sector by 8.1 per cent while credit to other activities rose by 15.5 per cent.

Analysis of the overall situation for commercial banks in the UAE at the end of 1995 indicates that the total of capital accounts and reserves of banks operating in the UAE reached Dh21.66 billion, an increase of 10.5 per cent over the end of 1994 figures.

The Emirates Industrial Bank 1995 Annual Report remarks that the UAE bank performance is worthy of note in the Gulf region as a whole with five banks present in the list of the ten best-performing banks within the GCC countries. All UAE banks, it states, now comfortably exceed the 8 per cent capital to assets ratio prescribed by the BIS (Bank for International Settlements) for commercial banks.

CENTRAL BANK ACHIEVEMENTS

The Central Bank has responsibility for organizing banking and financial markets in the country and remains committed to creating a stable economic framework in which trade and industry, as well as the individual residents of the UAE, will continue to prosper. In this context it issued a number of important decisions during the year. Resolution of the Board of Directors of the Central Bank, issued on 18 April 1995, regulated the financial sector, seeking to control activities of investment companies. The resolution of the Board, No. 164/8/94 aims at protecting investors' monies as well as ensuring that services offered by financial and investment consultants comply with recognized international standards. The resolution states that no person, whether natural or juridical, shall carry on the business of financial investment in the UAE unless such a person is licensed to do so by the Central Bank. The minimum required capital for investment companies was set at Dh25 million with provisions for increases according to the activities in which the company is engaged. The national shareholding in such companies shall be not less that 51 per cent of the paid up capital. Licenses may be granted to foreign investment companies to establish branches or representative offices if the Board deems such licensing as complementary to banking and financial services and in the interest of the national economy. An additional set of

criteria were laid down to ensure that only suitably qualified people are engaged in this area of business in the UAE.

A second resolution, No. 126/5/95, dated 25 June 1995, was passed in order to regulate financial and monetary intermediaries. According to this resolution, the business of the intermediary shall be confined to intermediating in the sale and purchase of domestic and foreign stocks and bonds, currencies and commodities, as well as intermediating in money market transactions. Only persons who have obtained a license from the Central Bank may undertake such business in the country.

DEVELOPMENTS IN BANKING

Whilst the number of national banks operating in the UAE remained unchanged, at 19, the number of branches and cash offices of national banks increased from 230 (191 branches and 39 cash offices) at the end of 1994 to 241 (204 branches and 37 cash offices) at the end of 1995. Meanwhile the number of foreign and commercial banks remained unchanged at 28 with 118 branches.

Banks and Insurance

	1994	1993	1992
No. of Banks	47	47	47
No. of Bank Branches	349	335	326
Currency (Dh. bn.)	6.0	5.7	5.1
Monetary Deposits (Dh. bn.)	13.2	12.5	9.9
Quasi Monetary (Dh. bn.)	54.7	50.3	54.6
No. of Insurance Est.	223	223	216
Premiums Paid (Dh. mn.)	2,247	2,013	1,649
Claims Paid (Dh. mn.)	824	764	740

Source: Central Statistics Dept., Ministry of Planning 1996.

LENDING RESTRICTIONS IMPOSED ON BANKS

The Central Bank imposed tough lending restrictions on commercial banks in 1995, many of which were over committed to trade and construction sector borrowers. Local banks responded by increasing their capital to counter the effect of a rule limiting lending to a private client to 7 per cent of a bank's capital, but the move was resisted by larger foreign banks, some of whom moved their larger loan facilities to offshore units in nearby Bahrain. The Central Bank also brought in regulations requiring insurance companies to increase their minimum capital to Dh25 million in three years, and to Dh50 million in six years.

PRIVATIZATION

The Governments of Abu Dhabi and Dubai committed themselves to off-loading shares in profitable state ventures, a move that analysts said looked like the first step towards ensuring a greater role for private investors in the planned stock exchange. The Abu Dhabi Government released a list of five state industrial ventures it intended to denationalize and increased the number of proposed industrial ventures open to the private sector to 51.

The Government of Dubai said that it would privatize EPPCO, which markets petrol and other oil products. The Abu Dhabi Government indicated private finance from both home and abroad would be involved in its plans for the downstream development of its oil and gas industry.

The annual meeting of the Council of Arab Financial Institutions held in April 1996 in Tunis, approved a UAE proposition for a $500 million programme for financing private sector projects in Arab countries.

SHARE TRADING

The first automated registration and trading system for shares in the UAE, Union Securities, was launched by Union National Bank in Abu Dhabi on 7 October 1995, paving the way for the establishment of an official UAE stock market. Whilst considerable progress was made during the period under review towards establishment of a stock market in the UAE, initial plans for opening a Bourse in 1996 were later postponed with a view to establishment in 1997. Meanwhile investment returns from traded shares averaged around 25 per cent during 1995, more than double the 10.5 per cent achieved in 1994.

FIGEX '95

The International Financial Exhibition, FIGEX '95, was opened on 9 October 1995 by Sheikh Sultan bin Khalifa Al Nahyan, Chief of Abu Dhabi Crown Prince's Court and Member of the Executive Council.

THE OIL AND GAS INDUSTRY

T HE UAE IS AT THE FOREFRONT of the world's oil, gas and hydrocarbon producing and exporting countries, and its capacity has steadily increased since H.H. Sheikh Zayed took over the reins of power in Abu Dhabi in August 1966. Although oil was first discovered in the UAE during the 1930s, it was not exported until the beginning of the 1960s. Its first oil flowed from the Umm Shaif offshore field in 1962, ever since oil-revenues have underpinned the country's vast development programme. UAE energy products play an important role in international oil markets and help the global economy develop and prosper.

The creation in 1971 of the Abu Dhabi National Oil Company (ADNOC) and of other national oil companies in the UAE, including the Dubai Petroleum Company, marked an important milestone in development of the oil industry. Another important development was the establishment in 1988 of the Supreme Petroleum Council, headed by Sheikh Khalifa bin Zayed Al Nahyan, Heir Apparent of Abu Dhabi and Deputy Supreme Commander of the Armed Forces. The SPC determines oil and gas policy in Abu Dhabi, and in this context fostered the ADNOC plan to raise its proven oil and

gas reserves through increased exploration and drilling, and through development of its production capacity, whilst creating new oil industries in an effort to maximize exploitation of the UAE's hydrocarbon wealth. At the same time, the UAE has a firm policy of adhering to its OPEC quota of 2.161 million barrels per day (bpd).Other milestones in the development of the UAE oil and gas industries were the opening of the important oil refinery in Al-Ruwais and establishment of the Abu Dhabi Gas Liquefaction Company Ltd (ADGAS).

EXPLORATION FOR OIL

A concession signed by Abu Dhabi in 1954 granted offshore drilling rights to the Abu Dhabi Marine Areas Company (ADMA). In 1962, Dubai gave an offshore concession to the Dubai Petroleum Company and a further concession was given by Sharjah in 1971 to the Al-Hilal Company. Oil was found in commercial quantities in Abu Dhabi in 1958, in Dubai in 1966, in Sharjah in 1972 and Ras al-Khaimah in 1983. Abu Dhabi is the largest producer of oil of the seven emirates. With the development of the oil industry in Abu Dhabi, it became necessary to create oil service companies ancillary to the concessionaires. The most important of the companies to be created was ADNOC in November 1971.

In 1983 an agreement between the Government of Umm al-Qaiwain and Deutsche Texaco was abandoned by the company. In 1984, other concessions were granted to two other groups. However, from that time until the present no important oil finds have been made in Umm al-Qaiwain.

Oil drilling began in Ras al-Khaimah in 1964 when Union Oil of California obtained a concession for drilling in all the territories of the emirate, but it abandoned the concession in 1972. In May 1973 a new concession covering 2200 square kilometres of the offshore territories of Ras al-Khaimah was given to a Dutch and an Australian company. They were later joined by other companies, and eventually the Government of Ras al-Khaimah obtained 50 per cent of the shares of these companies. Drilling began in 1975, and in July 1976 the drilling led to the discovery of oil in the Yabad field which is 25 miles off the coast. But circumstances delayed the development programmes and the company abandoned the work area in 1979.

The American company, Gulf, in 1978 signed an exploration agreement for the land areas of Ras al-Khaimah. In 1982 it abandoned part of the concession and then abandoned the concession entirely in 1987. Ras al-Khaimah gave two offshore concessions to Gulf Oil and International Petroleum of Canada, and in 1983 it was announced that Gulf Oil had discovered oil in the Saleh Field, 26 miles from the Ras al-Khaimah coast. Then in February 1984 there were ceremonies marking the beginning of production of the Saleh field which began to produce 5000 barrels per day and 25 million cubic feet of gas. At that point the Government of Ras al-Khaimah and the operating company at the Saleh Field agreed that the Government would own 50 per cent of the field. The average daily production of oil in Ras al-Khaimah was around

8500 barrels per day in 1984. This rose to 9117 barrels in 1985. There was little further development in Ras al-Khaimah oil production until H.H. Sheikh Saqr bin Mohammed Al Qassimi, the Ruler of Ras al-Khaimah, in 1996, signed an oil and gas exploration agreement with a group of American companies. This concession allowed them to explore and drill for oil and gas in the land and offshore areas of the emirate.

At the beginning of the 1970s the Rezeef Oil and Gas company searched for oil in the offshore areas of Fujairah. The concession area covered 28,000 square kilometres but it was allowed to lapse. Another search began in 1984 when the Government of Fujairah granted a concession to two groups of companies: one received a concession for an area of 2629 square kilometres of offshore territory and the other was given an area of 12,545 square kilometres on the northern borders of the emirate.

CRUDE OIL PRODUCTION

The first commercial oilfield was discovered in the Umm al-Shaif offshore area of Abu Dhabi in 1962, followed by an onshore discovery the following year. Dubai's Fatah oilfield was discovered in 1966, and the first shipment took place in 1969. The Margham field, also in Dubai, was discovered in 1982. As for Sharjah, oil was discovered there in 1972 in the Mubarak field and exports began in 1984. Meanwhile a second deposit, the Al-Saja land field, also in Sharjah, was discovered in 1980. In recent years, the UAE's oil production has been pre-determined, by agreement with OPEC, at 2.161 million barrels per day.

Abu Dhabi

Since it was established the Abu Dhabi National Oil Company (ADNOC) has been a partner in oil affairs with the foreign companies operating in the emirate. The initial basis for cooperation was that ADNOC, on behalf of the Government of Abu Dhabi, entered into formal partnership arrangements with foreign oil companies licensed to operate in Abu Dhabi, with ADNOC holding a 25 per cent share of the capital of these companies. Abu Dhabi's first commercial oil sales took place in March 1973. In December 1974, a second agreement was negotiated under which ADNOC raised the government share in the capital in the foreign based oil companies' local operations from 25 per cent to 70 per cent.

The emirate's first refinery became operational on the island of Umm al-Nar on 27 April 1980, with a refining capacity of 15,000 barrels a day, but almost immediately plans were laid for its expansion to raise its capacity to 75,000 barrels a day. Work on a second refinery began in April 1981, with this becoming operational in 1984 at 66 per cent of its planned capacity. The plant's operational status rose to to 88 per cent of planned capacity in 1985 and reached nearly 110 per cent in the first quarter of 1988. Meanwhile, work began on the construction of the Al-Ruwais Industrial Area refinery on the 15 March 1978, which became operational in July 1981. This is now considered to be the emirate's major refinery with a production capacity of 120,000 barrels of crude oil per day. Completion of the project made UAE not only self sufficient, but also an exporter, in refined products.

Abu Dhabi spent nearly $5.9 billion in 1994 on oil expansion projects, with $3 billion going into boosting refining output capacity and setting up of the country's first petro-chemical industry. ADNOC's new five-year plan (1996-2000) covers exploration and development in its land and sea concession areas, in addition to development programmes for some gas and oil fields which have recently been explored. The company's main land projects in Abu Dhabi include development of the Bab oil field and completion of the oil installations in the Dhabeya, Rumaitha, and Shanayel fields, as well as the oil and gas injection projects for increasing reserves and upgrading the electrical power in the Bab, Bu Hassa and Sahel fields.

Abu Dhabi Company for Onshore Oil Operations (ADCO)
The Abu Dhabi Company for Onshore Oil Operations (ADCO) was established in October 1978. In February 1979 it became responsible for the administration of operations in the concession area which covered 21,000 square kilometres. It also took over the 60 per cent of the shares owned by ADNOC. The remainder of the shares were distributed among six foreign companies. Exploration activities commencing in 1936 by the company's predecessor led to discovery of oil in commercial quantities in the Bab field in 1958, with exports of oil commencing from this field in 1963.

ADCO operates the Bab field, together with Asab, Bu Hassa, Sahel, Shah and Jarn Yaphour. A network of pipelines connects these fields to refineries at Ruwais and Umm al-Nar, as well as the Jebel Dhanna export terminal. Over time a collection of oil fields have been discovered in Abu Dhabi land areas and there remain a number of still to be explored areas which are expected to reveal oil and gas in commercial quantities in the future. The huge producing fields and the fields which have recently been discovered but which are not yet producing have undergone major development, particularly over the past ten to fifteen years.

With most of Abu Dhabi's crude oil production coming from land-based wells and the bulk of this being exported, a need arose for a suitable tanker loading facility. Construction of Jebel al-Dhanna port began in 1962 and was completed at the beginning of 1963 enabling the first shipment of 34,000 tons crude oil from the Bab field to be made from this port. Extension of port facilities, completed in 1971, included 13 tanks with a total capacity of 5.7 million barrels. The total oil export capacity became 1280 million barrels a day and the port was capable of receiving giant tankers on its fourth dock which could load up to 300,000 tons of oil. ADCO recently announced plans to expand capacity at the Sahel Field, currently producing 30,000 bpd, by 1998.

Abu Dhabi Marine Areas Operating Company (ADMA-OPCO)

In 1954 the Abu Dhabi Marine Areas Company Ltd (ADMA) was established. The company began survey operations in 1955 and made its first discovery of oil in commercial quantities in the Umm al-Shaif Offshore Field in March 1957, followed by the discovery of the Zakum Field in April 1963. Finds of lesser importance were discovered by other companies. On 9 December 1974 ADNOC obtained 60 per cent of the offshore concession rights of the ADMA Company Ltd.

The Umm al-Shaif Field was the first to be developed for production, beginning with 30,000 barrels a day. Development operations continued and eventually its production capacity rose to 200,000 barrels per day. The Zakum Field's production capacity is now estimated to be nearly 300,000 barrels per day.

A port at Das Island was constructed to handle oil production from the offshore fields with first shipments leaving from here on 4 July 1962. Thereafter, sufficient facilities and services were established on the island to cope with increased production.

ADMA-OPCO operates the Umm Shaif, Lower Zakum, Al-Bunduq and Abu al-Bukhoush fields. In October 1995 ADMA-OPCO announced preparation of long-term plans to develop Das Island, where all its oil and gas export facilities are located. The plan involves development of installations on the island over the next 30 years and runs parallel with ADMA-OPCO's projects to increase oil output capacity to face growing demand by Japan and its other main oil clients.

The Company for the Development of the Zakum Field (ZADCO)

ZADCO was established in 1977 with the aim of developing the upper part of the Zakum field in the land areas of Abu Dhabi which ADMA had relinquished. It began operations in the Zakum field in July 1977 and an ambitious plan was laid down with

the aim of bringing the production up to 500,000 barrels per day. Today it is one of the most important producing fields in the world. A joint-venture between ADNOC and ZADCO operates the Upper Zakum, Umm al-Dalkh, Satah and Arzanah fields with production from these processed on Zirku island.

Mubarraz Oil Company Ltd

The first well was dug in the Mubarraz field on 4 May 1969 with an initial production of about 3000 barrels per day. In late 1974 the concession for the area west of Mubarraz was given to the Mubarraz Oil Company Ltd which was established as a partnership

between the Maruzen Oil Company, the Daiku Oil Company and the Nippon Minerals Company. At the same time, the Mubarraz Oil Company signed an operations agreement under the terms of which it became the company which is responsible for the exploration and development of the concession areas. Oil was discovered in the Mubarraz Field in 1969. The field is located between the Zakum and the Bab fields at a distance of 50 kilometres from the city of Abu Dhabi. Mubarraz island, lying west of Abu Dhabi city, has become an important port for company operations which began oil production from the Mubarraz Field on 5 June 1973 with a production capacity of 20,000 barrels day. Facilities and installations were built on the island to be used for storing and exporting the oil from a floating dock.

Al-Bunduq Company

This company was established in 1970 and was granted a concession for the development of the Al-Bunduq Field. When the maritime borders between Abu Dhabi and Qatar were established in March 1969, it was agreed to split the Al-Bunduq field into halves between the two countries, whereafter commercial exploitation of the field began. However, ADMA of Abu Dhabi took over its development in the interests of both countries. ADMA relinquished its rights to the development of the Al-Bunduq field and on 23 July 1970 the Al-Bunduq Oil Company was established to exploit this area. A plan was laid down for the development of the Al-Bunduq Field to produce 30,000 barrels a day. Oil was transported from the central gathering platform at Al-Bunduq Field to Das Island where it was processed for export.

The Amiradahis Abu Dhabi Oil Company

In 1970,the Ocean Oil Corporation was granted a 3150 square kilometres concession to drill for oil near Arzana Island, north west of the city of Abu Dhabi. The company relinquished parts of the areas of its concession at different times. Finally, the name of the company became the Amiridahis Abu Dhabi Oil Company in March 1971. It found oil in commercial quantities for the first time with Arzana Well No. (1) in 1973. In 1976 it developed the Arzana Field and in 1985 there were other development operations in the field. The company began to produce in 1979 at a rate of 8900 barrels per day and in stages the production reached 11,500 barrels per day.

Total Abu al-Bakhoush Company

The Total Abu al-Bakhoush Company operates the Abu al-Bakhoush Field which lies about 180 kilometres northwest of the city of Abu Dhabi in the middle of the Gulf. The Total Abu al-Bakhoush Company is a subsidiary of the French oil company, Total. In 1979, oil was discovered on some levels of the Abu al-Bakhoush field after the company had drilled eight wells, beginning in July 1975. Production began in this field in July 1984 and the production increased gradually until, in 1985, it became nearly 65,000 barrels per day rising to 80,000 barrels per day in 1986. Oil was exported from a floating tanker near the production platform.

Dubai

Oil was first discovered in offshore regions of Dubai by the Dubai Petroleum Company on 7 June 1966. The field, declared to be of commercial scale, was given the name of *Fatah*. Rapid development led to first production on 6 September 1969, and to Dubai's first shipment of 180,000 barrels of oil on 22 September of the same year. During development of the Fatah field, a second offshore field was located some ten miles southwest of Fatah and development of this Southwest Fatah field led to production in October 1972. Meanwhile, another offshore field in Dubai waters, the Falah Field, was explored in 1972 and in spite of the its small size it began production in June 1978. Dubai's Rashid offshore field was discovered in 1973 and began production in March 1979.

The Dubai Petroleum Company, which operates the Fateh, Southwest Fateh, Falah and Rashid offshore fields, completed eight wells during 1995. The Fatah D development project, the first in the world to depend exclusively upon horizontal well drilling and water injection, began in 1993 with the aim of optimizing production from Dubai's hydrocarbon resources. As reserves become depleted the emirate's oil output has dropped back, showing a steady downward trend of 360,000, 310,000 and 300,000 barrels per day in 1992, 1993 and 1994 respectively. Faced with this situation Dubai is looking at the possibility of establishing itself as an international oil storage and blending centre similar to Singapore.

Development of Dubai's oil refinery, a private venture operated by the Western Oil Company , a subsidiary of the Indian Gadgil Western Group, situated in Jebel Ali, is an important development in Dubai's oil industry. Most of the refinery's products are sold as derivatives in Middle Eastern and Indian markets.

Sharjah

Oil activities began in Sharjah in 1969 when the Al-Hilal Oil Company received an offshore concession. Survey work under this agreement began in 1972 with its first exploratory well: Mubarak Well No. (1). Towards the end of 1972 the company

succeeded in finding oil at this site in commercial quantities: a first time for Sharjah, with the well flowing at 13,955 barrels per day. This was followed shortly afterwards by Mubarak 2 which initially produced 59,090 barrels per day of oil and 2.3 million cubic feet per day of natural gas; and by Mubarak 3 whose production was roughly similar to that of Mubarak 2. In 1975, the company found significant oil deposits at Mubarak 4. Meanwhile Sharjah's first shipment of oil took place in June 1974, making it the third of the emirates to become an oil producer after Abu Dhabi and Dubai.

Crystal Oil Company was granted an 850 square mile block for oil exploration off Sharjah in January 1974. This was followed in 1978 by a 2340 square kilometres land concession granted to the Amoco Company, also in Sharjah. The latter led to the emirate's first land-based oil discovery in the Al-Saja region in May 1980. Associated gas reserves of the same field were estimated to be 2 trillion cubic feet. The field was officially inaugurated on 20 June 1982 and the first shipment from it was exported on 21 July 1982.

The estimated production capacity of the Al-Saja field is about 80,000 barrels per day since the production of three wells amounted to 9000 barrels of light oil and 100 million cubic feet of natural gas.

Construction of the new oil refinery in the Port of Hamriyya in Sharjah is considered to be one of the most important developments in Sharjah's oil industry. Operation of the refinery will come under the supervision of a new company to be called the Sharjah Oil Refining Company Ltd. With a capacity of 40,000 barrels per day, the refinery will produce all products including aircraft fuel.

Production is expected to start at the refinery towards the end of 1996. The refinery, the first to be set up in Sharjah, is estimated to cost between $60 million and $70 million and would start with a refining capacity of 20,000 barrels per day, to be raised later to 45,000 barrels per day.

Ras al-Khaimah

The relatively small Saleh field, which lies off Ras al-Khaimah, presently produces only around 1000 bpd. There are still hopes of new discoveries in the emirate and in January 1996 an agreement was signed between Ras al-Khaimah and a consortium of US companies for oil and gas exploration throughout the emirate, to be carried out by Ras al-Khaimah Oil and Gas Company Ltd.

NATURAL GAS PRODUCTION

The UAE began the production of natural gas in 1983 when a gas liquefaction plant, the first of its kind in the Gulf region, was established for the offshore fields on Das Island. Later a land-based plant was constructed in the Al-Ruwais area in order to liquefy gas from Abu Dhabi's land fields. This was followed by a third plant in the Jebel Ali region and by a series of projects in the Habshan, Bab and Asab fields in Abu Dhabi, and by additional plants in Dubai and Sharjah. In 1991 the UAE's production of natural gas reached 32.86 billion cubic metres, a figure that had increased to 34.37 billion cubic metres in 1994. Gas production in the Emirates took on a new dimension in 1995 as a result of the execution of a number of huge projects. Natural liquid gas production stood at 275,000 barrels per day in 1991 and around 220,000 barrels per day in 1993 and 1994.

Abu Dhabi's Natural Gas
The Abu Dhabi Gas Liquefaction Company, (ADGAS)

As the first of its kind in the region, ADGAS was established with the aim of utilizing the huge quantities of gas which are released with the production of crude oil, and transforming it into a source of clean energy. Development of the gas sector has resulted in increased national income. Instead of burning off the gas, which is environmentally undesirable, gas production has provided a means to meet an important element of Japan's surging energy demands with a source of clean fuel. A 1982 agreement between the Tokyo Electricity Company and ADGAS provided for the

purchase by the Japanese company, each year, of nearly 2 million tons of natural liquid gas (methane) and nearly 800,000 tons of propane. The agreement became effective from the date of first production from the Das Island plant whose construction began in 1973 and took four years to complete. The first exports were shipped from the ADGAS plant to Japan in April 1977. A specialized fleet of tankers designed to ensure security and safety on the long journey of more than 6500 miles between Das Island and Japan was employed in the gas transportation. The receiving company in Japan was NIPCO.

Since establishment of the service the ADGAS fleet of tankers have made over 700 trips transporting liquid gas to NIPCO and a recent agreement, signed in

October 1990, provided that ADGAS would double the quantities of natural liquid gas to NIPCO over a period of 26 years, beginning in 1994 and ending in 2019. To enable ADGAS to handle the necessary increase in its production of natural liquid gas, it was decided to set up a third processing stream which would be the biggest of its kind for natural gas liquefaction worldwide. The project, which cost nearly $1.3 billion, was finally completed in April 1994 with production commencing in June of the same year.

The production increase and fulfilment of the NIPCO contract required construction of four new tankers for transporting the natural liquid gas, each with a capacity of 130 million tons. These were built by the Mitsui Heavy Industries Company and handed over to ADGAS on schedule at the beginning of 1994 when they began transporting liquid gas from Das Island to the Port of Tokyo. ADNOC also contracted with Finland to construct four other tankers for carrying liquid gas with a capacity of 135,000 tons. Two of these tankers have already been handed over to ADNOC, whilst the third and fourth ships will be handed over in March and June 1997.

Meanwhile a new development in relations between ADGAS and NIPCO emerged at the end of April 1996 when the two companies signed an agreement on a marine shipment program, stipulating that ADGAS would export to NIPCO 4.5 million tons of methane gas in 76 shipments during the period April 1996 through March 1997; constituting the largest number of shipments to Japan ever to be made in one year. The new agreement also called for the export of seven shipments of 315,000 tons of propane gas during the same period.

A contract signed by ADGAS and the Japanese company ITOCHU involves supply of 48 shipments of pentane plus from its Das Island plant over a three-year period. ADGAS was scheduled to deliver 400,000 tonnes of pentane plus under this contract during 1996. It was the first time in ADGAS' history that a long-term contract for pentane disposal had been signed. The company also entered into two contracts for the sale of its 1996 sulphur products. These contracts, valid for one year from January 1996, provide for the sale of an amount ranging from 240,000 to 420,000 tonnes.

ADGAS also began to cooperate with new customers in Europe and in 1995 the first shipments of methane and propane gas were sold to European companies. Consolidating its European business, ADGAS recently renewed agreements with European companies and signed a new agreement with a Spanish company to supply it with ten shipments of about 320,000 tons.

During 1995 ADGAS production reached 7.34 million tonnes, exceeding the target of 7.2 million tonnes, and the company sold more than one million tonnes of LNG to European buyers. Completion of the third process train on Das Island coincided with plans to set up complementary projects, including the expansion of the non-associated gas feedstock resources, upgrading the plant's control mechanisms and modernization of the fleet of tankers which transport the LNG from Das to Tokyo.

ADGAS's daily Liquefied Natural Gas, LNG, production in 1995 rose to 5.3 million tonnes, a new record for the company. The company's three units produced at an average of more than 17,000 tonnes a day and 172 tankers were loaded with LNG at Das Island in 1995. On 25 May 1996, production of LNG and other products hit their highest levels when 25,001 tonnes were topped and the single-week highest output was also achieved between 4 May and 10 May, when the level stood at 120,445 tonnes. Liquid sulphur also hit a record 7378 tonnes between 11 May and 17 May. Production of LNG hit a record 519,476 tonnes in May while propane output peaked at 77,193 tonnes. Sulphur from ADGAS's LNG complex on Das Island also reached its highest level of 28,654 tonnes in May.

According to the company bulletin, the Das Plant achieved 2 million man-hours in May and 'the safety target now is to work 3 million man hours.'

The Abu Dhabi Gas Industries Company (GASCO)

The Abu Dhabi Gas Industries Company, Ltd. (GASCO) was established in December 1978 to handle gas produced by land-based wells. ADNOC owns 68 per cent of its shares; the French company, Total, owns 15 per cent; Shell Gas owns 15 per cent; and the Bartex Gas Company owns 2 per cent. The project is considered to be the largest such project ever mounted in the UAE and one of the largest gas projects in the world. The four plants of the company went on stream in July 1981 and the first shipment of GASCO products were made on the tanker 'World Heritage' in March 1982. GASCO's activities expanded further in the early 1990s. In 1993 the company loaded 1300 ships safely without a single accident. Production rose to 38 million tons, with production levels during this period showing an increase of 20 per cent over previous periods. More recently GASCO has set out to double its production within the framework of a plan laid down by the Supreme Petroleum Council and ADNOC.

Completion of Habshan Gas Project

The major land gas project in the Habshan area was completed in early 1996 at a cost of $1.3 billion. The Onshore Gas Development (OGD) project at the Bab field has increased gas compression and processing capacity at the Habshan plant from 24 mcm/d to 53 mcm/d. Condensate and NGL production have also been raised to 130,000 b/d and 5900 tonnes per year (t/yr) respectively. Habshan can now handle 21 mcm/d of gas from the Thamama B and C reservoirs and 18 mcm/d from the F reservoir. In addition to supplying natural gas to power hungry utilities and general domestic users, the plant is also aimed at increasing oil supply from existing wells by injection of gas. Greater quantities of gas call for larger storage and processing facilities. GASCO is facing this challenge at its Ruwais plant with provision of new LPG storage tanks and further expansion of its natural gas liquids (NGL) plant.

Gas Project at the Asab Oilfield

In late March 1996, ADNOC announced plans to develop gas reserves at the onshore Asab oilfield. The project involves the building of a gas treatment plant with a production capacity of around 24.78 million cubic metres (826 million cu ft) per day and a pipeline network to carry gas to nearby Ruwais. Around 100,000 barrels per day of condensates (very light crude) will be produced by the project, which also includes gas injection into 29 wells. The project is one of the biggest gas ventures to be carried out by ADNOC and is expected to be commissioned in 1999.

Dubai's Natural Gas

Government-owned DUGAS is responsible for Dubai's gas industry which draws gas from fields in both Dubai and Sharjah. DUGAS's processing plant at Jebel Ali is conveniently situated for supplying various energy requirements of the Jebel Ali Free Zone. As demand has increased Dubai's own reserves have been insufficient to meet its needs and it has been forced to look elsewhere for supplies, firstly to Sharjah and more recently to Abu Dhabi.

Sharjah's Natural Gas

Sharjah's main natural gas reserves are on the offshore Mubarrak field operated by Crescent Petroleum, together with its

onshore Kahaif and Mo'ayyid fields. As mentioned above, gas from the Mubarrak field is transported via an undersea and on-land pipeline to the DUGAS facilities at Jebel Ali. An agreement to sell gas produced by the Saja field to the Emirates Oil Company was concluded in December 1982. The aim of this agreement was to pipe the gas to all the electrical plants in the Northern Emirates; a project which was completed in May 1984. Today the Saja gas-condensate field supplies an LPG plant operated by Sharjah Liquefied Petroleum Gas Company, and the Emirates General Petroleum Corporation which supplies feedstock to Ras al-Khaimah, Fujairah, Ajman and Umm al-Qaiwain. The new reserves recently discovered at Kahaif provided a 1994 output of about 28 mcm/d of gas and 6,460 b/d of condensate from three wells. SHALCO's processing plant is being expanded from 12.5 to 20.0 mcm/d in order to deal with the increased quantities of gas.

Amoco Sharjah at present extracts natural gas from three oil fields. It also operates gas treatment and liquefaction plants and gas storage facilities, in addition to coastal and marine installations in Sharjah. The major portion of Sharjah's natural gas is exported to Japan. In 1994, Amoco Sharjah expanded its facilities, especially the natural gas treatment plant, to provide a capacity of about 700 million cubic feet of gas daily. It then expanded other facilities to achieve a maximum average production of gas of more than 800 cubic feet daily. At the same time, the company became the focal point for importing natural gas in the Emirates over an extensive network of pipelines. This is a matter which has strengthened the position of Sharjah as a prominent producer of gas in the region.

In line with rise in the demand for gas in the Emirates, the company, in the last few years, has drilled more than 25 new wells among which are six which began to produce in 1994.

The Al-Saja developments, operation of the wells in the onland Kahaif field, and the expansion of the gas plant complex, have made Sharjah an important site for natural gas in the region.

Ras al-Khaimah's Natural Gas

Ras al-Khaimah has estimated gas reserves of 34 billion cubic metres. Associated gas produced from the Saleh field began in 1986 at a rate of 1.7 mcm/d which feeds a small gas processing plant. In January 1996 an agreement was signed between Ras al-Khaimah and a consortium of US companies for oil and gas exploration in the emirate, to be carried out by Ras al-Khaimah Oil and Gas Company Ltd.

Natural gas in the Emirates fuels electricity generating stations, water desalination and cement plants, where it is used instead of diesel oil. In addition to reducing the burden on the Federal Budget (which provides a 5 per cent subsidy on electricity) gas also has the advantage that it is a clean form of energy.

UAE GAS STATISTICS*

	1979	1984	1986	1988	1990	1992	1994
Reserves (bcm)	580	905	2962	5706	5675	5794	5794
Production (bcm)	6.1	11.0	15.2	17.4	20.1	22.2	24.5
Domestic Consumption (bcm)	4.4	8.2	12.3	14.2	16.9	18.8	20.2

*Source: BP Review of World Gas

OIL AND NATURAL GAS RESERVES

The total oil reserves of the UAE are 2.33 billion barrels, of which 50 per cent (116.8 billion barrels) is recoverable. Gas reserves are put at 354 trillion cubic feet. The United Arab Emirates has consolidated its position among the top countries in the world in terms of its oil and gas reserves, according to the BP Statistical Review of World Energy 1996. The annual report, produced by British Petroleum, now includes details on both oil and gas. According to the Review, the UAE ranks third in terms of proven oil reserves at the end of 1995, with 98.1 thousand million barrels, or 9.7 per cent of world oil reserves, permitting production at current rates for over 100 years. Most of the oil is in Abu Dhabi followed by Dubai, Sharjah and Ras al-Khaimah.

The top four, including the UAE, are said by the Review to have maintained their oil reserves at the same level since 1994, indicating that the amount of oil produced during 1995 was matched by the discovery of an equivalent amount of new proven reserves. The Middle East region, including the top four as well as Oman, Qatar, Syria and Yemen, each with less than 1 per cent of world reserves, account for a total of 64.9 per cent of world reserves, underlining the significance of the region.

The UAE and other Middle East states also figure prominently in the Review in terms of proven reserves of natural gas, the UAE, it is claimed, with 204.6 trillion cubic metres or 4.1 per cent of the world total. Most of the gas is located in Abu Dhabi followed by Sharjah, Dubai, Ras al-Khaimah and Umm al-Qaiwain.

PETROCHEMICALS

Refining
An average of 226,000 barrels of crude oil were processed daily during 1994 by the Al-Ruwais and Umm al-Nar refineries, both of which are owned by ADNOC. This represented 110 per cent of their designed capacity and led to production of around 11 million tons of petroleum products. Over the last two years this record has been improved upon. The average daily production of condensed products and chlorine of the Umm al-Nar Refinery is around 9720 barrels daily. Manufacture of chlorine continues to add to the revenues of the ADNOC companies with production amounting to around 11,250 tons along with 112,400 tons of caustic soda. The Abu Dhabi Water and Electricity Department were supplied with these products as were other local and foreign markets.

Expansion of ADGAS's utilities on Das Island, together with development of inland gas production in the Habshan district, increased the production of liquid sulphur and expansion of the Sulphur Station in Al-Ruwais was recently completed.

Privatization of Petrochemicals Industry
During April 1996 the Federal Cabinet studied proposals for the privatization of the petrochemicals industry. Following completion of infrastructural developments the intention is that the private sector will be encouraged to build on to these, establishing their own small and medium-sized industries. The main focus will be on non-labour intensive industries, involving high technology and low water consumption.

The Fertilizer Industries Company in Al-Ruwais
The Fertilizer Industries Company was established in the Al-Ruwais industrial area in October 1980. ADNOC and the French oil company between them own and operate the nitrogen fertilizer plant which was completed in September 1983.

SHIPPING

Marine transportation forms an essential ingredient of Abu Dhabi's oil and gas industries. ADNOC established three companies in this field: the Abu Dhabi National Tanker Company Ltd (ADNATCO) operates ten tankers to transport crude oil, refined products and sulphur. The National Gas Shipping Company Ltd (NGSCO) provides shipping services to ADGAS and manages the administration of the fleet of methane and propane gas tankers on behalf of the Liquid Gas Transportation Company. The Abu Dhabi Oil Ports Administration Company, ADPOC, operates facilities for loading oil in Jebel al-Dhanna, Al-Ruwais, Umm al-Nar, Das Island, Zarko Island and Mubarraz Island. The company also handles port maintenance

operations for the ports belonging to ADMA-OPCO and the oil terminals of ZADCO, and gives support whenever the matter so requires in combating oil pollution in the oil ports. ADNOC owns or leases some 38 ships.

SUPPORTING COMPANIES

The Abu Dhabi Drilling Products and Chemicals Company (ADCAR)

The Abu Dhabi Drilling Products and Chemicals Company manufactures and sells chemicals used in digging wells. It provides the services and support required for drilling operations and production in offshore areas. It also provides diesel fuel and water.

The National Petroleum Construction Company Ltd (NPCC)

NPCC operates a fleet composed of heavy loading craft, boat-cranes able to lift construction equipment weighing up to 2000 tons and pipe-laying vessels capable of laying underwater pipelines up to 152 centimetres (60 inches) in diameter. The company has also developed a workshop for manufacturing oil installations and pipe-coating. It is building a loading platform in the Musaffah Industrial Zone in Abu Dhabi which became operational in 1995.

The National Drilling Company (NDC)

The National Drilling Company owns ten rigs for drilling on land and ten for drilling offshore. It also owns five rigs for drilling water wells, two of which are being used for a study project for groundwater sources in Al-Ain. It owns a fleet of different kinds of heavy equipment which it uses in support of drilling operations.

The National Maritime Services Company (NMS)

The National Maritime Services Company owns 22 supply, maintenance and traans-portation vessels used to service and support oil and gas operations in offshore areas.

LOOKING TO THE FUTURE

ADNOC's recent development plan commenced execution in 1995 with construction of a pipeline for transporting gas from the Habshan region to the electrical station in Al-Marfa, a distance of 40 kilometres. Also in 1995 ADNOC began construction of the Jebel al-Dhanna gas pipeline scheduled to transport gas from Al-Ruwais to Jebel al-Dhanna, a distance of 23 kilometres. In June 1996, ADNOC completed the Bab/Al-Maqta/Al-Taweelah gas pipeline which has been built to satisfy gas production and consumption requirements until 2005.

In the first half of 1996, the company completed the Al-Ruwais port expansion project and expansion of the public utilities in Al-Ruwais. These two projects were dedicated on 26 June 1996. The aim of the first project is to expand the port for shipping petroleum products from the Al-Ruwais refinery and to fill the increasing demand of production from the inland gas development projects. The second project aims at raising the production capacity of the company's two electrical and water plants in Al-Ruwais and the growing requirements of its industrial development plan.

Progress continues as the UAE faces into the twenty-first century. Recently the Supreme Petroleum Council (SPC) under the chairmanship of Sheikh Khalifa bin Zayed Al Nahyan, the Heir Apparent of Abu Dhabi and Deputy Supreme Commander of the Armed Forces, issued directives to ADNOC to begin to design an expansion project to raise the capacity of the Al-Ruwais refinery. This project will lead to an increase in Abu Dhabi's exports of refined oil products. The project will include construction of an oil distillation unit with a capacity of 135,000 barrels per day, a distillation unit for condensed oil products with a capacity of 200,000 barrels per day, a unit for hydrogen breakdown with a capacity of 46,000 barrels a day in addition to the necessary storage and loading facilities. The SPC also agreed to an ADNOC plan to reduce the lead content in gasoline for automobiles; and to reduce the sulphur level in diesel fuels.

The SPC approved another project to diversify the ADNOC product range through construction of a petrochemical complex in Al-Ruwais, scheduled for completion at the end of 1999. This complex will be used for gathering gases which are released during production of polyethylene products. ADNOC chose the American Foster Wheeler Company to administer the engineering works for the expansion project which will cost nearly $1.8 billion.

Expansion of the Al-Ruwais refinery is next in line after the expansion of the Umm al-Nar refinery, completed in 1994. The capacity of the refinery will be 85,000 barrels a day. Three other small refineries are to be built in Dubai, Sharjah and Fujairah, along with an important oil purification centre in the region.

ADNOC also began work on the construction of a gathering centre for petrochemicals in Al-Ruwais which will usher the Emirates into the international petrochemical market after its gas production capacity has been expanded. ADNOC made contacts with 15 large international petrochemical companies in order to find a suitable partner for the Al-Ruwais project. The list was then reduced to four companies. Finally, the Supreme Petroleum Council chose the Borealis Company which is owned by a Finnish/Norwegian consortium to be the partners. ADNOC announced on 12 June 1996 that it will have 60 per cent of the shares in the project and 40 per cent will be held by Borealis. ADNOC also announced creation of a new company to market the product which is expected to go on stream in 2000. The annual production will be around 450,000 tons. ADNOC has set up two separate companies to handle the new production. The first company will be for the production of petrochemicals the other will be for marketing them. ADNOC confirmed that Borealis is considered to be the largest producer of polyethylene and polypropylene in Europe and the fifth largest producer in the world.

Given the range and size of these developments, and the proven ability of the UAE to handle such major projects there is no doubt that it will maintain its position as one of the world's leading oil, gas and petrochemical producers as well as one of its most innovative and forward thinkers in this highly competitive field. It will also continue to show wise judgement on use of the revenues to further expand and diversify its industrial base.

INDUSTRY AND TRADE

A L THOUGH THE UAE HAS the third largest proven oil reserves in the world, enough to drive an oil-based economy well into the twenty-second century, the oil-related portion of its Gross Domestic Product, GDP, is only one-third of the total GDP. Careful nurturing of its manufacturing, services and other sectors has paid real dividends in terms of creating a healthier more stable economy than one that is totally at the mercy of oil-price fluctuations. It is firm government policy to build upon the progress already made in terms of reducing the dependence upon oil through a policy of controlled diversification. In addition to its hydrocarbon resources the UAE has a number of other natural strengths which have helped to underpin its continued growth. These include its geographic location, lying approximately half-way between the burgeoning economies of southeast Asia and those of Europe, its long coastline, its winter-sun climate, its natural scenery and its intelligent, adaptable, warm-hearted and hospitable people.

The UAE's success in moulding such a vibrant economy owes much to the foresight and skills of its President, Sheikh Zayed, and of his colleagues on the Supreme Council of the Federation, who have consistently supported policies to create an atmosphere in which trade and industry can flourish.

Diversification has involved a number of highly imaginative and innovative developments aimed at encouraging investors to establish their enterprises in the UAE and at assisting local business people in making the most of all that the UAE offers in terms of both infra-structure and other support mechanisms. The major areas of non-oil manufac-turing industries involve aluminium, chemicals, rubber, beverages and paper. According to Ministry of Planning statistics, the local value-added component accounted for Dh 11.75 billion in 1994. Industrial centres at Ruwais, in Abu Dhabi; Jebel Ali in Dubai, and in Sharjah, Ajman, Fujairah, Umm al-Qaiwain and Ras al-Khaimah each have special packages of incentives for businesses to locate there.

Recent Development in UAE Manufacturing Industry

	1995*	1994	1993
Gross Fixed Capital Formation	5575	5310	5210
Gross Value Added	11810	11200	10600
Food, Beverages & Tobacco	900	825	814
Textile, Leather & Garments	680	645	525
Wood, Wood Prods. & Furniture	350	320	244
Paper, Paper Prods. Printing & Publishing	315	285	272
Chemicals, Petroleum Prods. & Plastics	6325	6045	6258
Non-metallic Minerals	860	830	819
Basic Metals	1070	1030	768
Metal Prods. & Machinery	1100	1050	750
Other manufacturing n.e.s.	210	170	150

Figures in million dirhams. * Provisional. Source: Emirates Industrial Bank Annual Report 1995.

INDUSTRIAL DEVELOPMENT

Much industrial development is centred on free-trade zones such as the one at Jebel Ali which now ranks as the fifth largest of its kind worldwide.

In the short space of ten years the Jebel Ali Free Zone has attracted over 900 international companies including many top flight names such as General Motors, AEG, Aiwa, BP, Ciba Geigy, Daewoo, and Heinz. Jebel Ali alone handled 1.88 million TEUs in 1995, making it the fourteenth largest port terminal worldwide. The remarkable success of Jebel Ali Free Zone has spawned a number of other special advantage trade zones in the UAE, whilst Dubai has taken the concept to its airport, the busiest in the region, on the north side of which a new free-trade zone is attracting high technology light industries.

In July 1996, the Government of Abu Dhabi announced the establishment of a $3 billion Free-Trade Zone which will include the building of huge storage facilities, a new port, airport and commodities' trading exchanges on Sadiyat Island, 7 kilometres south of Abu Dhabi city. The Board of Directors of the Free Zone Authority will be chaired by Sheikh Hazza bin Zayed Al Nahyan. The 3500 hectare Sadiyat Free Zone, which will be linked with Abu Dhabi city via a 6 kilometre-long bridge, is part of a long-term economic development plan for Abu Dhabi, and will include dedicated and specialized facilities for 67 commodities, including precious metals and gems, bulk materials such as grains, ores and oils and materials needing cold storage, such as foodstuffs.

It was stressed that Abu Dhabi's new Sadiyat Free Zone is not in competition with Dubai's Jebel Ali Free Zone. According to a senior official involved with the project: 'We are building a commodities trading and storing facility and not a free trade zone specializing in container handling like Jebel Ali'. It has been stipulated that all materials imported or exported from the zone will be exempted from any taxes and customs duties and that the Free Zone Authority will become a globally competitive enterprise and will be established and run as a private sector company that will be floated for private investors.

The oil sector inevitably dominates Abu Dhabi's industrial sector but the emirate is nevertheless applying its efforts to encourage other industries, from tourism to heavy engineering. Given that oil and oil refining are such vital elements in the overall picture, it is natural that industrial growth should be based, in the first instance at least, upon petrochemical industries which utilize petroleum products as feedstock. The hub of this activity is at the Ruwais industrial complex 230 kilometres to the west of Abu Dhabi city. The General Industries Corporation, which is responsible for planning and

regulation of Abu Dhabi's industrial development, recently announced plans for establishment of a petrochemicals complex to be situated next to the expanded Ruwais refinery, whilst nearby industrial areas have been created for iron and steel production, together with a number of light industries.

Companies operating in Sharjah do not have to be sited within the free zone area in order to avail of the emirate's liberal and attractive incentives, including zero rated corporate and personal taxes, 100 per cent foreign ownership plus full repatriation of profit and capital. It is not surprising that this policy has led to a 12 per cent annual growth rate in its industrial base.

Traditionally a boat-building centre, Ajman's industrial development has benefited from its maritime traditions with steel fabrication and ship repairs taking place at Arab Heavy Industries. Meanwhile the Ajman Cement Company supports the building industry and there are a number of light industries based in the emirate. The Ajman Free Zone is in the process of expansion aimed at increasing foreign investment.

The Fujairah Free Zone, next to the modern port, has around 50 companies operating within it, representing a total investment of over $100 million Although small, both Umm al-Qaiwain and Ras al-Khaimah have been focusing on development of their light industries and there are encouraging signs of growth.

A good measure of the buoyant nature of UAE trade is to be found in its freight figures which reveal that its 15 commercial seaports handled over 33 million tonnes in 1995, whilst over 630,000 tons passed through its airports.

RE-EXPORTS

Re-exports are technically defined as foreign merchandise which has been manifested to a UAE importer and then cleared by the UAE Customs Department before leaving the country again. In value terms (fob), re-exports grew from Dh6 billion in 1986 to Dh24 billion in 1995, whilst the re-export business itself has spread from its traditional heartland of Dubai to other centres of trade and industry, such as Jebel Ali, and to trade centres in Abu Dhabi, Sharjah, Ras al-Khaimah and Fujairah. Re-exports are playing an important role in the prosperity of the country and are having a substantial impact on the whole UAE economy. The GCC is the largest destination for re-exports from the UAE, followed by Iran, Hong Kong, the EU and India.

Contribution to GDP (Dh. billion)	1994	1995
Agriculture, livestock and fisheries	3.3	3.5
Manufacturing	11.7	12.5
Water and electricity	2.8	3.2
Construction	12.8	13.3

UNITED ARAB EMIRATES 1996

ALUMINIUM

Addressing the Seventh Arab
International Aluminium Conference,
Arabal '95, held in October 1995 under the
theme *The Aluminium Industry in the
Twenty-first Century*, Sheikh Hamdan bin
Rashid Al Maktoum, Deputy Ruler of
Dubai and Minister of Finance and Industry, said that the rapid growth of the primary
aluminium industry in the GCC region indicates the need to set up more downstream
projects in this sector.

*The strategic location of our countries between the East and West, as well as the abundance
of energy resources and the availability of modern facilities, plays an important role in
preparing this region to take the lead in re-
structuring the international aluminium
industry*, he said. In 1989, Dubai

Aluminium Com-
pany (DUBAL)
increased its pro-
duction by 40 per
cent, and in early
1995 it launched a
second expansion
phase scheduled to

increase production by 52 per cent, to more than 372,000 tonnes,
once it becomes operational in 1997.

SHIPBUILDING

The Abu Dhabi Shipbuilding Company, ADSBC, established by the UAE Government in 1994, announced a new joint-venture with Newport News Shipbuilding and Dry Dock Company, NNC. The new j-v company will be engaged in the maintenance, repair, inspection and the refurbishment of marine vessels.

Based in Mussafah near Abu Dhabi city, ADSB's first contract to overhaul six patrol boats for the UAE Navy is worth about Dh300 million and will take about four years. It involves the complete refit of the navy's six TNC-45 vessels which were built in Europe in the early 1980s. This will be the first navy overhaul project of its kind to be accomplished in the UAE. ADSB began operation at a temporary site in Mussafah industrial area, but is planning to build its own shipyard in the next two years.

CONSTRUCTION INDUSTRY

A report published in December 1995 by the Middle East Economic Digest, MEED, said that by regional standards, order books in the UAE construction industry are healthy and contractors can look forward to some sizeable opportunities in the near future. The report highlighted the fact that intense competition in the industry was stimulated by the fact that $4 billion worth of contracts were expected to come to the market in 1996. The rapid pace of building in the UAE has been fuelled by the Khalifa Committee, an official body named after its Chairman, Abu Dhabi Crown Prince Sheikh Khalifa bin Zayed Al Nahyan, that extends soft loans designed to spread oil income through the economy.

CEMENT INDUSTRY

The Dh592 million Ras al-Khaimah Cement Company was launched in October 1995, making it the fourth cement plant in the UAE. The Ras al-Khaimah White Cement and Construction Materials Company was engagaed in expansion during 1996, involving installation of a new kiln which was expected to increase the factory's capacity by 150,000 tonnes to a total figure of 450,000 tonnes per annum. The new kiln uses Japanese know-how and cost Dh140 million. Around 50,000 tonnes of the company's production is absorbed by the local market, while most of the remaining 250,000 tonnes is exported to the Gulf countries and the rest to Asian and African markets.

GOLD

An international campaign was launched during the Dubai Shopping Festival in February-March 1996 to promote Dubai as the 'City of Gold' and the biggest gold distribution centre in the world.

At present, the UAE is the world's second re-distribution point for gold, after Singapore, whilst the UAE and Saudi Arabia have the highest per capita annual consumption of gold, at 15 gms. The country's total annual demand for gold, including re-exports, is estimated at around 240 tonnes in 1995, projected to reach 300 tonnes in 1996.

CAR IMPORTS

The automobile market in the UAE has grown by an average of 5.7 per cent over the last 10 years. Imports increased by 89 per cent from 45,000 in 1989 to 85,000 cars in 1994. Re-exports through Dubai mirrored a similar trend with the market expanding by 270 per cent during the same period from 5000 units to 18,000 by 1994. Japanese cars account for 62 per cent of the UAE market, whilst US automobiles take 15 per cent, German 12 per cent, and South Korean 7.0 per cent.

OFFSET PROGRAMMES

The UAE Government's offset programmes have provided a means for companies selling highly technical goods and services into the country to also give something of more lasting worth in terms of transferring technology so that local industries can flourish. This policy has been applied to the petrochemicals industry with some notable success. The UAE is expected to spend more than $10 billion on the purchase of defence equipment by the turn of the century, opening the prospect of considerable stimulation of the local economy through the offset programme.

Plans for two pre-Offset ventures, both to be set up in Abu Dhabi, were revealed at the Dubai '95 Air Show in November 1995. McDonnell-Douglas announced its Nama Development Enterprises wing would establish a Dh65.7 million joint venture in Abu Dhabi with an export

potential of Dh150 million. The UAE Offset Committee, which controls all offset programmes by defence contractors to the Government, approved the joint venture which includes a refinery, associated process plants, storage tanks and buildings, with an annual capacity of 50,000 tonnes. The products to be manufactured are currently imported by GCC states.

UNITED ARAB EMIRATES 1996

Dubai Dry Docks takes large ships into its facility for repair and maintenance. It employs over 2700 people.

Meanwhile Pratt & Whitney announced that it was establishing a world class science and technology services company in the UAE, not only as a viable business in itself, but also as a means to create the basis for new ventures that will benefit from the offset programme in future. Teaming agreements with the Higher Colleges of Technology, the National University at Al-Ain and other institutions in the country were also planned.

WORLD TRADE ORGANIZATION

The UAE's admission to the World Trade Organization (WTO) in February 1996 marked a major step forward in the UAE's economic development and its role in the global economy. The UAE's status as a Founder Member of WTO was confirmed on 8 February 1996 when the world trade body officially accepted the UAE's membership in the organization after its Commodities Council approved its obligations schedule. The WTO replaced the General Agreement on Tariffs and Trade(GATT) after more than 100 countries signed a landmark pact in Morocco in 1994 to open their borders for trade between them.

AGREEMENTS WITH EUROPEAN UNION

Textiles: In December 1995 an agreement was signed with the European Union aimed at streamlining garment and textiles exports to Europe. The agreement covered administrative measures to organise the textile and ready made garment trade between the UAE and EU. Unlike a similar agreement concluded with the US, the accord with the EU did not include a quota system.

Oil: Discussions continued with the EU concerning its controversial proposals for a carbon tax. AGCC states repeatedly voiced concern about the proposed tax on the grounds that it would slow down growth in oil demand and depress their economies. The EU defended the tax as an environmental measure aimed at curbing the emission of carbon dioxide blamed for global warming, but AGCC countries and other oil producing nations have contended that industrial nations were only seeking additional revenues as crude oil is already heavily taxed there. In February 1996 the EU's previously strong support for such a tax faltered, partially as a result of strong AGCC opposition, and partially because it was realized that since EU member states can impose individual steps for environmental protection, there was little need for a separate EU carbon tax.

DOUBLE TAXATION AGREEMENTS

Double taxation agreements are the foundation for encouragement of trading and business connections between countries and the UAE has been active in reaching a number of new agreements in this area over the last 12 months. Among these were agreements with Poland, the Czech Republic and a number of other countries.

PATENTS

Steps taken by the UAE during 1996 are expected to help rid the UAE of patent pirates and improve the climate for industrial development in the country. Since legal protection for industrial and intellectual property was introduced three years ago (UAE Copyright Law No. 40 was introduced in 1992 and came into effect in early 1993, while the law governing patents No 44, was also introduced in 1992 and effected the following year) two problem areas have received particular attention, namely protection for pharmaceutical products and computer software. In February 1996 a spokesman for the pharmaceutical industry in the UAE said that patent pirates in the UAE were robbing pharmaceutical firms of more than $20 million per annum. The total pharmaceutical market of the UAE is estimated at around $200 million a year. According to the Business Software Alliance, BSA, the loss to software manufacturers is estimated at $266 million a year. The BSA claims that 93 per cent of software available on the UAE market is pirated and costs software manufacturers $39 million a year.

In June 1996, the UAE acceded to The Paris Convention for the Protection of Industrial Property, an international treaty guaranteeing the protection of patent rights for industrial property, including patents, trademarks and a wide range of other intellectual property rights. The Convention provides a general obligation that a national of any party to the Convention shall enjoy all of the industrial property rights in all other member countries granted by the laws of all such other countries. For example, the Paris Convention provides that, as a general rule, every trademark duly registered in the country of origin shall be accepted for filing and protected as in the other countries in the Convention. The Convention also acknowledges the right of the proprietor of a trademark to object in the event that an agent or representative attempts to register a trademark without the proprietor's authorization. Under the Convention, goods will be seized on importation in member countries if they unlawfully bear a trademark or trade name which is entitled to legal protection in that country.

Stricter enforcement of the existing laws are also expected to have a major impact. The Ministry of Trade and Economy and the Ministry of Information and Culture have taken a number of steps to enforce the laws and have achieved positive results. It is hoped that the UAE's commitment to the protection of intellectual property in general and computer programmes in particular will help to enhance international trust in the country, which, in turn, will pave the way for a better investment atmosphere in the country.

An aerial view of Abu Dhabi's Port Zayed.

UNIFIED CUSTOMS TARIFFS

The UAE has called on other Arab Gulf Cooperation Council states to take into consideration current liberalization trends and the provisions of GATT when unifying the GCC customs tariffs. In an official memorandum submitted by the Ministry of Finance and Industry to the AGCC General Secretariat, the UAE suggested classifying tariffs on imports, which could be put in three categories for customs purposes:

- goods which are exempted from customs duty such as vital consumer goods and industrial raw materials and spare parts;
- Essential goods on which a customs tax of 4 per cent would be imposed (most goods would fall into this category);
- all other goods on which an acceptable customs tariff should be imposed.

The Ministry emphasizes that increasing tariffs on imports will not comply with the rules of the World Trade Organisation, nor with ongoing trade negotiations between the AGCC and other economic groups, especially as four AGCC countries have already joined the WTO. The AGCC states are also trying to jointly set up free trade zones with the European Union and other economic giants such as the USA and Japan, the Ministry said.

The UAE favours the view of the AGCC Secretariat that the Maxwell Stamp Study will form the basis for discussing the unification as the Study was prepared following a decision by the AGCC Supreme Council. The Study suggests that tariff unification should be based on the average of customs tariffs in the AGCC states. It says the unified tariff would range from 4 per cent to 8 per cent on 10 different categories of products. However, the Secretariat supports the principle of average tariff, suggesting it should be 8 per cent, except on exempted goods.

TOURISM

A STRATEGIC GEOGRAPHICAL LOCATION, security, tranquillity, excellent shopping centres, guaranteed winter sun, top class accommodation, services and recreational facilities, including an ultra-modern sporting infrastructure, have all ensured that the UAE has become a centre for tourism since the 1980s. Tourists are also attracted by the UAE's heritage and culture, as well as traditional sports of camel, horse and boat racing, pearl diving and falconry.

Tourism Statistics

The UAE is placing more emphasis on promoting tourism in the course of lessening its reliance on the traditional oil industry and diversifying the sources of its national income. In an introduction to the Annual Statistical Report on UAE Hotels for 1995, issued by the Ministry of Planning's Central Statistics Department, Sheikh Humaid bin Ahmed Al Mu'alla said that thanks to the directives of H.H. President Sheikh Zayed bin Sultan Al Nahyan, Vice President, H.H. Sheikh Maktoum bin Rashid Al Maktoum and the Supreme Council Members and Rulers of the Emirates, the UAE has been able to grasp the realities of the age and place itself among those countries which focus on the tourism industry.

The Garden City of Al-Ain attracts growing numbers of visitors.

Information, Culture & Tourism			
	1994	1993	1992
Radio Stations	4	4	4
T.V. Stations	3	3	3
Daily Newspapers	8	8	8
Periodical Magazines	130	130	130
Sport & Cultural Clubs	35	34	34
Zoos	2	2	2
Public Gardens	93	93	93
Museums	7	7	7
Hotels	254	229	215
Rooms	17,834	16,285	14,682
Beds	30,105	27,526	25,355
Guests (000s)	1,919	1,665	1,466
Nights (000s)	5,674	4,823	4,046

The UAE has exerted a great deal of effort to attract tourists, especially among people visiting for conferences and exhibitions, and within a short span of time in the life of the country, it has become a central stopover and a significant attraction for businessmen and participants in conferences. This extensive promotion of the UAE as a tourist destination over the past several years has yielded positive results. The number of tourists visiting the Emirates increased significantly from 1.67 million in 1993 to 1.92 million in 1994. Sixty-five per cent of these tourists, or 1.24 million, came to Dubai, where they spent 3.37 million nights at its hotels, compared with 352,887 tourists, or 18 per cent, visiting Abu Dhabi and spending 1,138,222 bed nights.

Sharjah hosted 252,398 tourists, spending 960,112 nights and accounting for 13 per cent of the total number. Statistical studies show that 33 per cent of the tourists visiting the UAE in 1994 were Europeans, 28 per cent were from the Gulf countries, 26 per cent were Asians, 9 per cent were Arabs and 4 per cent came from the Americas. In order to cope with this influx, the number of hotels in the UAE rose from 229 in 1993 to 254 in 1994, an 11 per cent increase it said, adding that the number of hotel rooms were up from 16,258 with 27,526 beds to 17,834 with 30,105 beds. The number of nights spent at hotels increased from 4.8 million in 1993 to 5.67 million in

1994, an 18 per cent rise. The average duration of stay by each tourist also showed an increased, a good sign of tourism development paying-off, while the hotels' occupancy rate rose from 58 per cent to 61 per cent in 1994.

Total hotel revenues rose from Dh1.78 billion in 1993 to Dh2.01 billion in 1994. Dealing with the distribution of the hotels according to their ratings in 1994, there were 34 luxury hotels, 55 first-class hotels and 38 second-class hotels. Only 27 third-class hotels handed in the necessary data for the statistical study. Dubai had 191 hotels, representing 75 per cent of the total number in the country while Abu Dhabi come next with 34 hotels, 13 per cent of the total. Sharjah had 19 hotels in 1994, accounting for 8 per cent, Ras al-Khaimah and Fujairah with seven hotels represented 3 per cent, while Ajman and Umm al-Qaiwain, with three hotels each, accounted for only 1 per cent of the total number of hotels covered by the Ministry's study.

While the tourism industry in the UAE made rapid strides in 1995, even better results are expected for 1996, with ever-increasing numbers of Western tourists arriving, as well as a rise in the number of events taking place.

The most talked about event on the agenda was the Dubai Shopping Festival, held in February - March 1996, which drew visitors from the Gulf, Middle East, South East Asia and countries of the sub-continent.

During 1995, Germans remained the number one European nationality to visit the UAE, followed by the British, French, Swiss and Scandinavians. The number of South African visitors is also on the rise,

while a substantial number of Finnish tourists are coming to the Emirates. Americans have also shown an interest in visiting the country and a number of contracts have been reported between the UAE and American tour operators. Over 600,000 CIS tourists visited the UAE during 1995, spending over $1.5 billion to buy electronics, electrical appliances and automobiles.

Various new projects, including construction of new hotels and extensions to the existing ones, were undertaken throughout the Emirates, making them more attractive for tourists searching for sunshine and clear-water beaches. Plans for the Federal Tourism Board are also set to see light during 1996. This would streamline the promotion of tourism in the country and provide a platform to promote the UAE as a destination for tourism as as a whole.

ABU DHABI AND DUBAI

The Abu Dhabi National Hotels Company, established in 1975, and the Dubai Commerce and Tourism Promotion Board (DCTPB) play an important role in enhancing tourism in the country and both Dubai and Abu Dhabi have taken a number of steps to tap their tourism potential. The Abu Dhabi National Hotels Company (ADNHC) unveiled plans to add three new hotels in Bani Yas, Liwa and Mirfa to add another 500 rooms to the existing 2650 in its hotels in the emirate. The Dh180 million Abu Dhabi Golf Course, scheduled to be completed by the end of 1996, is also set to attract a lot of tourists from Japan and Europe. In addition, Abu Dhabi master plan for the next two decades includes establishment of entertainment parks and coastal resorts. Abu Dhabi's Lulu Island

project, which is presently under construction, promises to be one of the largest and most impressive tourism projects in the region.

DCTPB made significant progress in all areas of operations in 1995, its international marketing activities having successfully attracted a growing number of overseas tour operators to promote Dubai as a destination. The DCTPB's efforts were rewarded by Dubai winning the gold prize for the best destination in the Middle East at the 1996 World Travel prizes ceremony held in June 1996 in Las

Vegas, USA. It also won the silver medal for the third consecutive time for the best tourism and conference centre in the Middle East.

The first major expansion of DCTPB's overseas office network since 1990 saw the appointment of respresentation in Moscow, to cover the Russian Federation, and Johannesberg and Nairobi to cover southern and eastern Africa. The UK operation was upgraded from a consultancy to a full-fledged office. DCTPB is planning to build up its tourism promotions in the Scandinavian market during 1996, participating in leading travel trade fairs in Norway, Sweden and Finland for the first time. Dubai is expecting to complete the prestigious Chicago Beach resort redevelopment by 1998. A number of other hotels are also planned.

Dubai Municipality has a number of projects underway and at the planning stage, which should serve to enhance Dubai as a tourist destination. Among continuing projects is the upgrading of Khor Mamzar as a tourist site. A new museum for children was announced, aimed at enhancing children's attitudes and educating them on history, space and computers. It will also set up a number of parks in residential suburbs and build a large new zoo, besides restoring buildings and forts of archaeological interest dating to the eighteenth century.

Whilst a new garden was opened in Umm Suqeim on National Tree Day, expansion of Al-Khor Garden and construction of a large theme park were also under discussion. Restoration of a number of heritage monuments in Dubai was also undertaken, including the Al

Ahmediya Madrassa whilst a comprehensive plan has been prepared for reconstruction of Hatta village in order to make it a tourist attraction.

OTHER EMIRATES

Steps were also taken by other emirates to attract tourists. In September 1995, Fujairah, under the patronage of Supreme Council Member and Ruler of Fujairah H.H. Sheikh Hamad bin Mohammed Al Sharqi, announced the establishment of the Fujairah Tourism Bureau with the specific target of promoting in-bound tourism. The emirate also participated in the Arabian Travel Market in Dubai in May 1996, the most important tourism meet of the Arabian Peninsula, attended by 400 exhibitors from 48 countries. The Fujairah Government is planning several new tourist projects in Dibba al-Fujairah and the construction of three new hotels on the coastal strip between Rol Diba and Al-Faqueet, all richly scenic areas.

Fujairah's plans include installing a cable-car system in certain mountainous areas such as at Al-Wareeah, with its famous waterfalls - the Ministry of Agriculture and Fisheries are planning to build a dam in the area since the winter's rains on the eastern coast filled up the wadis of Al-Fai, Al-Abadelah and Zakt and greened the mountains.

Tree planting has already commenced at Wadi Zakt as part of the plan to change the area to a tourist resort. The first stage will include a restaurant and a coffee shop beside the lake waters. The opening of a 2.0 km road from the residential area of Wadi Zakt to the location of the new resort, will make it easier to reach. Being the only emirate located on the eastern coast of the UAE, Fujairah and its related areas along the coast are blessed by a series of mountains, falajes, natural water springs and valleys, in addition to several historical sites and green oases that could attract tourists.

The first phase of 'Dreamland', a 215,000 square metre aqua park, the largest in the world, is under construction in Umm al-Qaiwain and will open later this year. The initial investment in Dreamland is about Dh30 million. The second and third phases are expected to take about one year each to complete and the entire, three-phase project is scheduled to be completed by the end of 1998. Dreamland will have over 20 slides, most of them

exclusively designed for the waterpark. The park itself will have shaded areas and landscaping with artificial rocks, coffee shops, refreshment kiosks, snack bars and a wide selection of restaurants, shopping areas, private beaches, theatre etc. Among the attractions will be a 70-metre wave pool featuring 10 different types of waves. The park expects to receive over 500,000 visitors in its first season with the waterpark able to accommodate 7000 - 8000 people daily. A major advantage is that the park will be able to remain open for fully nine months a year, unlike in Europe.

Sharjah also increased its efforts to promote itself as a tourism destination and recorded a significant rise in traffic through its international airport, as well as road travellers from GCC countries. The magnificent beach in Sharjah city has proved a major tourist attraction, and the fact that Sharjah has two coasts adds to the attractiveness of its beach holidays. However, Sharjah has much more to offer besides sun and sand. Shopping visitors from the CIS frequently base themselves in Sharjah, whilst much is being done to develop conference and exhibition business. Sharjah Chamber of Commerce plans to build a 320 metre tower accompanying a 20,000 square metre exhibition hall.

A primary focus in Sharjah has been preservation of the local heritage as is evidenced by its extensive range of top-class museums, ranging from the state of the art Natural History Museum to the Archaeological Museum, Art Museum and Heritage Museum - the last two in a beautifully renovated old quarter in the city.

AGRICULTURE AND FISHERIES

They used to say agriculture has no future, but with God's blessing and our determination, we have succeeded in transforming this desert into a green land, Sheikh Zayed.

AGRICULTURE

WHO WOULD HAVE PREDICTED, 25 years ago that one would be able to walk through the fruit and vegetable stalls of London's Covent Garden and buy fresh strawberries, grapes, guavas and bananas, or fresh cut flowers, all grown in the UAE? Or that this desert land could support over 22 million date palms, making it one of the largest producers of dates worldwide with a single factory processing 14,000 tonnes a year? Or that UAE residents would take for granted that home grown citrus fruits, melons, mangoes, figs, cucumbers, carrots, cabbages, courgettes, celery, lettuce, marrows, aubergines, beans, maize, and tomatoes should be piled high on the stands in local markets throughout the UAE, let alone exported? Or that the Emirate of Abu Dhabi alone would plant more than 120 million trees by the time Sheikh Zayed celebrated his thirtieth year as its Ruler? Or that the extensive shade and evaporative cooling effect created by the leaf canopy would create its own microclimate, reducing local temperatures by several degrees centigrade? All this and much more form the backdrop to the UAE's agricultural revolution.

Significant achievements in the fields of agriculture and fisheries have continued to play an impressive role in achieving the UAE's declared objective of full self sufficiency in food production. Experiments have been carried out in growing many different fruit and vegetable plants and the most modern techniques have been adopted to refine cultivation of those species that show the greatest promise. Research undertaken at government experimental stations in Al-Ain, Al-Dhaid, Hamraniyah and Kalba have involved a wide range of techniques from mechanical fertilization of date palms to testing over 30 different strains of barley and wheat.

A great deal of the credit for the UAE's massive agricultural development rests squarely at the feet of the country's President, Sheikh Zayed, who has never lost his love of farming. He has personally invested heavily in the creation of large modern farms, such as those at Al-Jarf, an area of transformed desert where massive planting has created a forest of more than half a million trees; Al-Ajban with its 1500

mango trees, 5000 guava trees, 30,000 date palms and its numerous citrus fruit trees; or the island of Sir Bani Yas where Zayed has established a huge experimental farm and wildlife reserve on which apples, pears, oranges, pineapples, bananas and olives are all flourishing. Experimental coffee planting has also been recently undertaken there.

Zayed's personal example of what can be achieved in terms of water supply, irrigation and cultivation has proven a true inspiration for the entire country. His firm belief in the country's agricultural potential, despite the difficulties of high summer temperatures and low rainfall, have guided the government's policy of aiding agriculture. Not only have UAE nationals, willing to take up farming, been granted land to do so, they have also been generously assisted with financial grants, loans to purchase equipment, fertilizer and seeds, as well as technical advice and assistance. In addition the inexorable move from rural settlements to the main cities has been stemmed, in part at least, by schemes to provide modern housing and other facilities in proximity to new farming areas. Meanwhile home owners are encouraged to beautify their own surroundings by gifts of free plants, helping to soften the

impact of modern buildings and creating tropical gardens that few would have imagined possible prior to Zayed's agricultural renaissance.

Whilst the results of the UAE's agricultural revolution are highly impressive, this does not mean that everything has been done on a large scale. In fact, the average size of private farms in the UAE is only two or three hectares. Such farms make manageable family run units and it is the proliferation of successful small farms that is the basis for the country's steadily increasing food production. Neither are all the farms growing exotic fruits and vegetables; many are devoted to production of fodder for livestock, primarily alfalfa whose prolific growth rate allows up to 14 cuttings a year to be harvested.

Agricultural Production (000 Tons)

	*1994	*1993	1992
Plant Production Holdings	21,194	20,760	20,413
Area Cultivated (000 Hec.)	54.5	56.0	52.5
Vegetable Cultivated Area (000 Hec.)	13,101	13,848	12,805
Vegetable Production	957.0	537.7	486.9
Red Meat Production	16.6	15.5	14.5
Fish Production	108	95.5	95.0
Poultry Meat Production	21.9	16.7	15.7
Egg Production (mn. eggs)	223.2	230.0	217.7
Milk & Dairy Production	93.4	86.0	79.2

Traditional farming areas such as those in Ras al-Khaimah, Al-Dhaid, Falaj al-Mu'alla and Fujairah have been added to by many new areas where previous desert has been transformed into land that sustains trees, crops and livestock. Vast fields of cereals cultivated in fields around the Liwa oasis bear testament to the country's determination to take advantage of every opportunity that presents itself in the area of food production. To date over 100,000 hectares of desert have been transformed into cultivated land in the UAE and the process is continuing at a steady pace. Meanwhile the traditional areas have seen impressive agricultural developments with, for example, Ras al-Khaimah's Digdagga oasis farms supplying approximately 68 per cent of the UAE's vegetables.

Production of fodder has supported a growing dairy farming industry in the UAE with dairy herds of mainly Jersey cows in Abu Dhabi, Dubai and Fujairah contributing to a national annual milk production of more than 1000 tonnes. Cream, butter and yoghurt are also produced. In addition to dairy farming, livestock farming involving sheep, goats, cattle and camels provides fresh meat from over a million head of animals.

Intensive chicken and egg farming has been particularly successful in the Emirates, partially because it can be carried out in controlled environments, indoors, with the most modern techniques of husbandry. Umm al-Qaiwain was one of the first to enter this field and it produces over 1000 tonnes of poultry meat a year. Meanwhile, substantial poultry farms in Abu Dhabi, Dubai, Ras al-Khaimah and Fujairah are adding to these figures with, for example, the Ras al-Khaimah Poultry and Feeding Company at Digdagga capable of producing over a quarter of a million eggs per week. Overall poultry meat production in the UAE during 1995 reached 34,000 tons.

FISHING

Although the UAE's fishery, at 108,000 tons in 1994, produces more than the combined total for the other Gulf states, there are definite limitations on further growth of this sector, dictated by natural stocks and the necessity to sustain them. The introduction of modern methods, new boats, more efficient nets, powerful engines and sophisticated fish-finding equipment all make fishing a less problematic exercise but also place strains on the existing stocks. The Ministry of Agriculture and Fisheries is very much aware of the dangers of over-fishing and has taken important steps to control the level of exploitation so that breeding stocks can be maintained and fish will be available in future years.

One important approach has been that of insistence that fishing boats carry at least one UAE national on board. This serves the dual function of maintaining fishing as a national skill and also helps to prevent large scale slaughter of fish stocks with no eye to the long-term future. In an effort to further encourage local fishermen, UAE citizens can receive grants of up to half the cost of a new boat and necessary equipment. This policy has led to a relatively modern national fishing fleet of around 4000 vessels which land fish at purpose built fishery quays and supply modern markets in the main cities.

The prospect of dwindling local fish stocks and rising population has fuelled enthusiasm for fish-farming as a means to apply modern science to seafood production in a similar way to its impressive application on land. The Marine Resources Research Centre has been operating in Umm al-Qaiwain since 1984. It has focused on methods to commercially grow fish and shrimp in local conditions of high summer temperatures and salinity. More recently a number of commercial ventures in the aquaculture field have been announced, some of which fall under the offset programme.

The agriculture and fisheries sector continues to show growth throughout the UAE. In Abu Dhabi alone the sector earned Dh1.6 billion in 1994, up from 1993's Dh1.4 billion and Dh1.25 billion in 1992. Agriculture remains a high priority with thousands of farms in operation throughout the Emirates, funded by both the public and private sectors.

AGRICULTURAL UPDATE

Self Sufficiency

The UAE has already achieved 90 per cent self-sufficiency in dairy products, poultry, vegetables, fruit and animal fodder, and 24 per cent in animal products. Considerable expansion of its green belt and agriculture development has already been achieved and the focus is upon consolidation and further expansion with a view to achieving and maintaining complete food self sufficiency.

Water

The ADNOC administered water exploration project, described in the chapter on Infrastructure, has already yielded results in terms of deep reservoirs of

water suitable for irrigation (as well as potable water reserves). The discovery well, GWA-2, which reached a depth of approximately 1000 metres below ground level, revealed a 150 metre thick layer of limestone containing potable freshwater at about 300 metres depth, and a deeper 250 metre thick bed at just over 900 metres which is delivering around 100 cubic metres per hour of water with a salinity of 916 ppm which is suitable for agriculture.

As part of its policy to achieve self sufficiency the Ministry of Agriculture and Fisheries announced plans to build several new dams at various locations in the UAE with the first in Fujairah in an area which records the highest rainfall in the UAE. This and other dams in the scheme are aimed at enhancing replenishment of groundwater by preventing direct run-off to the sea after heavy rains. Major new dams were also planned for Ras al-Khaimah and Dibba, whilst 20 smaller dams were to be constructed in other parts of the country.

Boosted by such rainwater retention dams, sustainable underground aquifers now supply small farms, whilst effluent water is put to good use for horticulture. Abu Dhabi's mainland sewage treatment plant situated at Mafraq produces a daily flow of up to 190,000 cubic metres and supplies 90 per cent of the water required for the capital city's numerous public gardens. Water from the plant is pumped via a 32 kilometre long pipeline. Meanwhile seawater and low-cost energy are harnessed for large scale desalination with over 475 million cubic metres of water produced annually.

Dampener on Dates

Whilst most of the effects of the UAE's heaviest winter/spring rainfall in living memory were expected to bring positive results to the country's agricultural sector, there were also some losers along with the winners. The country's date palms were among the species that suffered a temporary set back as a result of persistent heavy rain in February and March 1996, leading to problems with fertilization of the trees: a necessary pre-requisite for date production. The rain caused pollen grains (fine, dust like-particles discharged from the male part of the flower) to be washed away, both from the stigma of its flowers as well as from the spadix (spike of flower around a fleshy axis) of female date palm trees.

Even though many date palms are artificially fertilized, generally between the middle of February and March, if rain falls within six hours of sprinkling pollen grains on the spadix, pollination is affected since the pollen grains tended to be washed off the plants, necessitating repeated efforts. The manual operation involves the farmer climbing up female palm trees at least three to four times during the fertilization season in order to place the male strands, laden with pollen into every spadix.

The Centre for the Extraction and Distribution of Pollens, situated in Digdagga in Ras al-Khaimah, is engaged in providing mechanized methods of pollination to farmers. At the Centre, strands from male trees are places in special drying rooms for about 48 to 72 hours, after which the pollens are extracted and mixed with wheat flour and other ingredients to increase their fertility.

The pollen is then 'dusted' (sprayed) on each female palm tree with the help of a 'pollinator', a process that eliminates the need for farmers to climb trees in order to sprinkle pollen grains into the spadix. With the help of the pollinator, at least 250 trees can be pollinated every day, as compared to 20 trees by the

manual method. The UAE's massive planting and farming of date palms has resulted in it possessing between 15 per cent and up to 20 per cent of the total number of date palms in the world.

Fertilizer Production

The ammonia unit of the Abu Dhabi Company for Fertilizers, FERTIL, produced a maximum daily output of 1269 metric tonnes in January 1995, whilst the company's total production during the same month stood at 39,165 tonnes. FERTIL, whose production is based upon gas from ADNOC's Bab, Asab and Thamamah field, sold 90,000 tonnes of urea in the local market in 1995.

Afforestation

In April 1996, the UAE celebrated its sixteenth Afforestation Week, an annual event that focuses on preservation of the environment and expansion of greenery in the country. Municipalities throughout the UAE planted new areas and undertook awareness programmes on the preservation of afforestation.

Poultry Farming and Marketing

The UAE's poultry farms produced 34,000 tonnes of meat in 1995, valued at Dh198 million. The production met 23 per cent of the country's consumption of 106,000 tonnes. There are five poultry farms in Abu Dhabi, three in Fujairah, two in Dubai and one each in Ras al-Khaimah and Umm al-Qaiwain. The UAE imported 91,000 tonnes of poultry meat in 1995, valued at Dh432 million, primarily from France, Denmark, Brazil and the Netherlands. Re-export of poultry meat, directed to the GCC, Arab and former USSR countries, nearly doubled over the past two years to 9000 tonnes, valued at Dh42 million in 1995, as against 5000 tonnes valued at Dh17 million in 1993. Local demand for poultry meat surged from 60,000 tonnes valued at Dh363 million in 1990 to 106,000 tonnes valued at Dh605 million in 1995.

INTERNATIONAL AWARD FOR SHEIKH ZAYED

In December 1995 the Director General of the UN's Food and Agriculture Organization, FAO, Dr Jacques Diouf, visited the UAE in order to present an award to H. H. President Sheikh Zayed bin Sultan Al Nahyan, in recognition of his achievements in greening the country's deserts. The award recognized that this had been achieved in a highly efficient manner, with an irrigation system that utilizes every available drop of water. Dr Diouf commented that the excellent farming techniques have helped rural areas to prosper, reducing the exodus to urban centres. Sheikh Zayed is the first regional leader to obtain such an honour from the FAO.

THE ZAYED AGRICULTURE CENTRE FOR THE REHABILITATION OF THE HANDICAPPED

A challenging project, which began its operations in the UAE in 1994, utilizes farming and the environment as a means to rehabilitate handicapped people. The Zayed Agriculture Centre for the Rehabilitation of the Handicapped is the first of its kind in the Gulf, and one of only a handful of such projects worldwide. It has been successful right from the beginning, owing much to constructive cooperation between the United Nations Development Programme, UNDP, the Ministry of Labour and Social Affairs and the Abu Dhabi Municipality and Town Planning Department. UNDP officials affirm that the centre provides a model for other countries interested in the welfare of their handicapped citizens to follow and enquiries have already been received from many countries seeking advice on, and details of, this fascinating project whose objective is to prevent segregation of the handicapped and offer them rehabilitation, together with a source of income and a new meaning to their lives. The scheme includes a conference hall, a mosque, a restaurant, a large store, a 5000 gallon ground water storage tank, two greenhouses of 30,000 metres square each and a nursery. The farm, manned by students whose ages range from 18 to 30, produces tomatoes, chillies, cabbages, okra, squash, aubergine, radishes and onions.

TRANSPORT AND COMMUNICATIONS

T HE ABILITY TO MOVE EASILY from place to place, and to communicate efficiently over long distances has always been a target for the bedouin of southern Arabia. The harsh reality of the desert created enormous difficulties which were partially overcome by domestication of the camel and by development of a social system which formed the core of bedouin culture. Much of this survived right up to recent times and is still part of local tradition although modernity has overwhelmed many of the old customs.

In 1971, when H.H. Sheikh Zayed was appointed as the first President of the United Arab Emirates, one of his priorities was to provide the emirates with an efficient inter-connecting system of roadworks that would ease the burden for people whose very lives depended upon an ability to move from place to place; and as a basic infra-structure around which other developments could follow. Road construction has continued at an impressive pace throughout the past 25 years, creating an ever expanding and improving network of dual carriageways and highways that have cut the time taken to drive from one city to another from days to minutes.

Sustained and dedicated efforts at constant improvements in the transport and communications sector have led to the present phase of rapid land, sea and air travel together with ultra modern telecommunications and participation in satellite technology. Over the last 25 years the UAE has gone from being one of the least developed countries in the world, in terms of its transport and communications network, to being one of the most modern.

Transport & Communication		1994	1993	1992
Paved Highways (km)		3,254	3,239	3,171
Vehicles (000's)		447	399	345
International Airports		6	5	5
Air Freight (000's Tons)		450	295	251
Passenger Traffic (000's)				
Air	Arrivals	4,024	3,527	3,345
	Departures	3,922	3,357	3,345
Land	Arrivals	1,107	937	892
	Departures	1,084	948	891
Commercial Seaports		15	15	15
Sea Freight (mn. Ton)		45	39	33
Telephone Exchange Lines (000's)		*707	*624	492
Telex Working Lines		4,028	4,371	4,756
Facsimile Lines		26,401	26,105	24,100
Post Boxes (000's)		116	100	94
Air Mail (000's)	Dispatched	83,451	74,517	65,800
	Received	57,369	54,860	51,200

LAND TRANSPORT

Abu Dhabi - Dubai Road Improvement

The one billion dirham Abu Dhabi-Dubai highway project is due for completion by the middle of 1997. The four-lane carriageway along a 78-kilometre distance will have four

major interchanges and a number of camel crossings. The project was initiated to facilitate free flow of traffic between Abu Dhabi and Dubai, which has risen at an average of 6.18 per cent during the last few years. An average of 40 accidents per month are reported on the existing two-lane highway.

Abu Dhabi - Al Ain Highway

The Dh1.2 billion Abu Dhabi - Al Ain highway is scheduled to be completed

136   UNITED ARAB EMIRATES 1996

by the end of 1998. In late 1995 the Abu Dhabi Government allocated Dh160 million for the first phase of a comprehensive project to improve and modernize the industrial area of Al-Ain.

Increase in Cars

The number of cars registered in Dubai has increased from just under 46,000 in 1985 to 146,000 by the end of 1995. The Structure Plan for Dubai Urban Area predicts that the population of the emirate will grow from the present 700,000 to about 2.2 million by the year 2011, fuelling further demand for transportation.

Northern Ring Road

Projects already identified include construction of a new ring road from Jebel Ali, passing through Sharjah so that north-south traffic is not forced into the Dubai bottle-neck. This is expected to substantially reduce traffic congestion and accidents. The multi-million dirham project is due for commencement in early 1997. The first phase, comprising the construction of a road linking Sharjah to the Dubai-Al Ain road, is expected to be completed by 1999, while the second phase will connect the new road to Jebel Ali.

SEA TRANSPORT

The UAE Commercial Fleet/Tonnage

Total fleet	**1,197,378**
Tankers	561,562
Bulk carriers	46,463
Container ships	211,720
Others	377,633

Source: Journal of Emirates Industrial Bank, February 1995.

Ports and Shipping

The UAE now has a total of 15 commercial ports which between them handle over 33 million tonnes of cargo a year. Virtually all of these are undergoing some form of expansion, together with constant customer driven improvements in services on offer.

Abu Dhabi

Mina Zayed

Mina Zayed's 21 berths are currently being visited by 50 leading shipping

lines. During 1995 the port recorded 2078 ships docking at the port compared to 1752 in 1994. Container traffic for the year increased by 96 per cent over the previous year, reaching 245,952 TEUs in 1995, compared with 125,416 in 1994. There was also a 65 per cent growth in the total cargo of 3,750,957 tonnes handled in 1995, compared with 2,270,670 tonnes in 1994.

During 1996 the Abu Dhabi Seaport Authority, under Sheikh Saeed bin Zayed Al Nahyan's chairmanship, earmarked Dh2.4 billion for the development of various projects at Mina Zayed and other ports under its jurisdiction. The Mina Zayed development plan includes a new container terminal with four post-Panamax gantry cranes, in addition to four regular gantry cranes for the existing berths, eight container stacking cranes, a 15,000-tonne cold storage, advanced handling equipment, a control tower and new administrative buildings. Additional warehousing space on 2.5 square kilometres of land near Mina Zayed is also being developed.

The Authority's development programme has attracted major shipping lines such as the Messina Line and an agreement signed in early 1996 has resulted in Integrated Container Feeder Services (ICFS) using the port as a regional hub for transshipment of goods to and from regional ports, as well as for trade with the Indian subcontinent. Mina Zayed is a 24 hour operating port which never closes, and its marketing philosophy is firmly rooted in satisfying customer needs. Documentation procedures have been simplified so that consignments can be cleared from the port within 20 minutes. Addition of the new terminal, which is now on the drawing board, will further boost Port Zayed's attractiveness to international shipping lines.

Mussafah Port

The Abu Dhabi Seaports Authority announced plans for development of a new port in Mussafah. Part of the Abu Dhabi Seaport Authority's Dh2.4 billion development plan, Mussafah Port, with its 380 metre long jetty, is expected to be operational by the end of 1997. It will be used particularly by international shipping lines engaged in transportation of scrap, steel products, heavy equipment and other industrial cargo used outside Abu Dhabi city in various industrial zones. It will have a capacity of 300,000 to 500,000 tonnes per year. The present access channel from Mina Zayed to Mussafah will cease to be used by shipping after completion of a new 25 kilometre long, 200 metres wide channel designed for ships up to 260 metres in length. There will also be an 800 metre anchoring area along the channel where four ships at a time can be docked.

Sadiyat Island

In July 1996, Abu Dhabi Government announced the establishment of a $3billion free trade zone which will include the building of a new port, as well as huge storage facilities, an airport and commodities trading exchanges on Sadiyat Island, 7 kilometres south of Abu Dhabi city.

Ras Sadr Fishing Port

The Abu Dhabi Government is building a $40 million fishing port at Ras Sadr, 35 kilometres northeast of Abu Dhabi city. The project involves dredging of a 350,000 square metre area, construction of breakwaters and provision of infrastructure.

Dubai

Dubai is a major trading hub for the whole region and its ports play a vital role in this, with more than 125 shipping lines using their facilities, making it a major world player in the field of marine-cargo handling. The Dubai Ports Authority & Jebel Ali Free Zone Authority are both chaired by Sultan Ahmed bin Sulayem who claims that Dubai's ports have shipping links to every international destination, worldwide. It is a remarkable achievement that today the emirate can lay claim to possessing what is probably the best port in the Middle East and one of the finest in the entire world. One of the Dubai ports' most recent innovations is the electronic manifest that eliminates the old paper-trail that could take up valuable administration time. The system provides important improvements in management of cargoes, enhancing speed of handling as well as collection of statistics. Development of Dubai's port facilities has taken place in tandem with major growth of the commercial sector in Dubai, with each sector depending upon the other for its own smooth operations. A classic example of this symbiosis is at Jebel Ali Free Trade Zone where efficient cargo handling and shipping facilities, combined with an attractive package of incentives, has resulted in the port zone becoming a base for almost a thousand national and multinational manufacturers and distributors.

The pattern at both Jebel Ali and Port Rashid is one of steady growth. Figures for the first two months of 1996, for example, showed total tonnage handled by the two ports increasing by 21 per cent over the same period in 1995, and reaching an impressive 5.3 million tons. Container tonnage showed a slightly larger increase, at 24 per cent, representing 61 per cent of Dubai Ports Authority total shipping volume. Jebel Ali port is now the thirteenth largest container port, worldwide, handling more units than Tokyo, Seattle or Shanghai. During the first two months of 1996 no less than 617 container vessels called at Dubai's twin ports, equating to a growth rate of 9 per cent over the same period in 1995. Overall, the DPA handled a record 2.07 million TEUs in 1995, compared to 1.88 million in 1994. Almost 40 per cent of the vessels calling at Dubai's ports in 1995 were container vessels, compared with around 34 per cent in 1994. Total tonnage handled by the two ports in 1995 rose by 12 per cent to 28 million tons. Recognition for Dubai Ports Authority's excellent achievements has also come in the form of international awards with the DPA being awarded 'Best sea port in the Middle East' by *Cargonews Asia* magazine, as well as the 1996 Asia Freight Industry Award.

Development plans include upgrading of facilities for handling general cargo and bulk minerals, installation of state of the art information systems, new warehouses and other infrastructural elements. At the time of writing, 23 gantry cranes are in operation, including two 51 tonne capacity highly sophisticated units; 34 yard cranes, 27 straddle carriers and 150 terminal tractors. By the year 2003 these figures will have increased to 30 gantry cranes and 31 straddle carriers. With so many containers passing through the twin ports they were natural locations for establishment of container repair yards, with one major facility of this kind at each of the ports.

Sharjah

Sharjah has a long record in shipping and was the first port in the entire Middle East to possess fully equipped container facilities at the Sharjah Container Terminal (SCT). Indeed, the Gulftainer Company, which commenced operations at Mina Khalid's SCT in 1976, celebrated its twentieth anniversary in June 1996, and is still operating the facility. Once the cargoes are landed rapid clearance and transport facilities are readily available at close hand with Speedtrux/Trucktainer, established by Gulftainer, now rated as the largest haulage company in the entire UAE. Meanwhile, Sharjah's impressive port on the east coast, at Khor Fakkan, provides valuable facilities for many ships that do not need to enter the Gulf. Gulftainer is also establishing a container repair facility.

Fujairah

From 1990 to 1994 the Port of Fujairah registered an annual growth of 10 per cent to 15 per cent. The port is one of the major and most modern container ports in the UAE. During 1995 Fujairah port handled 558,247 TEUs of containerized cargo. Total tonnage in 1995 was around 6 million tonnes of which container cargo represented around 15 per cent. Its expansion programme is already well underway with delivery of two Post Panamax Ship to Shore gantry cranes bringing its total complement of cranes and other handling gear to six ship to shore gantry cranes, 11 rubber-tyred (yard) gantry cranes, seven full container-handling fork lift trucks, and three empty container handling fork trucks.

Ras al-Khaimah

Mina Saqr, located next to the town of Ras al-Khaimah, is a deepwater port with several unique features. It can handle vessels up to 260 metres long and 11.5 metres maximum draught. Thanks to the development of a superb road network, the port is ideally situated for low-cost general cargo and container handling and it experienced a 35 per cent increase in its throughput in 1995. Not only can such cargoes be handled at less cost, but those destined for Dubai or Abu Dhabi also have the potential to link-up with fast road services and arrive earlier with a possible gain of 15 hours to Dubai and 28 hours to Abu Dhabi. Mina Saqr also has extensive storage facilities with 30,000 square metres of closed sheds plus 420,000 square metres of open space. Although the port is capable of handling 120 TEUs per hour and storing around 4000, its container facilities are still under-utilized and are being aggressively marketed. On the other hand its bulk handling facilities are heavily utilized with a major amount of trans-shipment taking place there.

RAIL TRANSPORT

The possibility of a GCC rail network was mooted during early 1996 and is receiving consideration by member states.

AIR TRANSPORT

Airports

In 1971 the old airport at Sharjah, the first in the UAE, which had provided such a vital refuelling base for Imperial Airways and BOAC, the fore-runners of British Airways, and had been an important operations headquarters for the RAF in Arabia, was handed over to the Emirate of Sharjah. By this time, however, the conveniently placed runway, which had originally been built in open desert on the outskirts of the main settlement, was becoming surrounded by new buildings that formed part of the rapidly expanding town. In 1977 Sharjah opened a new airport, about 10 kilometres northeast of the old one, further inland. Known as Sharjah International Airport, it played a vital role in bringing goods into the Emirates, fuelling the burgeoning demand that accompanied the surge in development of the 1970s and 80s. The airport has recently been extended and a free zone created in connection with it, further boosting its freight business. By 1994 the airport was handling 65 per cent of the UAE's sea-air cargo and 57 airlines were using its freight facilities.

Dubai too had an airport of its own by 1971, having received its first commercial jet in 1965. A new terminal building was constructed in that year, described as 'small and extravagantly pretty' (Alexander Frater: *Beyond the Blue Horizon*). Strategically placed as a convenient refuelling location for flights between Europe and Asia, and supporting greatly increased passenger and cargo transport in to the Emirates during a period of phenomenal expansion, usage of Dubai airport grew so rapidly that its facilities were soon placed under strain, and new ones were planned. This situation has continued right up to the present with forward planning, based upon steadily increasing figures for aircraft landings, passengers and freight, triggering new plans for development almost as soon as the cement has dried on the most recent construction phase. Thus, 35 airlines and 2.8 million passengers a year in 1980 had grown to 65 airlines and 6.3 million passengers in 1994, and plans for handling 12 million a year by 2000. In addition, its cargo village can handle 250,000 tons per year.

Dubai airport's complex operations are co-ordinated by a major organization in its own right, the Dubai National Air Travel Agency, DNATA for short, which is involved in both the marketing and operational sides of the business, ensuring smooth coordination and constantly striving for the highest possible standards. Already the Gulf's busiest airport, known and loved by passengers throughout the world, future plans will place it among the top worldwide in terms of both its aircraft and passenger handling facilities, not to mention its ancillary services such as an expanded duty-free complex and associated leisure centre.

Abu Dhabi has had three airport sites. The first was a strip of sand, marked out by oil-drums, just south of the town. This was still in use in 1971 by which time Bateen airport, not far from the Maqta bridge crossing to mainland Arabia, had been selected as a more suitable site for Abu Dhabi International Airport. This second airport remained in commercial use until the early 1980s, and continues to function today as a private and military air-base whilst Abu Dhabi's main passenger and cargo airport, at its present location, on the mainland, was opened for business in early 1982. A new Departure Lounge was opened in August 1995 when work on a new terminal building was also announced.

Other airports in the UAE include those of Fujairah and Ras al-Khaimah, both of which have experienced impressive growth in utilization since their establishment in the early 1990s. They have each benefited from increased trade with the CIS states of the former Soviet Union, particularly in the form of charter aircraft bringing passengers to shop in the UAE, but also as alternate depots for freight handling.

New Airport Developments
Over 11.6 million passengers and 637,000 tonnes of cargo passed through the UAE's airports in 1995. New airport developments intend to improve on these figures.

Dubai International Airport
Dubai International Airport currently handles around 7.3 million passengers per year and the figure is estimated to increase to over 12 million by the year 2000, necessitating a major expansion which started in earnest this year. Passenger growth rate at the airport is running at 10-12 per cent per year, compared to the normal rate of 4-6 per cent worldwide. The expansion of the airport is aimed at reaching a capability of handling 15.5 million passengers by the year 2003.

The expansion programme includes a satellite concourse of 100,000 square metres, which is under construction in front of the existing arrival and departure terminals, and is equipped with loading bridges providing direct access to 28 aircraft at one time, removing the necessity for bus transfers on most flights. An additional 22 gates are also to be built to the east of this concourse, increasing the overall simultaneous ground handling capacity to 50 aircraft. Other improvements for passengers at the airport include a business/conference facility, a family entertainment centre, a food hall with a range of restaurants and a new duty free shopping complex four times the size of the existing one. A 100 room transit hotel equipped with a health spa and swimming pool will replace the 12 room facility currently available.

An additional feature is a new Charter Terminal, also to be called the North Terminal, which will have a separate entrance from the Al-Towar area and will be fully

independent in all its handling and services. It will be used as a dedicated Hajj terminal during the pilgrimage season, and at other times will cater to charter flights from the CIS and extra-schedule flights during peak traffic occasions such as Eid and the summer holidays. Equipped with ten bays, big enough to handle Boeing 747 jumbo jets, the terminal will ease the congestion at the existing terminal. The new terminal will also house a bulk duty-free shop which will sell wholesale quantities of a wide range of products.

The expansion project involves development of the entire area around the airport, including a Free Trade Zone Business Park providing a million square metres for high tech industries on the north side of the airport; the Magic World amusement park, the first of its kind in the region; increased parking space for 2400 cars; and the Emirates Airline maintenance facility.

Cargo facilities at Dubai airport are also under expansion, following a doubling of cargoes passing through the airport over the past ten years. The Dubai Cargo Village, which reached its target annual capacity of 250,000 tonnes in 1994 - three years ahead of expectations, was extended to handle 350,000 tonnes per year in 1995. The airport is now engaged in further expansion of the Dubai Cargo Village capacity to 450,000 tonnes.

Regulations for Dubai Airport Free Zone

On 3 February 1996 Vice President, Prime Minister and Ruler of Dubai H.H.Sheikh Maktoum bin Rashid Al Maktoum issued a law in relation to Dubai Airport Free Zone stipulating that it is to be part of the Civil Aviation Department which will regulate the function of the zone. The DAFZ's functions will include the importing and storing of commodities to be re-exported or sent to the Customs Department. It will also include packaging of imported goods, establishment of light industries involving high technology, establishment of assembly plants for export purposes, as well as various other services such as banking, insurance and shipping. The law states that imports by the zone will be exempted from taxes, including income taxes. Neither will they be subject to any nationalization measures or other restrictions on their property. It also states that the firms and personnel working in the free zone will not be bound by the rules and regulations of the Municipality and Economic Department in Dubai. However, the law banned import of goods which are proved to be bad or unfit for consumption, those boycotted by the Government, products violating trade and industrial property laws, drugs and other related material and military items unless they are authorized by the competent Dubai authorities.

Abu Dhabi Airport

Abu Dhabi airport, having handled over three million passengers in 1995, has major expansion plans. The airport's US$400 million development will include a second runway and satellite building together with extension of both the passenger and cargo terminals. Work on these has already begun, with refurbishment of the passenger terminal and a new automated baggage handling system now underway. Meanwhile, the airport transit hotel was recently extended to house 20 rooms and a new fitness centre. A second runway, parallel to the existing main runway, is due to open towards the end of 1998, enabling the airport to handle the new large aircraft planned by Airbus

Industrie and Boeing. A new 11 gate second satellite, larger than the existing one with three stories and a basement, equipped with state of the art glazed loading bridges, is scheduled for opening in late 1999. Completion of these developments will enable the airport to handle seven million passengers a year. Those arriving at, or passing through the airport, will also have all their comforts taken care of since an airport leisure complex is being planned including a par three nine-hole golf course, a 200 room hotel 500 metres from the terminal, a swimming pool, tennis courts and an aircraft theme restaurant in a retired TriStar.

Abu Dhabi airport saw a 17 per cent increase in its cargo handling in 1995 with the total throughput exceeding 67,000 tonnes. Plans for expansion of cargo facilities at the airport include five additional parking stands and new warehouse space.

The comprehensive redevelopment is intended to turn Abu Dhabi International Airport into the Gulf's premier airport. The airport is keen to increase its role as a hub between Europe and Asia to cater for transfer business, which is seen as the future growth area as transit traffic is replaced by more non-stop flights.

Al-Ain International Airport
Al-Ain International Airport, opened on 31 March 1994, is also planning to expand to provide a 2400 square metre extension to the main terminal and three new buildings - a 4500 square metre dedicated cargo terminal, a flight catering unit and a building for ramp equipment. This new airport, the UAE's sixth international airport, is likely to play an increasingly important role for residents of the Al-Ain region and for promotion of tourism in this part of the UAE.

Sharjah International Airport
Sharjah airport handled just under 900,000 passengers in 1995, a slight fall over its all time peak figure of 1.1 million in 1993. Expansion plans include the addition of three to four more gates with accompanying loading bridges, whilst ramps to accommodate these have recently been extended. A new hangar, aircraft parking area and a new car park for 350 cars are presently under construction. Other improvements include increased immigration staff, new handling equipment and a general upgrading of utilities.

Lufthansa opened a dedicated terminal and warehouse at Sharjah airport in May 1993, making it the airline's regional cargo hub. Over 188,000 tonnes of cargo were handled at the airport in 1995 and facilities are being upgraded to cater for the large increase in cargo, 11 per cent of which is sea-air cargo. A free zone opened at the airport in September 1995, covering 1000 hectares.

Fujairah International Airport

In March 1996 Fujairah International Airport signed a contract to expand its Cargo Village by 35 per cent to meet the increasing demand from importers and tourists of CIS countries. The expansion project of the airport's Cargo Village involved an extension of around 2200 square metres. The airport handled a total of 33,000 tonnes of commodities in 1995, compared with 9500 tonnes in 1994, with most flights bound for Russia and the Ukraine. However, there was a slight fall off in passenger traffic in 1995, a phenomena that is regarded as a temporary pause in the growth statistics rather than a real downward trend since the emirate has strong tourism potential, having established a tourism board in 1995 and with a new resort hotel due to open in 1998.

Ras al-Khaimah International Airport

Ras al-Khaimah airport handled 126,498 passengers and 35,532 tonnes of cargo in 1995. The number of charter flights from the CIS declined in 1995, causing a 16.6 per cent drop in passengers. Cargo traffic, on the other hand, increased by 44 per cent.

Percentage changes in Passenger and Freight Traffic, 1994-1995

	1995 Passengers	Change	1995 Freight (tonnes)	Change
Dubai	7,102,984	+12.76%	315,804	+29.91%
Abu Dhabi	3,308,000	+3.19%	67,547	+17.22%
Sharjah	883,461	-3%	188,126	+81.7%
Ras Al-Khaimah	126,498	-16.6%	35,532	+44.5%
Al-Ain	114,300	N/A	3,595	N/A
Fujairah	103,776	-47%	26,785	+88%

AIRLINES

Gulf Air, formerly known as Gulf Aviation, was bought from BOAC in 1974 by a consortium formed by the Gulf states, including Bahrain, Qatar, Oman and the UAE. The company has grown to become one of the world's major airlines, serving as a joint national airline for the shareholding countries, but also developing its own distinctive style and a world-wide network (51 destinations in 1994). Its aircraft played a vital role in helping the UAE to develop its oil industry in the 1970s and 80s, both through carrying large numbers of oil workers, and also transporting urgently needed parts. In addition, it helped to create a national pride and interest in aviation, training UAE nationals in flying and other skills needed to run an airline. By 1994 Gulf Air was carrying five million passengers per year and was operating a fleet that included 18 Boeing 767-300s; 14 Airbus A320-200s, four Airbus A-340-300s and one Boeing 757F freighter.

Emirates airline was established by the Government of Dubai in October 1985. Its primary objective was to focus specifically upon the needs of Dubai itself, boosting business and tourism to the emirate. The airline has experienced impressive growth and gained a reputation for its high standards; a policy that has brought it numerous international awards and a considerable degree of client loyalty. Its routes have expanded from the Indian sub-continent in 1985 to Middle East and western Asia in '86 and Europe in '87. This was followed shortly after by flights to the Far East. It was the first airline, worldwide, to introduce a personal video in the back of every passenger seat throughout the aircraft, regardless of class. The airline has experienced a phenomenal growth over the past ten years, operating at a time when many airlines were experiencing very difficult trading conditions, exacerbated by the Gulf War.

Airlines: New Developments
Gulf Air

Gulf Air, partially owned by the UAE Government, continues to provide a crucial regional and international service, linking Gulf countries and providing direct flights to a growing list of international destinations. The UAE's long term interest in and support for the airline was reflected in 1995 with the appointment of its first UAE national as its president and chief executive. The role was filled by aviation expert, H.E. Sheikh Ahmed bin Saif Al Nahyan who is also Abu Dhabi's Under Secretary of Civil Aviation and a senior flight captain.

During 1995, the carrier transported a record 5.019 million passengers and 153,574 tonnes of cargo, but a combination of regional recession and increased competition were held responsible for a break in the post-Gulf War pattern of profits. A loss of US$159 million has stimulated a certain degree of retrenchment and consolidation, including some rationalization of routes that is likely to reduce the total number of destinations served to around 55. A review of the fleet requirements and priorities has also taken place, leading to plans for disposal of several aircraft and the possible return to service of others.

The airline operates a number of very successful strategic alliances, some of which are underpinned by equity holdings. For example, it owns 20 per cent of the Indian company, Jet Airways, whose passengers link up with Gulf Air at Bombay. The company was the first in the region to introduce a frequent flyer programme and this is under further development at present.

Gulf Air's shareholders are considering a partial sale of the company to the private sector, both as a means to introduce new capital but also to maintain the commercial focus of the airline in the increasingly competitive market in which it operates. Future plans also include increased penetration of the Far East market, with attention focused on China, Seoul and Tokyo, subject to successful negotiations for traffic rights and positive economic analysis.

Emirates Airline

In the 1994/1995 financial year Emirates reported a net profit of Dh95 million (US$25.9 million) on total revenue of Dh2.5 billion (US$683 million). Now in its twelfth year of operations, the airline operates to 90 destinations and has 36 non-stop flights per week between London and Dubai. Its fleet development, which has shown an average compound growth rate of 31 per cent a year over the last 10 years, includes introduction of three Boeing 777-200As in 1996, to be followed by four long range 777-200Bs in 1997, whilst the airline has options on an additional seven of these aircraft. The company's aircraft are all modern wide-bodied planes and the present fleet comprises six A300-600Rs, ten A310-300s and the three Boeing 777-200. As mentioned above, when the long range 777-200Bs are delivered Emirates will have the potential capability of running non-stop flights on routes such as Dubai-New York and Dubai-Australia.

Despite the fact that Dubai airport operates an open-skies policy, allowing any airline to land, Emirates, which is based in Dubai and owned by its government, must negotiate traffic rights with all overseas airports. Seventy-three scheduled airlines serve Dubai, which, in the words of Emirates' chief executive, "keeps us on our toes."

A new training centre equipped with Airbus and 777 flight simulators was completed by Emirates in 1995. The airline is also building its own maintenance facility at Dubai airport, a project scheduled to cost around US$60 million, and due to be operational in mid-1997.

CityLink

One of the latest and most innovative developments in the internal transportation system of the UAE is establishment of a sea-plane service between Abu Dhabi and Dubai whereby passengers board and disembark at the water's edge, close to the commercial and tourists centres of each city. CityLink, owned by Dubai-based Emitrex Aviation Services, established the new service in April 1996, using 12 seat Cessna Caravans. Flights between the two major cities take 30 minutes. Passengers flying from Abu Dhabi check-in at the Al-Ain hotel and fly from the Corniche, whilst those boarding at Dubai Creek check-in at the marina clubhouse.

With single fare at Dh195 (US$53) and return journeys costing Dh350 (US$95), the service provides credible competition for taxi or limousine services between the two cities. Passengers arriving in Abu Dhabi or Dubai may also receive a free limousine service to their first appointment.

Abu Dhabi Aviation

Partially owned by the Abu Dhabi Government, Abu Dhabi Aviation is a specialist airline which offers a wide range of services to the oil and gas industry, as well as crop spraying, tourist charters and the lifting of awkward loads. Following its purchase of Emirates Air Services' (EAS) operations in May 1994, the company's fleet is primarily helicopter based, with 26 Bell 212s, five Bell 206s and two Bell 412HPs 36 aircraft. In addition, there is a Dash 7 and two Twin Otters.

Emirates Air Services

The Advanced Group of Companies (AGC), which sold EAS's operations to Abu Dhabi Aviation in 1994, retained the company and its licences. It recently established a joint venture company, Airwork Advanced Group, with the UK company Airwork. This new company has contracted with the UAE and Kuwaiti Governments for maintenance of certain military training aircraft, and has established its own training facility for Hawk aircraft maintenance at Al-Ain airport.

Aerogulf
Aerogulf, based in Dubai, operates a fleet of Bell and MBB helicopters for charter work and sightseeing trips

Falcon Express
The company operates four Beechcraft 1900Cs and one Fokker F27 on feeder flights connecting with Federal Express' mainline freighters serving Europe, the sub-continent and the Far East.

DNATA

The Dubai National Air Travel Agency, part of the Emirates group, recorded net profits in the 1994/5 financial year of Dh50.56 million (US$13.8 million) on total revenue of Dh319 million (US$87 million). Recent expansion has included opening of a number of offices in London, Birmingham, Manchester and Glasgow. Meanwhile, a new subsidiary company, Mercator, in alliance with Swissair Information Systems, is offering automated data systems and services to the travel industry in the Middle East, Africa, the Indian sub-continent and the CIS.

AVIATION TRAINING

Dubai Aviation College, opened in 1991, aims to encourage local people to train in the aviation industry, including the fields of air traffic control, ground staff and engineering. A wide range of specialist courses in aviation subjects is offered with students coming from the UAE, neighbouring countries, Africa and Asia. The college is managed by Serco-IAL under contract to Dubai's Department of Civil Aviation. Training is also carried out at the Emirates/DNATA Training Centre which has flight simulators for both Boeing and Airbus aircraft. In addition, aviation engineering is taught at the Higher College of Technology in Abu Dhabi.

DUBAI AIR SHOW

Growth of aviation in the Emirates has spawned a secondary industry, that of aircraft marketing which reaches a climax every two years at the now world famous Dubai Air Show. Remarkably, the show is now in third place, after Farnborough in Britain, and Le Bourget in Paris, as one of the most significant international air-shows, on a global scale. The first such show was held as recently as 1986 and concentrated on civilian aircraft. The proposal, by H.H. Sheikh Mohammed bin Rashid Al Maktoum, that military aircraft should be included, transformed it into the major event that it has now become. The 1991 Dubai Air Show, held in November instead of January, as a result of Iraq's invasion of Kuwait, was a major event at which interest in military aircraft, that had been seen to perform so effectively during the conflict, were on show by their manufacturers. Even Lockheed's impressive Stealth Fighter was shown, but not for sale. Subsequent Air Shows, held in 1993 and 1995 were equally successful and Dubai has clearly made its mark as an essential venue on the aviation industry's calendar.

POSTAL SERVICE & PHILATELY

Postal services in the emirates which today comprise the UAE were initiated in 1909 when the first regional branch office of the Indian Postal Administration, then under British sponsorship and managed from Karachi, was opened in Dubai. Stamps used were Indian ones denominated in rupees and annas. Following the division of India, the office's operation was taken over by Pakistan and stamps were therefore overprinted with the word Pakistan.

On 1 April 1948 the British Postal Administration assumed responsibility for the postal administration in Dubai. British stamps were thus issued with portraits of the reigning monarchs, King George VI and later Elizabeth II. British control of this service ceased in 1963 and Dubai issued its first set of stamps on 15 June 1963. In 1961 it had issued a set for common usage by other emirates but since only Dubai had a post-office these were rarely used elsewhere.

Abu Dhabi's postal service was established on 30 March 1963 using stamps of the British Postal Agencies in Eastern Arabia. The emirate issued its own first stamp on 30 March 1964 and took over complete control of the postal service on 1 January 1967.

Post offices were opened in Sharjah, Ajman, Ras al-Khaimah, Fujairah and Umm al-Qaiwain during 1963 and 1964. These were linked to Dubai Post Office and mail travelled in and out via Dubai airport. At the same time each emirate began using its own stamps.

17

The combined postal service of the newly formed United Arab Emirates was established on 1 August 1972 under a Federal Decree and the General Post Administration was established under the Ministry of Communications. It decided to print the words United Arab Emirates over the stamps of the Emirate of Abu Dhabi, with these stamps being used in all emirates. The first new stamps of the UAE were then issued by the General Post Administration on 1 January 1973 with a set of 12 denominated values and a portrait of His Highness Sheikh Zayed bin Sultan Al Nahyan, President of the UAE and Ruler of Abu Dhabi.

U.A.E. الامارات العربية المتحدة

Postage

3 DH الذكرى الأولى لافتتاح متحف رأس الخيمة الوطني / ٣ دراهم
1st Anniversary of the Ras Al Khaimah National Museum

In 1985 the General Postal Authority was established under Federal Decree. The Authority has followed a balanced and conservative stamp-issuing policy which has gained respect in the philatelic world and has resulted in a great demand for the stamps of the United Arab Emirates by collectors both at home and abroad. Meanwhile, the postal service itself has been continually upgraded and improved, offering users a full range of efficient mailing services - a far cry from the time, not so long ago, when letters were carried by camel or dhow, taking weeks or months to reach their destinations.

1. First Commemorative and definitive stamps issued after formation of the United Arab Emirates (1.1.1973).
2. Centenary of Universal Postal Union 1874-1974 (5.8.1974).
3. 9th Arab Petroleum Conference (10.3.1975).
4. Traffic Week (1976).
5. International Literacy Day (8.9.1977).
6. Population Census (15.12.1980).
7. International Year of Disabled Persons 1981 (26.12.1981).
8. Arab 6th Gulf Football Championship (4.4.1982).
9. 10th Anniversary of Emirates Telecommunications Corporation (1.9.1986).
10. Emirates Airline First Anniversary 1986 (25.10.1986).
11. GCC Supreme Council Seventh Session (2.11.1986).
12. 10th Anniversary of the UAE University (23.6.1987).
13. 6th Anniversary of Abu Dhabi International Airport (2.1.1988).
14. 1st Anniversary of Ras al-Khaimah Museum (19.11.1988).
15. Sharjah International Airport (21.04.1989).
16. Football World Cup Italy 1990 (8.6.1990).
17. Twentieth National Day (2.12.1991).
18. EXPO 92 (20.4.1992).
19. Mina Zayed (28.6.1992).
20. GCC Supreme Council Thirteenth Session (1.12.1992).
21. Dubai Ports Authority (10.11.1993).
22. Environment Protection (10.10.1994).
23. Arab Gulf Twelfth Football Championship (3.11.1994).
24. Birds of the UAE (12.12.1994).
25. IDEX 95 (19.3.1995).
26. Fiftieth Anniversary of Arab League (22.3.1995).
27. Fiftieth Anniversary of United Nations (22.3.1995).
28. Census 95 (20.11.1995).
29. Hobie Cat 16 World Sailing Championship 1996 (27.2.1996).

29

UNITED ARAB EMIRATES

HOBIE CAT 16 WORLD CHAMPIONSHIPS 1996

50 FILS

POSTAGE 5 FILS بريد
UNITED ARAB EMIRATES الإمارات العربية المتحدة

150 FILS POSTAGE بريد
INTERNATIONAL YEAR OF DISABLED PERSONS 1981
الإمارات العربية المتحدة
UNITED ARAB EMIRATES

الإمارات العربية المتحدة
POPULATION CENSUS 1980
UNITED ARAB EMIRATES
15 FILS POSTAGE

UNITED ARAB EMIRATES
OIL PRODUCTION PLATFORM
10-3-1975
الإمارات العربية المتحدة
منصة إنتاج النفط
١٩٧٥/٣/١٠
125 FILS POSTAGE مؤتمر النفط العربي التاسع
9th ARAB PETROLEUM CONFERENCE ١٢٥

الإمارات العربية المتحدة
UNITED ARAB EMIRATES
Emirates
EMIRATES AIRLINES
1st ANNIVERSARY 1985-1986
175 FILS POSTAGE ١٧٥

دورة كأس الخليج العربي السادسة لكرة القدم
Arab Gulf
6th Football
Championship
POSTAGE الإمارات العربية المتحدة UNITED ARAB EMIRATES 75

60 FILS 1874 1974 العيد المئوي للاتحاد البريدي العالمي
CENTENARY OF UNIVERSAL POSTAL UNION ١٨٧٤ ١٩٧٤
POSTAGE بريد
UNITED ARAB EMIRATES الإمارات العربية المتحدة

3 DHS الإمارات العربية المتحدة
1977-1987 ١٤٠١ - ١٤٠٧
UNITED ARAB EMIRATES
10th ANNIVERSARY OF THE U.A.E. UNIVERSITY

الإمارات العربية المتحدة
UNITED ARAB EMIRATES
1976-1986
3 DIRHAMS

U.A.E. الإمارات العربية المتحدة
140 FILS ١٤٠ أسبوع المرور ١٩٧٦/٤/١
TRAFFIC WEEK 1-4-1976

U.A.E. الإمارات العربية المتحدة
8th SEPT. 1977 ٨ سبتمبر ١٩٧٧
١٣٩٧
POSTAGE بريد
اليوم العالمي لمحو الأمية
3 DIRHAMS INT. LITERACY DAY

الإمارات العربية المتحدة
UNITED ARAB EMIRATES
GCC SUPREME COUNCIL 7TH SESSION (ABU DHABI NOV 1986)
STATE OF QATAR
POSTAGE بريد
50 FILS ٥٠

الإمارات العربية المتحدة
UNITED ARAB EMIRATES
6th ANNIVERSARY
ABU DHABI INTERNATIONAL AIRPORT
50 FILS POSTAGE بريد ٥٠

15

UNITED ARAB EMIRATES الإمارات العربية المتحدة
مطار الشارقة الدولي ١٩٧٩ - ١٩٨٩
SHARJAH INTERNATIONAL AIRPORT 1979 - 1989
50 FILS

16

UNITED ARAB EMIRATES
الإمارات العربية المتحدة
UAE
FOOTBALL WORLD CUP
ITALIA 90
POSTAGE 1 DH

18

الإمارات العربية المتحدة
UNITED ARAB EMIRATES
EXPO '92 اكسبو '٩٢
2 POSTAGE DIRHAMS AL-JAHLI CASTLE AL-AIN

UNITED ARAB EMIRATES الإمارات العربية المتحدة
"MINA ZAYED"
ABU DHABI
175 POSTAGE FILS ١٧٥ 20TH ANNIVERSARY

20

الإمارات العربية المتحدة
United Arab Emirates
G.C.C. SUPREME COUNCIL 13th SESSION
POSTAGE ABU DHABI DEC. 1992
50 FILS ٥٠

21

الإمارات العربية المتحدة
UNITED ARAB EMIRATES
DUBAI PORTS AUTHORITY
250 POSTAGE FILS ٢٥٠

22

UNITED ARAB EMIRATES الإمارات العربية المتحدة
ARABIAN LEOPARD
50 POSTAGE FILS ENVIRONMENT PROTECTION

24

UNITED ARAB EMIRATES الإمارات العربية المتحدة
MEROPS ORIENTALIS
50 POSTAGE FILS ٥٠ BIRDS OF U.A.E

23

الإمارات العربية المتحدة
UNITED ARAB EMIRATES
POSTAGE
50 FILS ٥٠

25

الإمارات العربية المتحدة
United Arab Emirates
95 UAE
IDEX ايدكس
INTERNATIONAL DEFENCE
EXHIBITION & CONFERENCE
ABU DHABI 19 - 23 MARCH 1995
1 DH.

26

الإمارات العربية المتحدة
UNITED ARAB EMIRATES
50
50th. ANNIVERSARY OF THE ARAB LEAGUE
1 DH.

27

الإمارات العربية المتحدة
UNITED ARAB EMIRATES
50
50th. ANNIVERSARY OF THE UNITED NATIONS
250 FILS ٢٥٠

28

الإمارات العربية المتحدة
UNITED ARAB EMIRATES
CENSUS 95
250 FILS ٢٥٠

TELECOMMUNICATIONS

ETISALAT's board approved the launch of two telecommunications satellites, following feasibility studies for the multi-million dollar scheme. The first satellite, EMIRSAT, scheduled to be launched in 1998, will be used to transmit telephone data and television programmes and will be exclusively used by ETISALAT: the other, THURAYYA, will provide a regional system serving mobile telecommunication systems on a fixed orbit around the globe, and providing roaming voice, data, fax and location demarking facilities covering a large number of Arab states, India, Pakistan, Iran, Turkey, East Europe and the Mediterranean and Red Sea, the Arabian Gulf and Arabian Sea. In the UAE it will help to provide telecommunications

services to rural and remote areas and islands, as well as benefiting mining and oil research firms. The UAE is already a subscriber to two Arab satellites currently in orbit. The Arab Satellite Organization, ARABSAT, which owns the two, plans to launch a third one to meet growing demand.

ETISALAT launched several new services at the start of 1996, including Calling Line Identification Presentation, CLIP, which will combat nuisance calls; the Calling Card service, a talk globally play locally feature; an Automated Bill Payment service and a Fax-on-Demand facility. At the same time the company also introduced automatic monthly bill payment, using a machine similar to the ATM.

ETISALAT has continued to work on

installation of a fibre optic network which is now considered to be one of the most up to date networks of its kind worldwide. Etisalat's extension of the network, which links the UAE, Qatar, Bahrain and Kuwait through a submarine cable, will enter service in mid-1997.

ETISALAT is also a subscriber to a number of international cable systems providing digital links with most parts of the world, particularly financial centres in the East and West. Prime among these are the FLAG cable and Se Me We 3, which will enter service in 1997 and 1998 respectively. In addition, the UAE will also be linked with Saudi Arabia through a territorial fibre optic cable.

Net profits of ETISALAT increased from Dh1.24 billion in 1994 to Dh1.44 billion in 1995. A total of Dh593 million capital expenditure was spent on ETISALAT's fixed assets in 1995. The UAE now has the highest telephone density in the region with 29 lines per 100 people. Residents spent a total of 2280 million minutes or 1.58 million days on the telephone in 1995. Domestic traffic, i.e. the total time spent on local calls within the UAE, increased by 217 million minutes from 11779 million minutes in 1994, corresponding to a 12 per cent growth. Traffic volume from international calls registered a phenomenal growth of 73 million minutes from the 428 million minutes recorded in 1994, placing ETISALAT twenty-eighth among the major telephone

administrations in the world and second in the Gulf region. The total number of subscribers rose by 57,206, reaching a total of 672,330 lines by the end of 1995, corresponding to a 9 per cent increase over the preceding year. The UAE has direct international telephone services with some 238 countries.

ETISALAT's mobile telephone services remained its fastest-growing business activity in 1995 with the GSM system attaining a record growth of 204 per cent over the preceding year. GSM subscribers, who at the close of 1995 totalled 128,495, reflecting an increase of 41 per cent since 1994, can now also use their phones in a growing number of countries worldwide, including most of Europe, Africa, Asia and Australia.

Introduction of ETISALAT's Internet service opened up the vast information resources throughout the world to users in the UAE.

ELECTRICITY & WATER

DEMAND FOR ELECTRICITY IN THE UAE increased by 40 per cent in the past five years while the installed capacity rose by 30 per cent. Total energy generated in the UAE increased by 8.96 per cent in 1994 to 23,402 million KWH from 20,806 million KWH in 1993. The 1993 level was itself 12.03 per cent up on 1992. This rate of growth is an indication of government support for industrial diversification. In March 1996 a decision was announced by Abu Dhabi Crown Prince and Deputy Supreme Commander of the UAE Armed Forces Sheikh Khalifa bin Zayed Al Nahyan to form a committee to study the privatization of the Water and Electricity Department.

AL-AWIR POWER STATION

In early February 1996 the Dubai Electricity and Water Authority, DEWA, announced the award of a Dh1.08 billion ($295 million) contract for construction of a new power plant at Al-Awir, 25 kilometres from Dubai city. The project involves construction of a 600 megawatt power station with 400 kilowatt sub-station and installation of six single cycle gas turbines, with the option of turning them into combined cycle later. Japan's Mitsubishi Heavy Industries Ltd and Mitsubishi Corporation won the

contract which will bring Dubai's installed capacity to 22,600 megawatts from the existing capacity of 1540 megawatts. The first phase is scheduled to come on stream in June 1997, the second by October 1997 and the third by February 1998.

SOLAR POWER

An Abu Dhabi-based local company, Gulf Solar Company, announced plans to manufacture solar electrical arrays to provide power during emergencies and in remote areas in the UAE. The 1000 watt array called SOLAGEN charges a battery bank and then converts electricity from DC to AC with a 3600 watt inverter.

In February 1996 the Abu Dhabi Water and Electricity Department, WED, announced it was considering making use of solar energy for the desalination of seawater after the success of an experimental project in Umm al-Nar. The solar desalination experiment produces about 20,000 gallons of desalinated water daily and has been in operation for around ten years. The project is the outcome of the technical cooperation between the Abu Dhabi Government and the Engineering Advancement Association of Japan. The Umm al-Nar facility, with its simple heat collectors, has eliminated the need for a boiler, which is often difficult to operate and maintain in rural areas. Solar distillation is also attractive because it eliminates the need to transport large quantities of heating oil to remote islands and locations.

WATER

By the year 2015, water consumption in the UAE is expected to reach 600 million gallons per day (mgd). The maximum domestic water demand in the Emirate of Abu Dhabi alone is expected to reach 250 mgd over the next 15 years.

DESALINATION

The UAE possesses one of the best developed desalination production and distribution systems in the world. Massive investment in coastal desalination plants has helped to transform a previously harsh and barren region into one that lists greenery as a major characteristic and one that supports the massive socio-economic development that has been in progress over the past 25 years. Sixty to seventy per cent of total water supplies are desalinated - a figure that will rise even higher as new projects come on stream and the demand continues to increase at a rate of 10 per cent each year. Developments in this sector during the next 15 years are likely to bring an increased capacity of over 1.137 million cubic metres a day of desalinated water.

The UAE's first desalination plant was established in 1960 with a capacity of 12,500 gallons per day and using the multi-stage flash, MSF, system which has become the standard for all the large distillers presently working in conjunction with the main power stations in the country. During the 1970s large new plants were built at the Abu Dhabi Power Station, while new stations were set up at Umm al-Nar, Taweelah, Jebel Ali and Sharjah, all using MSF distillers. Developments continues and an eight-unit station at Jebel Ali has recently been completed with a production capacity of 60 mgd, as well as a six-unit station of 76 mgd at Taweelah. The latter units are said to be the largest in the world and will each produce 12.7 mgd.

At present, 16 mgd of desalinated water is supplied through a pipe system towards Al-Ain. In addition, two new pipes with a total capacity of 40 mgd are currently being built to take water from the Taweelah 'B' station in Abu Dhabi to Al-Ain. These pipes are scheduled to enter full service in 1997 and will help to take the pressure off groundwater resources in the Al-Ain region. Extra water required for Abu Dhabi will be produced by further extension of the Taweelah station, making it the biggest in the UAE. At Mirfa, a 16 mgd station which will pump water to Madinat Zayed and Liwa is also under construction.

On 20 March 1996, Chairman of the Abu Dhabi Water and Electricity Department, Sheikh Surour bin Mohammed Al Nahyan, signed a contract for the supply and installation of two desalination units for Ras al-Khaimah. The Dh105 million project is financed by Sheikh Zayed bin Sultan Al Nahyan to meet the water needs of the Emirate of Ras al-Khaimah. The project, to be implemented within 23 months, will have a production capacity of 3.0 million gallons.

Sharjah's 1996 budget for its Department of Water and Electricity was approved in March at around Dh1.01 billion. In April 1996 Supreme Council Member and Ruler of Sharjah H.H. Dr Sheikh Sultan bin Mohammed Al Qassimi signed a contract for the importation and installation of a water desalination unit to be installed at the emirate's Al-Laya desalination plant, with a capacity of 5.0 million gallons per day.

Large desalination plants in the UAE

Site	Utility	Design	Number of	Start-up
Umm al-Nar	WED	384,600	16	1979
Abu Dhabi City	WED	57,700	4	1977
Taweelah A	WED	130,900	4	1990
Taweelah B	WED	345,600	6	1995/96
Mirfa A	WED	73,600	3	1996
Jebel Ali D	DEWA	163,600	8	1979/80
Jebel Ali E	DEWA	127,300	4	1988
Jebel Ali G	DEWA	272,700	8	1993
Dubai	Dubal	136,300	5	1978/80
Aluminium Laya	SWEC	98 ,200	4	1981

Source: Development of Desalination Plants in the UAE: Past and Present, November 1995, Water and Electricity Department, Abu Dhabi.

GROUNDWATER EXPLORATION

H.H. Sheikh Zayed has always had a strong interest in freshwater resources of the UAE and has closely followed the work that has been undertaken for groundwater exploration during the past quarter century. Whilst most of this has been concentrated on shallow-depth aquifers, Sheikh Zayed has continually stressed that many of these were first discovered hundreds or thousands of years ago and were tapped into by people inhabiting areas such as Al-Ain and Liwa. The major challenge, he emphasized, was to locate deeper aquifers that have not been previously discovered.

Following the UAE President's call for further action in this field, important progress took place during 1995 and 1996, with an agreement signed in October 1995 between ADNOC, Deutsch Gesellschaft Fur Technische Zusammenarbeit (GTZ) Gmbh and

Daimler Benz Aerospace. The first phase of the plan, scheduled to last one and a half years, involves satellite scanning of areas expected to have large water deposits, followed by site exploration by ADNOC engineers using special sensors, and finally the digging of 10 deep experimental water wells in Liwa and Al-Ain regions. If efforts to locate significant deep reservoirs though use of satellites meets with success, the UAE could achieve savings worth billions of dirhams.

The first deep reservoir discovery under this programme took place in May 1966, approximately 20 kilometres east of Al-Ain city. It was a strong affirmation of Sheikh Zayed's conviction that such deep wells do exist and can be tapped into in order to boost freshwater supplies. The discovery well, GWA-2, reached a depth of approximately 1000 metres below ground level, having penetrated two main beds of limestone. The first of these, which is 150 metres thick, lies at about 300 metres depth and contains potable freshwater of 916 ppm which is delivering around 100 cubic metres per hour. The second deeper, 250 metres thick, bed lies at just over 900 metres and its water is suitable for agriculture. Assessment of the volume of water held in these important aquifers is still being undertaken, whilst new wells are also being drilled. In addition to the actual discoveries of deep wells, an important element of the project has been the training of UAE nationals in the technologies involved in this work. ADNOC's extensive geological research in the UAE has been of great importance to the project and the application of the latest survey techniques, including satellite imagery, has extended the team's capabilities and the overall coverage of the groundwater survey.

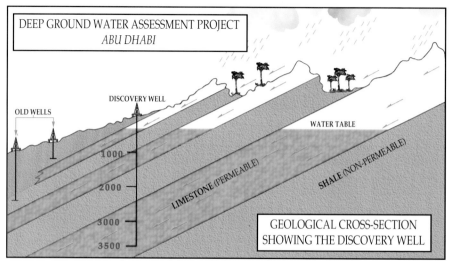

DEEP GROUND WATER ASSESSMENT PROJECT
ABU DHABI

OLD WELLS
DISCOVERY WELL
WATER TABLE
1000
2000
3000
3500
LIMESTONE (PERMEABLE)
SHALE (NON-PERMEABLE)

GEOLOGICAL CROSS-SECTION
SHOWING THE DISCOVERY WELL

HOUSING

SINCE ITS FORMATION the UAE has been concerned with providing adequate housing for its burgeoning population. In the course of the last 25 years, tens of thousands of houses have been built and furnished with all necessary services such as schools, hospitals, roads, electricity, water, recreational and other facilities required for a modern city. The Ministry of Public Works and Housing is responsible for the construction of federal housing schemes. Municipalities and specialized housing councils carry out regional projects.

The Ministry of Public Works and Housing distributed more than 17,000 houses to citizens in the Northern Emirates up until last year, while work is underway on the construction of 2000 houses for UAE nationals, financed by H.H. Sheikh Zayed bin Sultan Al Nahyan. The Ministry finished the first stage, consisting of 1259 houses, at a cost of Dh500 millions.

In Abu Dhabi, the number of housing units drastically increased both in urban and rural areas. According to latest statistics from the Planning Department, housing units increased from 117,000 in 1991 to 139,802 by 1995. Last year, Abu Dhabi Municipality distributed 690 housing units to nationals at Al-Marfa, Al-Rahba and Al-Nahda cities.

The Department of Social Services and Commercial Buildings plays a pivotal role in building construction. The idea behind this scheme is for the Government to finance and construct buildings for UAE nationals on their own land under instructions issued by H.H. Sheikh Khalifa bin Zayed Al Nahyan, with financial guarantees to recover the

U.A.E. Housing Census 1995

Emirate	Vacant	Occupied	No. of Buildings
Abu Dhabi	13,378	139,802	73,988
Dubai	7,082	102,849	49,419
Sharjah	7,546	71,712	46,586
Ajman	3,794	18,002	12,238
Umm al-Qaiwain	1,048	5,965	7,221
Ras al-Khaimah	3,544	27,177	28,301
Al-Fujairah	1,142	11,095	11,293
Total U.A.E.	**37,534**	**376,602**	**229,046**

Source: Ministry of Planning (Prelim. Results, Housing Census 1995)

construction costs from the proceeds of these buildings which are managed by the Department. The investment in this project reached Dh14 billion, covering 5500 buildings and 45,000 housing units. A special corporation for housing loans plays an active role in financing housing schemes. H.H. Sheikh Khalifa bin Zayed Al Nahyan allocated 500 million dirhams last May, being the fourth installment of money donated for housing schemes.

TOWN DEVELOPMENTS

Major town development and housing projects were undertaken throughout the UAE during the period under review. Such projects included a new township west of Shahama City and Rahba agricultural lands in the Emirate of Abu Dhabi where the proposed project stretches from Bel Ghilim island towards the north along the Umm al-Nar - Shahama highway, a region previously characterized by sand dunes, rocky hills and sabkha mud-flats. Abu Dhabi Municipality undertook a major land-reclamation project prior to development. As part of a plan to establish an integrated city in Mussafah, 77 commercial buildings were constructed there during 1995, providing 894 residential units. Over the past four years, 158 commercial buildings, providing more than 1517 residential units, have been constructed in the area at a cost of Dh347.9 million. An additional 437 projects involving commercial buildings were under construction in April 1996, at a total estimated cost of Dh1.55 billion. Upon completion they will provide more than 5244 residential units.

A new integrated township with all necessary amenities is scheduled for construction in the suburbs of Al-Ain city and levelling of the land for the construction of 100 houses has already been completed. A total of 551 houses are under construction in different areas of Al-Ain city and the Public Works Department recently completed construction of 859 houses. In 1996, Dubai Municipality budget earmarked Dh150 million for various local housing projects for its citizens.

EDUCATION

Education is like a lantern which lights up your way in a dark alley. Sheikh Zayed.

ARABS, FROM THE EARLIEST TIMES, have had a strong tradition of literacy, rooted partly in the obligations of a Muslim to daily prayers and recitation of the Holy Qur'an which was invariably the first book that a child learned to read. Schooling was relatively informal, a *Mutawwa* or tutor, usually taught children, the sexes separating at seven according to Islamic tradition. It wasn't until the beginning of the oil era in the late 1950s that formal systematic education in purpose-built schools, first for boys and then for girls, started to appear. When the UAE was formed, only a tiny minority of children had access to schooling, and of those, the majority were boys. The formation of the Federation in 1971 brought a real focus on education. Gradually, kindergarten, elementary, intermediate and secondary schools were established in urban and rural areas. The spreading of educational facilities throughout the country, coupled with the introduction of legislation making education compulsory, at least until the completion of the intermediate stage, means that all children, boys and girls, are given the opportunity to go to school.

The process of overseeing a complex and sophisticated educational system is supervised by the Ministry of Education, in conjunction with the Ministry of Higher Education and Scientific Research. In 1995, a new educational policy was approved by the Cabinet, emphasizing the true Islamic upbringing and aiming at enhancing national unity, inculcating collective responsibility among the community, stressing the significance of productive work and comprehensive development, in addition to preparing UAE society for the ever-changing future. The following table illustrates the remarkable progress achieved in education:

SCHOOL TYPE	1972-73		1995-96		% increase
	Schools	Students	Schools	Students	
Government Schools		40,193		295,333	363%
Classes	1290		11,259		363%
Schools	132		615*		774%
Teaching and Admin staff	2368		25,289		365%
Kindergartens	16	3276	75	19,291	
Elementary Schools	91	30,495	316	152,742	
Intermediate Schools	11	2453	123	74,798	
Secondary Schools	5	1225	88	46,948	
Tech. Second. Schools	5	333	7	1554	
Private Schools	400		390	185,289	

*In addition, in 1996-97 25 new schools are planned throughout the State.

The zone-wise figures from the Department of Data and Research at the Ministry of Education show there are 246 schools with 124,480 students in Abu Dhabi, including 104 schools with 54,446 students in Al-Ain and 38 schools with 10,940 students in the Western Region, as well as 369 schools with 170,854 students in Dubai and the Northern Emirates. The figures include 89 schools with 39,214 students in Dubai, 71 schools with 33,662 students in Sharjah, 35 schools with 17,797 students in Ajman, 21

schools with 7210 students in Umm al-Qaiwain, 86 schools with 38,405 students in Fujairah and 86 schools with 24,565 students in Ras al-Khaimah.

By the end of the academic year 1995/96, 15,939 students were examined for the General School Certificate, whereas 184,460 students were examined for upgrading to upper classes.

THIRD LEVEL COLLEGES

The UAE University was opened in Al-Ain in 1977 and a number of other specialized third level colleges, such as the Higher College of Technology, Ajman University College, Dubai Islamic College and Dubai Medical Sciences College, were also established.

UAE University's fifteenth batch of students, comprising 1347, graduated this year, bringing to 16,000 the total number of students graduated since its formation Meanwhile the Higher Colleges of Technology graduated 153 students, bringing their total number of graduations to 694 students, representing an average annual growth rate of 35 per cent. Of the 153 students from this year's HCT graduation class, 122 are from the Business Programme, which includes Business Administration, Office Administration, Information Systems, Accounting, Banking and Finance. A total of 31 students graduated from Engineering Technology, including Electronic Engineering - both Industrial and Computer; Aviation - Avionics, Airframe and Engines; and Chemical, Civil and Mechanical Engineering Technology.

As a result of the rapid expansion of the Higher Colleges of Technology's admission policy, the number of students at the eight colleges rose to 4534, among whom 1843 are enrolled in the diploma degree and 691 are registered for the Higher Diploma Programme: the number of students first enrolled in the colleges was 240.

The Colleges are constantly striving to organize new courses which will cater to the development needs of the state. In 1995, the Colleges of Higher Technology and Dubai Custom Authority jointly organized a Diploma in Transport and Trade to graduate personnel specialized in customs and cargo services. In addition, the International Campus of Technology, which is an affiliate to the Centre of Applied Research at Abu Dhabi's Higher College of Technology, was opened. The Centre, costing more than 1 million dirhams, was established in collaboration with the global telecommunications company, AT&T. The Centre holds training courses for the maintenance of optical fibres networks and systems and telecommunication equipment in general. A Systimax 'Intelligent Classroom' has been installed by AT&T. This involves a 6m x 12m classroom setting, a sophisticated, computerized system which increases the effectiveness of the teacher's instructions and speeds up the students' assimilation of information. A camera installed on top of each computer transfers each student's image to the teacher's screen, so that even when communicating at a distance they can have access to each other through video-conferencing by which teachers and students will be able to exchange information, notes and remarks on the spot. This is believed to the world's first such classroom and will soon be followed by similar classes in all the UAE's HCT, including the two new ones to be opened in the Emirate of Fujairah in 1998.

Sharjah Airport's ELOUFQ College celebrated, in 1995, the graduation of its fifth batch of students, 150 graduates specializing in tourism services, business administration, commercial information services and computer services. Ajman University also celebrated the graduation of its first 8 groups, comprising 587 students.

ADULT LITERACY

Adult literacy has been given considerable attention through the launching of a comprehensive campaign in 1989 for eradicating illiteracy. A successful programme has resulted in a decline of adult illiteracy to 15 per cent, compared with 95 per cent in the past. Ministry of Planning statistics listed 140-adult literacy centres catering to 19,000 people, in comparison with 98 centres for 11,000 students in 1972. The UAE is endeavouring to completely eliminate illiteracy by the year 2000. Due attention has also been given to special education classes and centres for teaching Qur'an, at which the number of students has risen from 800 in 1989 to 4750 in 1996.

UNITED ARAB EMIRATES 1996

VOCATIONAL TRAINING PROGRAMME

To encourage nationals to benefit from their free time and develop their potentials and skills, the UAE People's Heritage Revival Association, EPHRA, is launching a National Occupational Project, NOP, involving the establishment of 11 vocational training centres throughout the Emirates. These will offer various forms of vocational training - including car repairs, smithery, electrical installation, carpentry, designing, air-conditioning, construction, agriculture, computers and handicrafts - and will be established in each emirate in co-operation with both governmental and non-governmental organizations. They will be divided into three sections, one each for men, women and children.

The children's section will have an intensive training programme devoted to pupils of preparatory and secondary school age who, in addition to the vocational training, will receive religious, social and cultural education. The programmes for men and women will focus on the development of skills that could generate an income: professional, vocational education has been lagging behind the progress witnessed in various other fields in the country. The NOP is needed for several other reasons, including the Emiratization of professions (vital for the development and stability of society); the importance of introducing programmes to keep the youth busy during leisure time; providing the disabled (10 per cent of society) with the chance to receive training and education to help them be part of a productive work force; giving prisoners a chance to utilize their long hours of loneliness and boredom, and helping nationals whose main jobs are insufficient to meet the high cost of living.

It is also hoped that the NOP will educate Emiratis who have their own businesses on how to run them successfully. In the future, NOP centres would come to rely on self-generated profits while marketing committees would promote the products produced by those acquiring skills through the NOP, using them to further expand the project.

NEW TECHNICAL SCHOOLS

The Federal Council of Ministers approved, in its meeting on 11 March 1996, a report from the Ministry of Finance and Industry on the financial allocations required for the implementation of a project to develop technical education in the country in co-operation with a specialized German institute. The project includes the construction of nine industrial and commercial schools at a cost of Dh52million. Construction work will start this year and is expected to end by the year 2000.

UAE-UNESCO PACT

UAE Minister of Education Hamad Abdul Rahman Al Madfa and UNESCO Director General Frederico Mayor recently signed a Memorandum of Understanding covering the fields of education, higher education, scientific research, culture and information and a National Commission for Education, Culture and Science. It was agreed that UNESCO would contribute to the development of secondary and technical education, basic and pre-school education. Both sides agreed that UNESCO will help in implementing the recommendations included in the report of the International Commission for Education in the twenty-first century. They also agreed to sustain co-operation in the field of activities pertaining to education in early childhood, the production of material for this stage and assistance for teachers and social workers in the field of early childhood and family environment.

On matters of higher education and scientific research, the two sides have agreed to co-operate in the following fields:
- to improve the quality and suitability of higher education;
- to provide technical assistance to facilitate the diversification of education, both open and distance learning;
- to strengthen the links between higher education and the labour market;
- supporting the UNESCO programme of universities twinning;
- establishing a UNESCO chair in a specialization to be defined later;
- promoting co-operation between universities;
- developing education, training and research activities;
- UNESCO to give support to a UAE scientific research centre; and
- to provide the necessary expertise for setting up a National Commission in oceanography, an international hydrological programme and a Man and Biosphere Programme, MAB.

UNITED ARAB EMIRATES 1996

HEALTH

IT IS HARD TO BELIEVE THAT the only person a resident of Abu Dhabi could turn to for medical treatment 40 years ago was the master of the local religious school, Darwish bin Karam, who combined his teaching with a wide range of other social services including barber, marriage counsellor, and traditional herbalist healer. There was no doctor and no hospital. In fact Abu Dhabi remained without a hospital until 1967. Inevitably many people died of illnesses that could have been treated and cured if the facilities for health care had been available. When the older residents of the UAE take stock of all that has been achieved since the foundation of the Federation, many of them have personal memories and regrets over the deaths of family members whose fate might have been different had they enjoyed the benefits of today's UAE. Many also reflect that today's young people take too much for granted the superb health care facilities that have been created in such a short space of time. At the same time there is a deep appreciation for the fact that revenues from oil have been spent for the benefit of all the UAE's people and that health-care has remained a top priority of the government, inspired and led by its President, Sheikh Zayed. Despite federal budgetary constraints, the UAE Government continues to dedicate a significant part of its wealth to the healthcare system: in 1994 Government expenditure on healthcare was Dh2.55 billion.

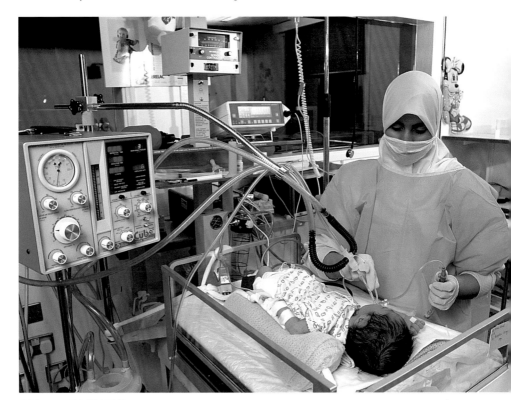

Just what these developments mean in terms of the lives of UAE citizens can be illustrated by the fact that average life expectancy has increased from 60 in 1970 to over 73 years old today, whilst infant mortality figures have dropped from 6.8 per cent to around 2 per cent, and are still falling.

Summary of Development of Health Services

Item	Unit	1972	1993
Hospitals	number	16	46
Beds		1252	6113
Health Centres		11	127
Private Clinics		50	857
Maternity & Child Centres		1	10
Central School Health Clinics			10
Outpatients at Health Centres	million	1.5	43
Doctors	number	264	3718
Nurses		616	8270
Government spending	Dh. million	86.1	2,369

HEALTH INDICATORS

	UAE	Developed countries
Life expectancy at birth in 1960 (years)	53	57
Life expectancy at birth in 1992 (years)	74	70
Fertility rate (% in 1992)	4.2	2.7
Infant Mortality Rate (deaths per 1000 live births; 1960)	145	83
Infant Mortality Rate (deaths per 1000 live births; 1994)	9.46	38
Under five Mortality Rate (deaths per 1000 births; 1994)	13.43	37
Births attended by trained personnel (%; 1983-93)	99	86

Data compiled from UN sources

FACILITIES

Among the UAE's growing list of hospitals, the largest are the Mafraq General Hospital in Abu Dhabi, the Tawam and the Al-Jimi hospitals in Al-Ain, and three large hospitals in Dubai: the New Dubai, the Zabeel East and the Rashid Central. There are also general hospitals in Sharjah, Ras al-Khaimah and Fujairah, as well as health centres throughout the country. During recent years, many small private hospitals have been established and there are now

752 private out-patients clinics. Of note is the 1993 opening of an advanced 120-bed centre for the care of the elderly and impaired, in Abu Dhabi. This formed part of a series of similar projects that have included a prosthesis unit, also opened in 1993, and a 150-bed psychiatric hospital opened in late 1995. New projects include development of a centre for herbal and traditional medicine, a new paediatric hospital, and an emergency hospital in Abu Dhabi with 613 beds.

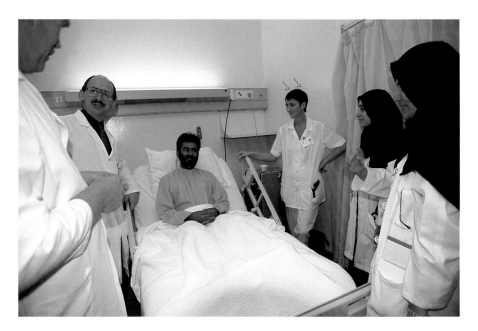

HOME FOR THE AGED IN AJMAN

The multi-million dirham project for the aged, designed to accommodate 50 elderly people, was opened in Ajman by Sheikh Ammar bin Humaid Al Nuaimi, Crown Prince of Ajman. The new building offers a wide range of facilities, including a section for physiotherapy and creative activities for the elderly inmates. Whilst tradition and custom in the UAE calls for elderly people to remain with their families, there are nevertheless circumstances where the elderly do need such facilities.

MENTAL HOSPITAL

The third and fourth stages of the newly-inaugurated mental hospital in Abu Dhabi were completed during early 1996. The new sections include a General Physiotherapy Unit and an Addiction Therapy Centre. These additions essentially represent a transfer of facilities and expertise from the existing units at the Abu Dhabi Central Hospital. The new hospital already has an integrated physiotherapy ward which is regarded as one of the most modern in the world and there are also three specialized clinics for general psychotherapy and treatment for serious mental diseases, making the hospital a pioneer in this field in the UAE. A new Out Patient Department was added, along with an emergency service that is focusing its efforts on helping to resolve conflicts between psychiatric patients and their families within the confines of their own homes.

HEALTH PROJECTS IN AL-AIN

Al-Ain has been upgrading its health service facilities in development projects valued at around 1 billion dirhams. The projects included a new radiology unit at the Tawam Hospital that is part of the overall expansion in the hospital and other medical units, a consultative clinic complex, college of medicine, housing complex for nurses and doctors and other facilities.

PRIVATE MEDICAL INSTITUTIONS REGULATED

H.H. President Sheikh Zayed bin Sultan Al Nahyan issued Federal Law No. 2 for 1996, containing 30 articles, and banning the issuance of licences for private clinics, health centres and hospitals to non-nationals. However, the law permits expatriate medical practitioners to become partners with nationals in such establishments. Nevertheless, only those who have practised medicine for at least five years in the country as specialist doctors, or for two years as consultants, will be eligible to become partners in ventures of this type. A grace period of one year for the existing medical institutions to regularize their status under the new law was granted. Management of private medical institutions must be undertaken by a licensed doctor, whereas the management of polyclinics, private hospitals and sanatoriums may be undertaken by a person specialized in hospital management.

178

ISO 9001 ACCREDITATION

Two Abu Dhabi medical facilities were awarded the ISO 9001 accreditation. The two centres were the Corniche Hospital in Abu Dhabi city which belongs to the Government of the emirate, and the Ruwais Hospital and Satellite Clinics, which belongs to the Abu Dhabi National Oil Company. They were assessed on the basis of

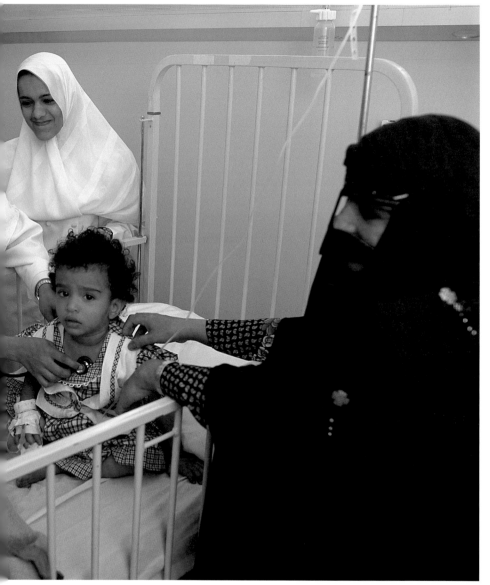

the internationally recognized British Standards Institute criteria for total hospital services. It is believed that they were the first in the Middle East to have successfully gained such accreditation for the scope and range of services provided and it was of particular interest that both facilities are government owned, rather than held by the private sector. The Corniche Hospital is a specialized facility providing maternity care for all women in Abu Dhabi. The one in Ruwais is a general acute care unit catering to ADNOC Group companies' personnel and their dependants in the emirate's Western Region.

CHILDREN'S RIGHTS

The UAE Government has been working to implement the UNICEF Child Rights' Charter, affirming the child's right to live, to grow and to be cared for mentally and physically. The Charter states that governments should work to reduce the malnutrition rate and eliminate fatal and dangerous childhood diseases. A complete vaccination programme, immediate and effective medical treatment for respiratory inflammations, protecting children against diarrhoea and malnutrition, and avoiding accidents at home and at school were the main issues of special concern to medical bodies all over the world and in the UAE.

According to the UNICEF's 1996 edition of the 'Progress of Nations' report - published annually and ranking the countries of the world according to their achievements in child health, nutrition, family planning and women's rights, the UAE has made enormous strides in improving the health of its children by boosting measles immunization from 58 per cent in 1988 to 90 per cent in 1994 - an increase of 32 per cent. Only in the last 15 years has protection been extended to the majority of children in the developing world. The UAE also scored high in the provision of health services and child nutrition among the Middle East and North African countries, topping the list in the standard of child nutrition. In fact, no malnutrition cases were spotted in the UAE in children under five years of age.

PARENTAL CARE OF IMPAIRED CHILDREN

In November 1995 Supreme Council Member and Ruler of Sharjah H.H. Dr Sheikh Sultan bin Mohamed Al Qassimi inaugurated a symposium on 'Parental Care of Impaired Children'. The symposium aimed at effectively promoting the cause of the handicapped. The five-day meeting, attended by 41 delegates from GCC member-states, was organized by the Executive Office of the Council of GCC Ministers of Labour and Social Affairs in cooperation with the Ministry of Labour and Social Affairs and the Sharjah City for Humanitarian Services.

MEDICAL RESEARCH

Since the establishment of the Faculty of Medicine & Health Sciences in Al-Ain in 1986, development of medical research in the school has been substantial. The infrastructure required for modern medical research has been gradually implemented and includes the construction of 1500 square metres laboratory space, the purchase of state of the art research equipment, the appointment of trained research technicians and a process for research funding based on scientific evaluation.

Several major research themes are currently being pursued in the Faculty of Medicine & Health Sciences relating to the health problems of the United Arab Emirates. These include research into the mechanism, diagnosis, and treatment of diabetes mellitus, cancer research, herbal medicine, gastrointestinal diseases, molecular genetics, perinatal medicine and public health problems. Significant progress has already been made in each of these areas as witnessed, amongst others, by a remarkable increase in scientific publications. For example, in the past eight years the number of international medical research publications originating from the UAE has quadrupled due to the output from the medical school which now features as one of the major biomedical research institutions in the region.

Muscle Mapping

In the context of the research efforts of the Faculty of Medicine & Health Sciences, several research projects are achieving remarkable results. An example of one such project is the study of normal and abnormal propagation of electrical impulses in smooth muscle. These electrical signals dictate the contraction of several organs in the human body such as the stomach, intestinal tract, and the uterus. Similar to the beating of the heart, which must contract in a regular and controlled fashion in order to pump blood to the rest of the body, so must also the stomach and the intestines contract on a regular basis to facilitate digestion and absorption of food. The pregnant uterus forms a special case in the sense that this organ, during pregnancy, must remain silent in order to avoid premature delivery whereas during labour, the uterus must suddenly and forcefully contract for birth to take place.

In the Department of Physiology in the Faculty of Medicine, a unique technology has been developed which makes it possible for the first time to record the electrical activity from the surface of smooth muscles from 240 different sites simultaneously. From these signals and with the help of a complex computer programme developed locally, propagation of the electrical signals in these organs can be reconstructed.

Cancer Research

Research work on the role of melatonin in predicting or regulating cancer is being carried-out in the UAE as a first attempt by any Arab country in this very advanced field. Dr Mai Hussein Shouman, who is working in the Medical Research Office, Department of Curative Medicine, Ministry of Health, stated that an initial study on

12 patients having breast and brain cancer showed the level of melatonin to be very high compared with persons who do not have cancer. Melatonin is a chemical substance in the blood, released by the pineal gland in the brain. It is a natural substance which is produced at night and is known to induce sleep. Studies are being carried out all over the world on its relation to the presence or absence of cancer. The UAE studies are of particular significance to cancer research since, if confirmed, melatonin could act as a predictor or an alarm for the body's system and might also be used in the treatment of cancer patients.

Meanwhile healthcare professionals in the UAE are leading the way in the early detection and treatment of breast cancer. Hospitals such as the Tawam Hospital in Al-Ain are showing impressive results. Consultant and head of the Nuclear Medicine department of the Tawam Hospital (Dr Abdul Rehim Suhaili) recently presented the results of hospital research undertaken on 45 breast cancer patients who were treated at the hospital. He also outlined ongoing research on breast tumours and the use of nuclear medicine in mammography.

The Al-Khaleej Health Centre in Abu Dhabi has also achieved an impressive early detection record of breast cancer since it began mammography a few years ago. The centre handles between 10 and 25 screenings a day and emphasizes education and self-examination in order to make women aware of the benefits of early screening and detection.

MALARIA

Malaria cases among UAE nationals dropped by 12.8 per cent over the past ten years, due to preventative measures taken by the Ministry of Health's Malaria Control Programme. Expatriates account for 96.3 per cent of malaria cases, while the figure for nationals stood at 3.7 per cent in 1994. Malaria was detected in expatriates from over 35 countries and only one out of 12 cases detected among infants was found to have been transmitted locally. A total of 178 cases, including 15 nationals, were reported among children less than five years of age.

Natural breeding grounds of the anopheles mosquitoes, which transmit the disease, are limited in the UAE and further reduced during the summer. Some 83,005 potential breeding grounds in the UAE were identified and checked in 1994, of which only 1493 showed the presence of the anopheles mosquitoes. Malaria detection and control is performed mainly at government health centres and clinics which detected over 98 per cent of 1994's 3308 malaria cases.

WORKSHOPS ON SMOKING

Workshops were held for medical staff of the Ministry of Health to study new techniques to encourage heavy smokers to abandon their habit. The programme was organized by the Ministry with the collaboration of the UAE University. The UAE and other Gulf states have taken several measures to check smoking, including tariffs on tobacco and banning staff of public departments from smoking in the offices.

AIDS CAMPAIGN

The UAE AIDS Control Programme has been recognized worldwide as a pioneering model. A public awareness campaign against AIDS, with the slogan 'Together Against AIDS' was undertaken by the UAE Government during December 1995. The Red Crescent Society, in association with the Julphar Pharmaceutical Company, organized various activities to educate the public about the dangers of the disease, the factors that can cause it and the measures to be taken to prevent it. Young people were especially targeted, with a series of informative lectures arranged in schools and other educational institutions, including the Higher Colleges of Technology. Educational leaflets and posters were also widely distributed.

DRUG ADDICTION

The UAE Government is making serious and committed efforts to eradicate drug addiction through a series of drug rehabilitation programmes. In the Emirate of Sharjah the Addict Supervising Programme was started by Sharjah Police Department under the directives of H.H. Dr Sheikh Sultan bin Mohammed Al Qassimi, Ruler of Sharjah. While those addicted to drugs are supervised by police officers, they undergo weekly blood tests and physical and mental rehabilitation. The aim of the project is to ensure that those who enter the programme leave with no traces of drugs in their system. The programme includes counselling which encourages addicts to use their will power to overcome the mental, emotional and physical addiction to drugs. The programme has yielded positive results and increased awareness of the problem of drug addiction.

On 9 March 1996 the UAE Cabinet agreed to establish a higher committee which will define strategies and programmes to confront the drug problem, protect society and enhance international cooperation in this field. The committee is chaired by Deputy Prime Minister Sheikh Sultan bin Zayed Al Nahyan and was set up in accordance with recent instructions from Sheikh Zayed to make a serious effort to combat the drug menace.

The Government also approved that the UAE should be a party to the draft of the Arab Agreement for Combating Drug Trafficking and Narcotics. The new measures complement the amendments to the UAE's anti-drug laws, approved by Sheikh Zayed on 9 April 1995, paving the way for introduction of the death penalty for drug dealers and increased penalties for drug offences.

HEALTH SURVEY

The UAE began a major family health survey in 1995, aimed at providing base-line data for future planning in the health sector. The first part of the survey, completed in October 1995, involved collection of data from 6000 national households in both urban and rural areas in the country, using 60 interviewers and 20 supervisors. The entire survey, which will provide the first major base-line data, was scheduled for completion in late 1996. Based on the report, the Ministry of Health will prepare a plan of action to tackle highlighted problem areas.

184 UNITED ARAB EMIRATES 1996

WOMEN IN THE UAE

To MANY FOREIGNERS Arab women remain enveloped in mystery. This is hardly surprising since much of this external image of the Arab woman is coloured by myths derived from a misunderstanding of history, and ignorance about Arab culture and traditions, as well as about the precepts of Islam. Indeed misconceptions concerning the position of women in Arab society bear little resemblance to reality. Unlike their Western counterparts, Arab women have always had the right, guaranteed by Islam, to own property and to inherit it, and there have been women of great prominence and influence in Arab society throughout history. They have never been seen as mere adjuncts to their menfolk.

Today with the rapid spread of education, Arab women are coming to play an ever-increasing role in all aspect of society, including government and commerce. In few places is this more obvious than in the United Arab Emirates, whose women, with the active support of their fathers, husbands and brothers, are contributing fully to the building of one of the most rapidly developing states in the region.

The expanding role of women within UAE society over the last quarter of a century is largely due to the underlying commitment of the UAE Government to the progress of women in all fields, a commitment made plain from the earliest days of the UAE Federation by President Sheikh Zayed. It was never true, of course, that the country's women simply stayed at home. In the traditional society that existed before oil, women played an active role in agriculture in the mountains and in the desert oases. Some women also played a major role in the running of tribal affairs, though it was generally behind the scenes. The mother of Sheikh Zayed, Sheikha Salamah, for example, was to a very considerable extent responsible for the way in which her four sons worked together from the late 1930s onwards, for over 30 years, to help bring the Emirate of Abu Dhabi through the hardships of the world economic depression and the Second World War, and in to the beginning of the oil era.

Time-honoured tradition meant, however, that as the country began to develop, and as its menfolk moved to take advantage of the newly-provided opportunities, there was a danger that the UAE's women might be left behind.

LEGAL FRAMEWORK FOR EQUALITY

The right of women to effectively participate in the development of society is enshrined in the UAE Constitution which was adopted when the Federation was formed in 1971. The Constitution guarantees equality between men and women. It lays down, for example, that the principles of social justice should apply to all, and that women are equal with men before the law. They enjoy the same legal status, claim to titles, access to education, the right to practise professions, the same access to employment, health and family welfare facilities. In accordance with the rights and privileges laid down in the state religion, Islam, on which the Constitution is based, the rights of women with regard to the inheritance of property are also guaranteed.

The Constitution notes: *The family is the basis of society which shall be responsible for protecting childhood and motherhood. Laws shall be formulated in all fields to observe this protection and care, in a way which safeguards the dignity of women, preserves their identity and secures for them the conditions appropriate for a prosperous life and suitable work which is in accordance with their nature and capabilities as mothers and wives and as workers.*

Sheikha Fatima commented that the constitutional support for women . . . *stems from the teaching of the Islamic religion and the heritage and traditions of the UAE, as well as the prudent view of President His Highness Sheikh Zayed bin Sultan Al Nahyan. It gives women the opportunity to reach the highest echelons of education, penetrate all fields of work, establish a foothold in society and assert their belief in their own abilities and justify the faith of society in them.*

The guarantees laid down in the UAE Constitution have been carried through effectively into legislation passed since the establishment of the state. For example, the Labour Law, governing employment, prescribes equal pay for equal work. As recently as July 1996, Sheikh Zayed incorporated the International Labour Organisation agreement NO 100 for 1951, governing the implementation of the principle of equal pay for equal work, into federal law. Moreover, UAE legislators have taken into account the fact that certain special conditions apply to women, in particular, the requirement for paid maternity leave, special paid leave for periods of mourning prescribed by Islamic Sharia law, as well as special leave to accompany a parent or child abroad for medical treatment. The latter applies also to men, however it is usually taken up by women. While these conditions are at least comparable to those existing elsewhere in the world, the officially supported UAE Women's Federation is currently campaigning for amendments to the law, to provide further support. One focus of the campaign is for the Civil Service Law to be changed to promote further employment of women in Government. A second is for the period of maternity leave to be doubled, while the third is for the introduction of leave of up to two years, on reduced salary, for mothers to nurse their infant children.

WOMEN IN EDUCATION

Education is the real wealth which we should preserve and care for. A girl has the legal right to proper education. Sheikha Fatima bint Mubarak.

When the Federation was formed, only a tiny minority of children had access to schooling and of those, the majority were boys. A comprehensive educational policy has seen the number of schools in the UAE rise from 129 in 1972-73 to 615 in 1995-96. After a relatively slow start, Ministry of Education statistics indicate that the UAE's female students have seized the opportunities for schooling, avidly outstripping their male counterparts. Girls now outnumber boys at virtually all levels of education. This becomes most noticeable at secondary stage where students can drop out. Overall, the number of girls in government schools more than tripled in the decade between 1981/2 and 1991/2, from 64,724 to 194,545, far ahead of the growth in the population as a whole and underlining not only the increased availability of opportunities for education, but also the thirst of the UAE's girls to make the best possible use of those opportunities. This trend continues.

As far as third-level education is concerned, since the creation of the Emirates University in 1977, and the Higher Colleges of Technology in 1988, the percentage of female students has slowly, but steadily risen. In 1980/81, women accounted for half of the students at the University, but figures have now reached nearly 70 per cent. In 1996, more than 1500 students from the University and the Higher College of Technology graduated, 324 males and 1023 females from the University, 57 males and 96 females from the HCT.

Sheikha Fatima commented: *What has been achieved . . . is a matter of pride and delight for every citizen. Women have proved their superiority, and their serious commitment to education. They have become an ideal for their sisters to follow. They demonstrate the values and teachings of Islam. They have shown how to meet the expectation of their country. But none of this could have been possible without the support and encouragement of President Sheikh Zayed bin Sultan Al Nahyan.*

But it is not only in the higher echelons of education that women have availed of the tremendous opportunities open to them. Although the expansion of education in the 1970s made major inroads into illiteracy among the young, it remained a major problem among the older generation, especially women. As late as 1980, for example, 77.6 per cent of women and 51 per cent of UAE men over the age of 45 were still illiterate. By 1995, male illiteracy in the total population 10 years and over was down to 17.4 per cent For women, the comparable figure was 11.3 per cent in 1995.

Women's societies have been instrumental in helping women to overcome the problem of illiteracy. Abu Dhabi's Women's Association is in charge of running the Centres for the Eradication of Illiteracy Among Women. In fact, the UAE Women's Federation, chaired by Sheikha Fatima has spearheaded the campaign, having adopted the objective of full literacy among the country's women by the year 2000. Working in collaboration with the Ministry of Education, and in consultation with its member organizations around the country, the Federation prepared a detailed campaign which aimed at not only the eradication of illiteracy, but also set up a comprehensive health, social affairs and cultural programme.

Adult education centres offering women formal schooling from primary to secondary stage have also been established. In addition, to fulfil the need for vocational training for women, in collaboration with the United Nations Development Programme (UNDP) and the International Labour Organization (ILO), a special vocational training centre was established in 1978 by the Ministry of Labour and Social Affairs and the UAE Women's Federation, with a programme that paid special attention to the preservation and revival of traditional handicrafts. Learning from that experience, the Government has subsequently established a number of other centres around the country which, quite apart from their value in preserving the country's traditions, also help to generate income for those who work with them. This was later followed by another UNDP project in association with the Abu Dhabi Women's Association to establish a specialized vocational training centre, which provides opportunities for those women who have not yet completed a literacy programme.

WOMEN IN EMPLOYMENT

Educational opportunities, coupled with a percentage increase of women in the population, has meant that there are greater numbers of women entering the workforce. The percentage of women in the labour force has risen from a mere 5.3 per cent in 1980 to 12 per cent in 1995.

Many women are employed in the Government sector, particularly in traditional areas such as education and health, although they are now spreading across the entire federal civil service, accounting for around 40 per cent of total employees. Women represent 100 per cent of nursery school teachers, 55 per cent of primary school teachers and 65 per cent of intermediate and secondary school teachers, the latter figure related to the greater number of female students.

In the health services, women account for 54.3 per cent of the total number of employees, both UAE citizens and expatriates. One of every three doctors, pharmacists, technicians and administrators is a woman, as are 81 per cent of the nursing staff. This has, in part, been due to the success of the country's colleges of nursing in attracting UAE girls into a nursing career. In the future, the same may well be true of doctors produced by the Faculty of Medicine and Health Science of the Emirates University, which is attracting far more female than male applicants.

Of the growing number of women seeking employment, however, many are qualified to enter a wide variety of other careers beyond education and the health services. Graduates in disciplines such as the arts, engineering, the sciences and communications, computer technology, office and business administration have chosen careers in commerce, banking and the oil industry, as well as in administration in both the Government and the private sector.

The employment of women in the civil service is particularly marked. By the end of 1993, women filled 39.8 per cent of all Government posts, comparable with their share of the population at large, and held 27.1 per cent of the higher posts at a decision-making level. Although none have yet reached the rank of Ministerial Under Secretary (there are three Assistant Under Secretaries), UAE

Female % Share of Labour Force		
Emirate	1994	1995
Abu Dhabi	8.5	9.6
Dubai	9.4	11.7
Sharjah	11.3	14.5
Ajman	9.9	20.2
Umm Al-Qaiwain	12.3	17.7
Ras Al-Khaimah	12.8	16.2
Al-Fujairah	10.8	13.6
Total U.A.E.	9.6	12.0

Source: Ministry of Planning.

women are well-placed to have an effective impact upon the development of the country's political, economic, educational and social policies. This process is helped by the active involvement of women in media, as presenters, writers and editors, through television and radio programmes and magazines specifically devoted to topics of interest to women, and through more general types of media.

Women are also breaking new ground in the police and the armed forces. The number of policewomen has grown rapidly, and they can now be found performing a variety of functions, from criminal investigation to customs control. Uniquely amongst the six member states of the Arab Gulf Cooperation Council UAE women can now join the armed forces. The breakthrough was achieved at the time of the 1990-91 Gulf War, when the women of the Emirates demanded the right to undergo basic military training to equip them to defend the state, if necessary.

With the approval of President Sheikh Zayed and with the enthusiastic support of the UAE's First Lady, Sheikha Fatima bint Mubarak, a special basic training programme for women was established. The results were so successful that it was immediately decided to create a special women's corps within the armed forces, and a training college named after one of the great female heroes of Arab history, Khawla bint Al Azwar, was created. The first batch of 59 women graduated from the school in 1992 after a six-month practical and theoretical military training course.Today, hundreds of young UAE women are working, side by side with their brothers, in the armed forces, filling all types of posts except those involving front line combat.

Access to education and to opportunities for employment is a key part of the Government's strategy for developing the human resources of the state, one, moreover, which is based upon the objective of offering equality of opportunity to both men and women. However, despite the Government support and the enviable achievements of women in education, their share in the workforce is still relatively weak, partly because of constraints placed on female employment by social attitudes and realities, as well as indirect cultural influences. Some UAE men, for example, are opposed to women working at all, while others will approve of female members of their family only working in areas of activity in which they do not come into contact with men. On the other hand,  women from aristocratic families, who have a better chance for higher education, often fail to realize their full potential. Most educated women prefer jobs more suited to their social status rather than jobs consistent with their qualifications or ability. Nevertheless, these attitudes are changing.

WOMEN'S HEALTH

As already indicated in the chapter on health, Government investment has had a significant effect in improving the quality of health care and health education, with a consequent impact on women's health, child care and infant mortality. The extensive medical services in the state include three hospitals devoted specifically to women, as well as mother-and-child care centres and clinics. Smaller decentralized advice centres were instituted in the early 1980s. Hundreds of thousands of mothers and children now visit the centres every year, in part a reflection of the growing female population, but in part too an indication of the benefits to be gained from the greater availability of advice provided by the decentralized units.

One easily-detectable result has been in the decline in mortality rates among young children, infant mortality, for example, declined from 80 per 1000 in 1980 to 32 per 1000 in 1985, dropping again to less than 10 per 1000 in the 1990s, while the rate of mortality among mothers on delivery is now around two per 100,000, a rate comparable to the lowest international levels.

The Ministries of Health and Education collaborate closely on the improvement of children's health, with several school health centres, and over 450 individual units in schools, which are of benefit not only to the children themselves, but also to their mothers. In addition, with the assistance of the United Nations Development Fund, UNICEF, the Women's Federation and the Government are actively engaged in the spreading of health education among the country's women, with particular emphasis on raising the quality of health care for pregnant women and for young children. Promotion of health education is also undertaken through the media, where the country's television and radio stations devote special programmes to the topic, while newspapers and magazines allocate extensive space to these issues.

According to UNICEF's 1996 edition of the 'Progress of Nations' report - published annually and ranking the countries of the world according to their achievements in child health, nutrition, family planning and women's rights, a higher percentage of girls attend primary school in the UAE than in any other Middle Eastern of North African country. The report points out that as well as being a right, education for girls is one of the most powerful levers of progress since girls' education is closely linked to wider opportunities for women, fewer maternal and child deaths, better child health and nutrition. The report also ranks the UAE as a leader in general women's health, with the table of maternal deaths - during pregnancy or childbirth - showing that the UAE had fewer fatalities than almost any other country in the Middle East and North Africa.

SOCIAL WELFARE

The interests of UAE women and their children are also the responsibility of the Ministry of Labour and Social Affairs, in particular its Social Affairs section, itself headed by the country's top female civil servant. The Ministry pays welfare assistance to those in need, including widows and divorced women, as well as to the poorer members of society.

The Social Security Law, which came into effect in 1977, lists the following categories of people as being entitled to financial assistance from the state, if required:

- the totally disabled
- widow-spinster-orphan-those of a limited income
- married students
- the elderly
- divorcees
- women separated from their husbands
- the families of those serving prison sentences
- those married to foreign nationals

The underlying philosophy behind the Social Security Law is that the state guarantees to help individuals and families who may face particular problems, while at the same time trying to help them once again to become productive members of society. In implementing the terms of the Law, the Ministry takes pains to explain its objectives to applicants, and also helps, where possible, to find employment for those able to work.

Over the course of the last decade and a half, the total number of people receiving assistance has fallen but, at the same time, the average payment per recipient has increased sharply, in response to the rising cost of living. While the percentage of men and women varies slightly from emirate to emirate, over the country at large, women represent by far the larger percentage, accounting for 60.6 per cent of all recipients, compared to 39.4 per cent men. Of the total population 5.74 per cent of women and 2.49 per cent of men are in receipt of social assistance. While this is partly due to the lack of educational and employment opportunities for women in the past, compared to men, the discrepancy is also an indication of the efforts being made by the Government to ensure that the women of the Emirates are provided with all necessary help to ensure that they are able to play the fullest role possible in society.

As part of those efforts, the Ministry of Labour and Social Affairs is also responsible for the management of a network of Social Development Centres which were established with the purpose of contributing to the social and economic development of the country's women, particularly in rural areas, with the objective of preparing them to play a fuller part in the fast-changing life of the state.

Their activities include the offering of help both in the home and outside in the wider world. They are responsible for the first stage of assessment of any application for the receipt of the welfare assistance provided by the Government to the indigent and needy, and also play a role in helping to offer advice in a variety of social and domestic problems, as well as helping the courts in civil court cases involving private individuals.

As already outlined, a wide range of educational, recreational and social activities are organized by the Social Centres, often in collaboration with the various Women's Associations. The centres also act as the focal point for the preservation of much of the traditional heritage of the UAE's women through their heritage work groups, where women gather to continue the making of traditional handicrafts, which are then sold to the public, helping to provide some additional income for the artists. A network of nurseries and play-groups ensures that the children of participants are well looked after during activities and classes.

While the Ministry of Labour and Social Affairs devotes most of its attention to the welfare of the citizens of the UAE, it also supports the various associations of expatriate women living in the country, amongst the most well-established of which are those from the Egyptian, Jordanian, Sudanese and Indian communities.

Focusing on their own nationals, these community groups are engaged in a variety of activities which include the running of nurseries and kindergartens for small children, thus permitting their mothers to go out to work. Several of them also run special schools for the disabled and the mentally and physically handicapped.

UAE WOMEN'S FEDERATION

The UAE Women's Federation was established in 1975, at the initiative of Sheikha Fatima bint Mubarak, to bring together under one umbrella all of the women's societies in all seven emirates. The very first of the federated societies was formed in Abu Dhabi three years earlier on 8 February, a memorable day in the history of Emirati women. The initiative for its establishment, too, was taken by Sheikha Fatima who felt that it was only by organizing women that a real start could be made in their emancipation and development. The response of Abu Dhabi women to Sheikha Fatima's call was, to say the least, enthusiastic. It was she who articulated the aspirations of the Emirati women and channelled these into a constructive institution, clearly setting out its objectives. The decision subsequently to link the societies in a Federation was based on the success of that first venture.

Essentially, the aim of the Federation, like that of the founding Society, is to develop on a national scale the appropriate opportunities, in all aspects of life, for the country's women to achieve the full realization of their capabilities. Its founding principles laid down the following objectives:

• Developing women's image and self-esteem so they are able to play their part in the country's development in line with Muslim traditions.
• Making them socially and culturally active.
• Encouraging education and eradicating illiteracy among adult women.
• Conducting evening classes for their further education.
• Ensuring that social services and care reach women and their families.
• Planning activities to raise cultural standards.
• Helping women take better care of their families.
• Enhancing coordination and liaison among social welfare organizations.
• Building strong links with international women's organizations.

The Federation currently has the following member associations: the Abu Dhabi Women's Development Society, the Dubai Women's Development Society, the Sharjah Women's Development Society, the Umm al-Mou'meneen Society in Ajman, the Umm al-Qaiwain Women's Development Society and Ras al-Khaimah Women's Development Society.

Depending on the geographical size of the emirate, the individual societies may have more than one branch, and there are now a total of 31 branches of the six societies, many operating in remote areas of the country. The Abu Dhabi Women's Development Society, for example, has a branch, with its own extensive premises, on the island of Delma, around 180 kilometres west of Abu Dhabi city.

The individual societies have their own wide range of educational, training and recreational activities. All have well-equipped libraries, three societies also publish magazines, *Sawt al Mara'a* (Woman's Voice) in Sharjah, *Al Fajr al Jadid* (New Dawn), in Umm al-Qaiwain, and *Dourat al Emirat* (Jewel of the Emirate), in Abu Dhabi, while the Sharjah Society runs the only chess club for ladies to be found anywhere in the country, which represents the UAE in Arab and international competitions.

The Federation, which is funded by the Government budget, is specifically granted its own autonomous legal character by law, and is empowered to represent the country's women, of all communities, in discussions with Ministries and other Government departments and institutions. It is also responsible for suggesting new legislation, or amendments to existing laws.

In turn, the Women's Federation conducts its own programme of research on topics of importance to local women, and liaises with Government institutions to obtain the necessary statistics and information. The Women's Federation has also been at the forefront of efforts to deal with social problems with potential damaging effects, such as the high cost of dowries and marriage ceremonies which instigated the setting-up of a Marriage Fund to help alleviate the situation. Upon orders from Her Highness Sheikha Fatima, An Office of National Women's Affairs has been established at the Abu Dhabi Women's Society's main branch in Bateen to serve as a private office in charge of listening to national women's problems and finding suitable solutions to them. For example, the Women's Federation has been at the forefront of a public campaign designed to educate parents of the potential dangers of placing the upbringing of their children largely or wholly in the hands of maids and nannies from a different culture.

The UAE Women's Federation has also taken the global perspective into account. In fact it has participated in all of the major international women's conferences of the last couple of decades, beginning with that held in New Mexico, in 1975, followed by Copenhagen in 1980, and Nairobi in 1985, paving the way for the 1995 conference in Beijing. Taken together with the active co-operation between the various organizations and institutions in the Emirates concerned with women and the specialized agencies of the United Nations, this active development of links with the rest of the world has added significantly to the ability of the country to enhance its own programmes for women. However, this does not mean that the UAE necessarily takes on board all the recommendations of these international gatherings.

Mohammed Issa Al Suweidi, Under Secretary at the Labour and Social Affairs who headed the country's 40-member delegation to the Beijing women's conference commented, following the conference, that there were countries where women did not enjoy the same rights as in the UAE. The UAE supported all recommendations emanating from the Beijing conference that extend such rights to these under-privileged women, he said. However, he emphasized that the UAE is wholly opposed to recommendations that go against the Sharia. In particular, the country is totally against abortion, unless the mother's life is in danger, as Islam prohibits destruction of life. The UAE also rejected the conference's definition of a family, which included man-man and woman-woman units, as that is both against the Sharia and natural human instincts, he commented.

There is no doubt that women in the United Arab Emirates have made great strides in development, in a manner that takes fully into account both the international objectives of the women's movement and the unique circumstances of the country itself. This progress has been achieved with the assistance of a clear-cut Government policy of women but has, at the same time, had to tackle the inbuilt culture and traditions of local society. As in other countries, men still have an advantage in terms of political, economic and social power, but equality of opportunity, and in attitude, is fast developing. Many challenges still remain. Looking back, however, the women of the United Arab Emirates can feel pleased at the considerable progress made in the 25 years since the establishment of the state.

SPORT

THE UAE HAS BECOME SOMETHING of an international capital for sporting events and this has been reflected by steady increases in both sporting facilities and national enthusiasm for outdoor pursuits. Aerobic fitness through regular exercise has been greatly encouraged by the UAE Government and facilities have been provided in all the major cities, both in terms of sporting arenas, pitches, training tracks and gymnasiums, but also on a larger scale through municipal developments that provide lengthy and safe walking, running, skating and cycling routes away from the main traffic, frequently along peaceful, tree-lined avenues and corniches. A dedication to excellence that is apparent in many areas of the UAE's development is also apparent in the field of sports. In addition to world-class facilities that are the envy of many international sportsmen and women, a number of UAE sportsmen have gained world-class recognition for their own achievements including, among others, world champions in bowling and powerboat racing together with several international chess masters.

Sporting policy is formulated by the Ministry of Youth and Sports while separate sports federations help to co-ordinate activities of individual clubs and associations.

There are over 30 well appointed sporting clubs that offer facilities to thousands of members throughout the UAE. The jewel in the crown of UAE sporting venues is undoubtedly Abu Dhabi's coliseum-like Zayed Sports City which accommodates 65,000 spectators and is equipped for international events, both indoors and outdoors and can easily be turned into a full-fledged Olympic Village. The centre also houses the headquarters of the Ministry of Youth and Sports and the UAE Soccer Association.

1996 OLYMPICS IN ATLANTA

The UAE competed in four events at the 1996 Olympics in Atlanta - athletics, swimming, shooting and cycling - represented by Mohammed Mahkoum Al Aswad (athletics: 100m and 200m); Khuwaider Al Dhaheri (swimming: 100m freestyle), Nabil Tahlak (marksmanship: 100m air rifle) and Ali Saeed Darwish (cycling: road race, time trial).

SPECIAL OLYMPICS

The UAE team won 28 medals at the Special World Olympics held in the USA. This provided a strong endorsement of Sheikh Zayed's continued encouragement of handicapped people in the UAE and his support for all efforts to foster their integration and development within UAE society.

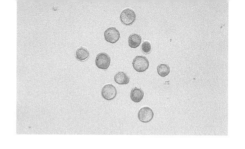

CAMEL RACING

Camel racing is a competitive traditional sport that has spawned its own industries of camel-breeding and training. As with so many aspects of the UAE's devel-opment the most up to date technologies have been employed to improve both camel stock and their training. One such example of this dedication to purpose is the Embryo Transfer Research Centre for Racing Camels established in 1989 under the patronage of H.H. the Crown Prince of Abu Dhabi, Sheikh Khalifa bin Zayed Al Nayhan. This

project's initial research resulted in the world's first embryo transfer calves from racing camels being born early in 1990. Since camels only have a calf every two years the technology allows a top racing camel to 'donate' embryos to other surrogate camels, allowing one female to have multiple offspring each year while remaining non pregnant herself. To date there have been some remarkable results with one female, Misakin, producing 12 offspring in one season, a feat that would take a minimum of 24 years under normal conditions. Camels produce up to 30 embryos at a time and these may be transferred immediately to waiting recipients or can be stored indefinitely in liquid nitrogen. In February 1995 the world's first frozen embryo transfer baby was born, having been stored initially at - 196 °C and then thawed for transfer to complete its 13 month gestation in a 'new' mother. The Al-Ain based centre remains dedicated to improving the reproductive knowledge and efficiency of the camel in its quest for the production of faster camels. With over 130 embryo transfer babies due at the end of 1996, the Centre is continuing to build on its successes.

Child jockeys have been banned in UAE camel racing and tests are carried out on winning camels to ensure that neither steroids or other drugs have been administered. The racing season begins in September and runs through most of the winter months. Races with around 25 to 30 registered camels are classified according to their age-classes and care is taken to ensure that very young camels are not entered.

HORSE-RACING

The Emirates are justifiably famous for their contribution to international horse racing. One of the major developments of recent years has been the practice of training horses raced on the international circuits in the UAE during winter months. In particular, Dubai's Godolphin establishment (named after one of the original three Arabian thoroughbred stallions from whom all modern racehores are derived) is an incredibly impressive stabling and training facility that has become winter home for some of the world's finest race horses.

The unique advantages of winter horse training in the Emirates were first brought to the attention of the world's racing community in 1994 when the Godolphin-trained filly Balanchine won the Oaks at Epsom followed by the Irish Derby. In the following year a horse trained at Godolphin's Al-Quoz stable, Lammtarra, took the Derby, the King George VI and Queen Elizabeth Diamond stakes at Ascot, as well as the Prix de L'Arc de Triomphe at Longchamp. Also in 1995, another Godolphin horse, Moonshell, won the Oaks and Classic Cliche together with an impressive romp home to cross the line first at the St Leger. A tally of international race winners that have recently over-wintered in the UAE includes Dumaani, So Factual, Heart Lake, Red Bishop, Vettori, Darike and Flagbird.

It is now widely recognized that the Emirates offers a unique combination of excellent stables equipped with state of the art training facilities in a safe, clean environment together with top class trainers; access to world-class veterinary facilities (Dubai has an internationally-renowned Equine Hospital to which horses are brought from all over the world); and a climate which is ideal for developing peak equine health and fitness.

Jockey Jerry Bailey atop horse Cigar celebrates victory in the Dubai World Cup 1996.

Dubai possesses two state of the art racetracks; the left-handed flat track at Nad al-Sheba and a right-handed track with an uphill finishing stretch at Jebel Ali. Over a billion people, around the globe, watched the world's richest-ever horse race, the $4 million Dubai World Cup, held in March 1996 at Dubai's Nad al-Sheba floodlit race-track. Created by General Sheikh Mohammed bin Rashid Al Maktoum, Crown Prince of Dubai and UAE Minister of Defence, this unique world championship race has further consolidated the UAE's status as one of the most important horse racing venues in the world. Sheikh Mohammed has over 500 horses in stables across Europe and America and has always visualized Dubai as becoming a place where East meets West at the horse races. The great American wonder-horse Cigar successfully beat a strong four-horse home challenge, led by the indomitable Halling. A light drizzle softened the course somewhat, providing conditions under which Cigar has proved himself on a number of previous occasions.

In addition to hosting the world's richest horse race in March 1996, Nad al-Sheba hosted the World Jockeys Challenge in 1993, 1994 and 1995. Jockeys who rode there are reported to have described the track as one of the best, if not the best, that they had ever raced over.

Abu Dhabi also has excellent and impressive horse breeding, training and racing facilities, especially after the recent upgrading of its main race track situated in the grounds of Abu Dhabi Equestrian Club. The latter, with its 500 stables, equine swimming pool, indoor riding school and immaculate show ground offers state of the art facilities in all areas of equine activity. The first Pure-bred Arabian Horse Show to be held in the UAE was staged at the Abu Dhabi Equestrian Club on 8 March 1996, organized by the UAE Equestrian Racing Federation in association with Emirates Arabian Horse Society and the Abu

UNITED ARAB EMIRATES 1996

Dhabi Equestrian Club. The concept was very much in line with Sheikh Zayed's own strong interest in the Arabian horse and in the application of modern technology as a means to enhance equestrian activities throughout the UAE. The Show had nine breeding classes together with five speciality classes in which horses were judged for characteristics such as the most beautiful head, their ability to move freely to music, and as traditional mounts in which riders wore Arabian dress. The success of Sheikh Zayed's own stables was particularly apparent at the show with many of the winning horses coming from the Royal Stables which presently contain approximately 200 horses.

Sharjah also has recently modernized horse racing facilities and is taking an active role in promoting an interest in horse racing, both nationally and internationally.

With so much talk of large stables and major equine centres in the UAE it is well to record that there is still room in the sport for relatively small operators. Here is one brief story to illustrate the point. Khalifa bin Dasmal, the Dubai Racing Club's Steward and a 'small-time' owner scored a major success when his horse Shaamit won the 1996 Vodaphone Epsom

General Sheikh Mohammed bin Rashid Al Maktoum won the 4th place in the second Desert Giants Marathon held from Ras al-Khaima to Jebel Ali in January 1996. Sheikh Tahnoon bin Mohammed emerged winner.

Derby in early June. Commenting on his impressive win Khalifa said, 'Initially I was thrilled to have an entry in the Derby and then we were hoping for a good finish. Shaamit's victory has swept me off my feet! It all seems like a dream. This is one of the happiest moments of my life. It's unbelievable.' Dasmal has never been a big horse owner and despite now having bred and owned a Derby winner doesn't plan on increasing his stable, which comprises three horses. The Dasmals are a popular sporting family in Dubai. Khalifa is a former UAE national tennis champion, as is his son Salem. Both his daughters, Leila and Ameena, and his younger son Mohammed are champion showjumpers while his wife is the backbone of the Dubai Equestrian Centre.

In November 1996 the World Arabian Horse Organization held a major conference in Abu Dhabi, the first time that it had met in any of the Gulf countries.

FOOTBALL

The UAE Football Association was established in 1971 and joined FIFA in 1972, followed by both the Arab Football and the Asian Soccer Federations in 1974. The UAE F.A., whose Silver Jubilee coincides with that of the twenty-fifth National Day celebrations, is presently chaired by H.H. Sheikh Abdulla bin Zayed Al Nahyan, Under Secretary of the Ministry of Information and Culture.

The national team put up an excellent performance at the qualifying stages for Olympic selection. By obtaining 8 points and achieving the first position in its group which included Iran and Turkmenistan, the UAE Olympic Team qualified for the final Asian qualification round. It played 14 preparatory matches, eight of them before the first round and the other six in preparation for the Malaysian finals. It defeated the Sarajevo Team 2 - 1, drew 1 - 1 with a Romanian team, and also drew 1 - 1 against the Korean Goldstar Team. It won against a Ukrainian team 1 - 0 and played Saudi Olympic before leaving for Singapore on 4 March 1996.

Olympic Team Results at the first round

Teams	Results	Date	Venue
UAE v Turkmenistan	2 - 1	23/09/95	UAE
Iran v UAE	1 - 1	29/09/95	Iran
Turkmenistan v UAE	1 - 1	05/10/95	Turkmenistan
UAE v Iran	1 - 0	22/10/95	UAE

Opening Ceremony of 12th Gulf Cup Football Championship held at Sheikh Zayed Sports City, Abu Dhabi, November 1994. Saudi Arabia won the trophy.

The UAE is justifiably proud of the outstanding performance by its international referee Ali Bu Jassem at the World Cup finals in the USA in 1994. Bu Jassem, one of the most distinguished Arab, Gulf and Asian referees, and UAE roving ambassador in the international soccer arena, was chosen to run a critical and decisive match between Sweden and Bulgaria to determine the third position in the tournament finals.

Football remains the most popular spectator sport in the UAE. Promotion of the sport through football clubs at schools and colleges, as well as at local, regional and national levels has paid dividends in terms of raising the standard of the game in the UAE. Twenty-six football clubs, each with around 150 players, are currently affiliated with the UAE Football

UAE vs Bahrain in action at the 12th Gulf Cup Football Championship held in November 1994 in which UAE beat Kuwait. Saudi Arabia won the trophy.

Association. UAE soccer fans are unlikely to forget the Singapore Qualification Rounds for the 1990 World Cup where their National Team gained its passport to Italy. It did so by scoring 2 - 1 against China, reaching scoreless draws with North Korea and Saudi Arabia, and one all draws with Qatar and South Korea.

In 1992 the national football team came fourth at the Asian Cup held in Hiroshima, whilst it took second place at the 1995 Gulf championship played at the Zayed Sports Centre in Abu Dhabi.

The First Division is a hotly contested league of 10 teams whose games draw big crowds in the UAE. The 1996 First Division Cup was won by Sharjah.

Preparations are presently underway for hosting the Asia Cup Finals 96, in December of this year, with the participation of 12 national teams, including the UAE. Ten teams will qualify from the first rounds, plus the former champions (Japan) and the host country (the UAE). The competing teams will be distributed into three groups, to play matches in Abu Dhabi, Dubai and Al-Ain. The UAE is no stranger to hosting major football tournaments, with past experience gained through staging such events as the highly successful and much acclaimed twelfth Gulf Cup, held in late October and early November 1994, the December 1991 Arab Clubs' Cup, the fifth Cup of Cups for Asian Football in January 1995 and the Emirates International Football Tournament held earlier this year.

BOWLING

Ten pin bowling is well catered for in the UAE with some state of the art bowling alleys and some keen clubs. An international bowling centre has been financed by Sheikh Khalifa bin Zayed Al Nahyan to be built in Abu Dhabi in time for the 1999 World Cup. The UAE Ten Pin Bowling Team won the GCC fourth Men's Championship held at the Abu Dhabi Tourist Club last autumn; and UAE national, Mohammed Khalifa Al Qubeisi, was chosen for the second year running as the world's best ten pin bowler. Mohammed has been involved in the world bowling scene for some time, having won the first world championship held in Mexico in 1989. He played a series of exhibition matches at the 1996 Olympic Games in Atlanta.

BOAT RACING
TRADITIONAL AND MODERN

Although the UAE's traditional long-boats are not quite as long as in the past, the shortened versions of these unusual craft nevertheless create an impressive picture as their tightly packed crews labour at their oars, propelling their boats through calm inshore waters under the appreciative gaze of both national and expatriate spectators. The race itself is the culmination of days of preparation of both vessel and crew. Whilst strong young men train to do battle at sea, their older colleagues take a special interest in their boats and oars, making continual adjustments to oar handles, blades and to the oiled surfaces of the wooden hulls. National pride in the customs and skills of a bygone age is a priceless attribute of the UAE's cultural heritage that has been preserved as a result of Sheikh Zayed's strong belief in building upon past strengths. Pearl-diving and sailing may no longer form essential ingredients of the UAE's survival but the character building influences of this previous era are nevertheless valued and appreciated by a new generation who remain in touch with the sea and maritime skills.

The Dubai Open Race for Sailing Boats of category 60 feet held in June 1995. Won by Boat no. 30, Muhadad, owned by Salem Saeed Bulahij.

Along with the rowing races, traditional sailing races are also held at regular intervals during the period from October to April. Here even greater attention is paid to the wooden boats and their massive rigs. Competition is strong and every effort is made to improve performance of the essentially one-design craft. Among the latest innovations is the introduction of carbon-fibre gaffs and booms which are tastefully disguised as wooden spars.

Modern sailing is an increasingly popular sport in the UAE. From dinghies such as Lasers, Toppers and Kestrels to their faster and more exciting multi-hulled counterparts, the Hobie Cats, club racing is both competitive and great fun. Whilst larger sailing vessels are also catered for, with a number of offshore races, the turbulent waters of the shallow Gulf, together with some strong tides, provide strong challenges for yachtsmen. A less conventional but nevertheless extremely popular form of sailing, windsurfing, also has a strong following in the Emirates with the Abu Dhabi Boardwalkers Club holding weekly competitions throughout the summer.

Powerboat racing is one field in which the UAE excels at the international level and it has played a key role in hosting a series of major events including world championship races. Saeed Al Tayer's world champion win in 1995 was sadly marred by the tragic accidental death of fellow team member Hamed Buhaleeba at a race in southern England. The Victory Team continues to compete in the Class One World Offshore Championships, and the Formula One World Championship for circuit boats.

Action from Hobie Cat 16 World Championship held at Mina Seyahi, Dubai. Brazilians Claudia Cardosa and Frederico Monterio (not shown) won the title.

The UIM Class II & III World Offshore Championship held in Mina Seyahi, Dubai., October 1994. Title won by Phil Duggan and Tony Galligure of Abu Dhabi Duty Free.

Saeed Al Tayer and Felix Serralles of Victory Team celebrate after winning the World Offshore Powerboat Championship at Mina Siyahi, Dubai, November 1995.

Nick Price and Greg Norman at Dubai Desert Classic Golf held in January 1995. Fred Couples of America won the trophy.

GOLF

Twenty-five years ago golfers keen to practise their sport in the UAE were restricted to playing on oiled sand and putting on 'browns' rather than greens (a pleasure that can still be enjoyed at Dubai Country Club). It is thus a remarkable achievement that the UAE has at least eight golf clubs with more courses under development. The fact that two of these courses host international events such as the Dubai Desert Classic, attracting world-class golfers who have nothing but praise for the fairways and beautifully manicured greens, seems little short of a miracle. Such events have made Dubai's golf courses particularly well known to competitors and the public at large since they are televised on major sports channels. The 1996 Desert Classic saw the prize purse raised to a million dollars and attracted 10 of the top 12 Ryder Cup stars together with some of the best golfers from Asia. Meanwhile the Dubai Creek Golf and Yacht Club played host to one of the four major events that combine to make up the Asian PGA tour - a competition that carries with it over US$5 million in prize money.

UAE golfers have now taken to the game with enthusiasm and are making their own waves on the regional tournament circuit. The UAE golfing team, led by Ismail Sharif, took first prize based on handicap at the 1995 GCC championship held in Dubai. Other team members were Khalid Al Halyan, Secretary General of the UAE Golf Association, and Walid Al Attar. Walid went on to win the ProAm tournament.

The UAE Golf Association is committed to encouraging golf from junior level right up the ranks. Taking a professional approach to its work it has its sights firmly set on building up the national team to a level where they can take on top international

Dubai Creek Golf Club.

Emirates Golf Club.

players. Their efforts will be greatly assisted by the continued commercial and governmental support for golf in the Emirates and the development of additional golf courses such as the new 18-hole course near Abu Dhabi, built at a cost of around Dh64 million, as well as by the golf village which is part of a massive tourism development project underway at Ghantout. Also in 1996, Dubai Golf and Racing Club added an extra nine-holes to its existing course, raising it to championship standard; and Emirates Golf Club developed a second 18 hole course.

TENNIS

Tennis is popular as both an amateur sport in the Emirates and as part of the professional sporting scene. The Dubai Tennis Open is one of the major events that attracts superb players, from among the top 50 in world rank. The US$1 million annual tournament, officially recognized by the Association of Tennis Professionals, is sponsored by Dubai Duty Free and played on courts at a new all-purpose tennis centre, built at a cost of Dh20 million, situated at Dubai Aviation Club.

Abu Dhabi also plays host to major tennis events such as Le Meridien Abu Dhabi Tennis Open.

Prize Ceremony of Dubai Tennis Open 95 held at the Aviation Club Tennis Stadium in February 1995. Wayne Ferreira won the title.

CRICKET

Sharjah is the capital of cricket in the UAE with the Emirates Cricket Board, its official association. Not only does Sharjah host local and national cricket matches but it is also home to some major international events on the cricket calendar. The 100th international in the Pepsi Cup was held at the Sharjah cricket stadium in April 1996. The UAE's cricket team triumphed against Holland in their World Cup League match held in Lahore on 1 March 1996.

CHESS

The game of chess in the UAE received a powerful push following UAE national, Saeed Ahmed Saeed's winning of the World Junior Chess Championship in Mexico, in 1979. Chess has continued to develop as a popular game in the UAE and some excellent players have been discovered. In 1995 UAE national and International Chess Master, Talib Moosa,

Basit Ali of Pakistan batting against India during Pepsi Sharjah Cup cricket, April 1996. South Africa won the cup.

was placed seventh at the World Junior Chess Championship, held in Hali, Germany with participation of 80 players from 75 countries.

Sheikh Hamdan bin Mubarak opening the Chess Tournament at Abu Dhabi Cultural Foundation, August 1995.

Dubai International Rally held in December 1995. Won by Mohammed bin Sulayem and his Victory Team.

SWIMMING

The UAE swimming team won the GCC silver medal, while freestyle swimmer Saif Mohammed Jabir won the GCC gold medal in the 1500 metres event, the first time this has been won by a UAE national.

Marlboro Car Rally held in Abu Dhabi, March 1996.

MOTOR RACING

Motor racing in the UAE is synonymous with the name of Mohammed bin Sulayem, widely recognized as the best driver throughout the Arab world and one of the best rally drivers worldwide. With his performances at the prestigious Dubai International Rally in danger of becoming predictable - he recently logged his ninth win there - Mohammed has taken to the international circuit, leaving greater opportunities for other skilled UAE drivers such as Sheikh Suhail bin Khalifa Al Maktoum and Khalifa Al Motaiwi.

SNOOKER

The UAE has some world-class snooker players in people like Mohammed Al Joker who had the top break in the 1994 World Amateur Championship. The UAE team also chalked up its fourth successive win at the GCC Snooker Championship.

SQUASH

The UAE's undisputed top squash player remains Sheikh Ahmed Mohammed Hasher Al Maktoum who has been repeatedly declared national champion and is an excellent ambassador for the game. Squash is a most popular game in the Emirates with over 45 teams playing in different leagues.

John Higgins vs Steve Davis during Dubai Duty Free Snooker Classic, October 1994. Higgins beat Davis. Alan McManus won the title.

 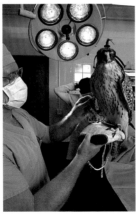 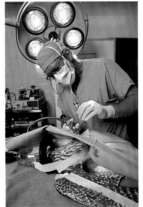 

FALCONRY

The traditional sport of falconry in Arabia is accompanied by strict rules of conduct concerning care for the wild birds, and by a highly sophisticated infrastructure of supporting facilities ranging

from falcon hospitals where birds are treated for a wide range of ailments, to centres for captive breeding and research into the falconer's traditional prey: the houbara bustard. But it is the traditional aspects of falconry that endear it to UAE nationals who find in it a means to link up with their previous bedouin lifestyle. The sport brings them close to nature and the desert environment, enhancing appreciation for the natural world, and through that creating an underlying support for wildlife conservation in all its forms.

Action shot of 7UP 17th Gulf Waterski Championship held at Al Jadaf Drydocks in November 1995. Ahmed Al Qassimi won the Championship.

Action at UIM Aquabike World Championship 1995 held at DIMC, Mina Seyahi in December 1995.

SCUBA DIVING

Although not a competitive sport, scuba diving is one of the most enjoyable ways to cool off in summer or winter. The UAE's warm, relatively clear and safe waters are ideal for learning to dive as well as offering interesting adventures to more experienced divers. There are a number of diving clubs that provide both training and organized diving.

WATER-SKIING

The best lady water-skier in the Gulf region, twelve year old Tanya Niebuhn, resides in the UAE. Water skiing, promoted by organizations such as Dubai Water Sports Association is undertaken at very high competitive levels in the Emirates where facilities for training are excellent.

JET-SKIING

One only has to walk along a corniche in any of the coastal cities of the UAE, in order to see jet-skiers testing their skills against the waves. In fact the UAE has some of the world's top proponents of this modern sport and last year the world championships were held here.

SPORT-FISHING

One of the best kept secrets of UAE sport fishermen is that the Emirates offer superb game fishing for marlin, sailfish, dorado, barracuda, kingfish and tuna. Tales of 300 lb marlin caught in UAE waters are not necessarily of the fisherman variety but are more likely to be the real thing. There is a tendency however to play down just how good the sport fishing can be, perhaps to discourage too many others from spoiling the fun. Competitions are, however, organized by several of the marine clubs and strict rules are applied to ensure conservation of game fish stocks.

OTHER SPORTING ACTIVITIES

In addition to the sports discussed above there are a number of games, adventure and minority sports with strong followings in the UAE. These include rugby, hockey, dirt

Rugby action in game played at Dubai Exiles ground between Arabian Gulf and Kenya RFU. Arabian Gulf beat Kenyan RFU. March 1995.

GCC Youth Basketball Championship. Qatar vs UAE at Al Ahli sports club. Qatar beat UAE and won the trophy. October 1995.

biking, dune buggy riding, go-karting, hang gliding, dune surfing, caving, marksmanship, parachuting, cycling, and darts.

Middle East 24 Hour Pro-Kart Endurance Race held in Dubai, March 1996. Assarain Oman (not shown) won the race.

INFORMATION AND CULTURE

IT IS UAE POLICY TO ENCOURAGE a free press, subject only to normal constraints under-pinning the spiritual, moral and political integrity of the country and its people. Sheikh Zayed has provided the guiding force in this movement, emphasizing that the Arab mass media should help to advance the basic needs and aspirations of the Arab world, supporting its calls for unity, stability, peace and justice, and encouraging brotherly dialogue as a means to solve disputes that arise between nations. Zayed has stressed that, whilst the mass media has been granted freedom, along with this comes responsibility to serve the best needs of its people. Islamic values are at the very core of the UAE media's guiding principles, especially with regard to its teachings on tolerance, fraternity and moderation.

RADIO AND TELEVISION

Transmission from UAE TV Abu Dhabi began on 6 August 1969, initially in black and white, changing to colour on 4 January 1974. Over the ensuing years a number of relay stations have been established, greatly extending the range of the signal. The second channel was introduced in 1984 and the service was the first in Arabia to present filmed news reports. Dubai Television began its transmission in 1974 and has the distinction of being first in the Arab World to have introduced teletext as 'Gulfax',

which it did in 1985, producing 1200 pages in Arabic and English. It is also the first television service to broadcast its programmes in Arabic from London, via a local cable network, and its satellite channel is considered the most successful among the Arab channels now available worldwide. UAE television from Sharjah began its transmissions in 1989 and introduced a second channel in April 1996. The first transmission of UAE TV from Ajman was made during early 1996 and work was continuing to establish the full new service by the end of the year.

Establishment in 1995 of the UAE Television and Broadcasting Corporation, based in Abu Dhabi, was an important milestone in the UAE's efforts to upgrade its mass communications network.

There are four radio broadcasting stations in the Emirates, situated in Abu Dhabi, Dubai, Ras al-Khaimah and Umm al-Qaiwain. Abu Dhabi's station commenced its broadcasts in February 1969 and has gone from strength to strength, providing a balanced selection of news, music, drama and cultural programming. Emirates FM was introduced by the station in 1996, and offers an up to date selection of programmes. UAE Radio from Abu Dhabi is also transmitted by short-wave, reaching great distances and listened to by many people who have an interest in the region.

PRESS

News gathering and dissemination throughout the region has been greatly assisted by the Emirates News Agency which commenced transmission of its special news service in 1977 and sends news reports, pictures and information to the world's media, in English and Arabic, for approximately 18 hours per day. In all it covers over 222 destinations.

In the field of UAE newspaper publishing the Al-Ittihad Corporation for Press and Publications is one of the pioneering organizations in the country. It publishes the *Al-Ittihad* newspaper in Arabic and *Emirates News* in English, together with the weekly *Zahart Al-Khajeel* and *Majid* magazine. In Dubai the Al-Bayan Corporation for Press and Publications produces *Al-Bayan* newspaper together with a weekly *Sports and Youth* magazine, a weekly supplement, and the *Emirates Today* magazine. Meanwhile, the *Khaleej Times*, also based in Dubai, publishes its English language daily newspaper, a weekly magazine, special supplements, *Young Times Magazine* for children and *Al Hadaf* - a sports magazine published in Arabic. *Gulf News* is another Dubai-based newspaper and the company also publishes a *Gulf Weekly* magazine together with the *Junior News* magazine for children.

The Sharjah-based company, Dar Al-Khaleej for Press and Publications, publishes a daily newspaper, the *Khaleej*, together with its weekly *Al Shurouq* magazine and several other periodicals. In March 1996 it launched its weekly *Economist* magazine followed by launch of a new English daily in April, *Gulf Today*. In addition to the above mentioned publications there are approximately 60 other magazines and periodicals published in the UAE, covering a wide range of professional, cultural, scientific, leisure and sporting interests.

CULTURE

The United Arab Emirates has taken steps to preserve its cultural heritage in a multitude of ways. Not only do government agencies and state-owned corporations provide sponsorship for major events in the arts, but there has also been substantial capital investment in many different areas of cultural heritage from preservation of historic monuments to establishment of modern facilities for storage and classification of documents relating to the UAE. Many festivals involve performances in the fields

of music, dance and literature as well as exhibitions of paintings, sculptures and other art forms. Visiting performers and travelling exhibitions are greatly encouraged and form a powerful ingredient in the UAE's cultural menu which reaches far beyond its own boundaries, embracing aesthetic, poetic, literary, and other creative works from a wide range of ethnic roots. Across this great range of cultural activities there can be discerned the guiding presence of the UAE President, Sheikh Zayed, and of his colleagues in the Supreme Council of the Federation, all the members of which have demonstrated their keenness to preserve their strong heritage whilst showing appreciation for current artistic and cultural works. A prime example of this commitment is provided by the fact that each emirate in the UAE has been recently engaged in upgrading its museums or building new ones.

At government level responsibility for promoting cultural activities, functions and institutions rests with the Department of Culture at the Ministry of Information and Culture. It helps to sponsor a fascinating cultural melange including drama, literature, poetry, art, music, singing and dancing, especially by participants in over 27 folklore associations who have staged performances at many Gulf and Arab festivals, including events held in Cairo, Damascus, Tunisia and Qatar.

CULTURAL INSTITUTIONS

The Abu Dhabi Cultural Foundation plays a most valuable and deeply appreciated role in the cultural life of the UAE, and particularly that of Abu Dhabi. Situated in the same compound that contains the Abu Dhabi's main fort, it contains a large exhibition area, several lecture rooms, smaller exhibition centres, a large and well organized library, together with administrative offices for staff who are concerned with arranging various exhibitions, events and promotional activities for music and the arts. The Foundation was visited in February 1996 by Director General of UNESCO, Frederico Mayor, who expressed his admiration for all that had been achieved there.

Two recent major events at the Foundation have been the Jerusalem Festival, in autumn 1995 and the sixth Abu Dhabi International Book Fair in April 1996. A selection of the works of H.H.Sheikh Zayed and poems by General Sheikh Mohammed bin Rashid Al Maktoum, Defence Minister and Crown Prince of Dubai, formed part of an Islamic heritage exhibition, held under the patronage of Sheikha Fatima bint Mubarak, wife of the President, at the Cultural Foundation on 3 December 1995. Entitled 'Whispers from the Emirates' the exhibition featured poems displayed in the form of traditional embroidered calligraphy, blending fine fabrics and natural colours with the evocative verses.

Also in December 1995, the Arabian Leopard Trust, in conjunction with the Foundation, held a month-long series of activities aimed at awakening public awareness regarding the factors that are driving the Arabian leopard to extinction. 'Artists to the Rescue' was a collection of 35 works by Abu Dhabi's amateur and professional artists. The works were auctioned on 20 December in order to raise funds for the ALT.

A nation-wide exhibition showcasing the talents of handicapped UAE nationals was inaugurated on 2 March 1996 at the Foundation. After three days the exhibition moved to Dubai, Ras al-Khaimah and Fujairah. Held at the behest of President H.H. Sheikh Zayed bin Sultan Al Nahyan, the exhibition aimed at promoting art as a means to assist handicapped people to gain confidence in their abilities and to play meaningful roles in the development and progress of the UAE.

Over 110,000 people visit the Cultural Foundation each year and over the past 12 months it has published more than 20 titles under its own imprint, including the Emirates Encyclopaedia. The Documentation Centre, situated behind the Abu Dhabi Cultural Foundation, in the magnificently renovated fort building, contains one of the largest, if not the largest collection of manuscripts dealing with the UAE and the whole of the Gulf region. A dedicated staff are engaged in cataloguing and filing references on everything from politics to wildlife. It is a fascinating place to visit, right in the heart of downtown Abu Dhabi, and yet a haven of peace and tranquillity, reminiscent of the cloistered halls and corridors of an old English university.

The Dubai based Culture and Science Forum was established in 1978 in order to promote cultural activities in the emirate. It is involved in organizing a series of cultural symposiums and exhibitions as well as publishing material on the UAE's cultural heritage, literature, science and contemplative studies. The Forum also administers the Sheikh Rashid Award for Scientific Excellence, for which science masters and Ph.D. graduates are eligible. In December 1995 the Forum celebrated the eighth season of the Sheikh Rashid Awards scheme, presenting prizes to 28 Ph.D. holders, 76 M.Sc. degree holders and a similar number of masters graduates in military sciences.

Sharjah has gained a particularly strong reputation for its cultural activities and it has established a large number of centres there to provide facilities for those engaged in cultural pursuits, together with exhibition and display facilities where members of the public can learn from, and gain inspiration from, creative works, both ancient and modern. The Sharjah Culture and Information Department was established in 1981 with the aim of helping to coordinate the activities of other cultural institutions based in the emirate. It is fitting that Sharjah should be the headquarters for the UAE Authors' and Writers' Union whose publications now number over a hundred. In early November 1995, the Sharjah Art District was opened by H.H. Dr Sheikh Sultan bin Mohammed Al Qassimi, Member of the Supreme Council of the Federation and Ruler of Sharjah. Located in the centre of old Sharjah city, in the Showeiheen area, the two centuries old district includes a number of renovated historic buildings, one of which houses the Sharjah Art Museum. A Special Art Group club facility, donated by Dr

Sheikh Sultan with the aim of assisting in the integration of handicapped artists into society, is also a feature of the district.

The seventh Sharjah Theatre Festival took place in April 1996, attracting actors, directors, playwrights and theatre-goers from all over the country. Eleven theatrical groups from the different emirates staged 12 different productions. Organized by the Sharjah Department of Culture and Information, the festival began with a local play *Al-Bushtakta*, written by Ismael Abdulla and directed by Habib Ghuloom. Actors, actresses and critics were also invited from Qatar, Kuwait, Bahrain, Lebanon and other countries.

H.H. Sheikha Jawaher (wife of Dr Sheikh Sultan) Chairwoman of the Sharjah Women's Society, inaugurated a conference on women's culture in the UAE which began on 5 May 1996. The four-day gathering, organized by the UAE Women's Writers Association, brought together a large number of female authors and researchers from the AGCC. Papers on culture and the role of women in cultural development were presented. The gathering was intended to highlight the role of women in the cultural and educational development of AGCC societies, as well as women's responsibilities in preserving the identity and culture of local societies in the face of cultural invasions.

The Jumma'a Al Majed Centre for Cultural Heritage provides a wide range of facilities for researchers and scholars working on documents and manuscripts concerning UAE and Gulf history. In February 1996 the centre, in collaboration with the UAE University and Abu Dhabi Cultural Foundation, hosted a symposium on the writings of geographers and travellers in the Gulf region. This was accompanied by an exhibition of around 400 books on the subject, together with some rare maps, and participants debated to what extent western historical authors could be regarded as accurate when it came to their reporting of local and regional affairs.

NEW MUSEUMS

On 8 November 1996, H.H. Dr Sheikh Sultan bin Mohammed Al Qassimi, Ruler of Sharjah, inaugurated the Desert Park in Sharjah which includes a natural history museum and a Green Garden containing various species of UAE plants. Taxidermy of all the animals, which were never killed for this purpose, but died natural or accidental deaths, was undertaken by wildlife expert Christian Gross. The museum is an important educational tool as it can teach both young people and adults useful information about animals, birds, plants, geology and other aspects of the UAE's natural world.

On 14 November 1995 H.H. Dr Sheikh Sultan bin Mohammed Al Qassimi inaugurated the Sharjah Heritage Museum, together with a number of other heritage projects in Sharjah, including the traditional Al-Arsa Souk, the Islamic Antiquities Hall at Sharjah Archaeology Museum, and the second Archaeology Exhibition. Dr Sheikh Sultan said that the buildings were renovated not just to attract tourists but also to let the younger generation see how their forefathers lived and to build a greater awareness of their heritage.

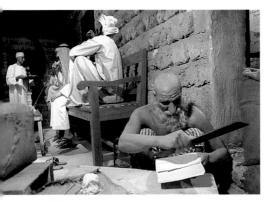

BOOKS & LITERATURE

Many new publication of relevance to the UAE were launched in 1996, the following is a sample:

Perspectives on the United Arab Emirates

This is a book written by experts with the general reader in mind. Containing chapters on palaeogeography, archae-ology, history, heritage, politics, social development, trade and industry, foreign relations and regional security it is an academic reference that will become essential reading for many people who are involved with the United Arab Emirates. The book is published by Trident Press of London, UK.

UAE: Chronicle of Progress 1971 - 1996

With 560 pages of text and pictures this is a big book on a big subject. Based upon research into newspapers and other published materials, the book provides a day by day account of major events in the United Arab Emirates from the beginning of its formation. It also

contains a fascinating collection of historic photographs and comprises a valuable addition to the serious literature on the Emirates. It is published in English and Arabic by Trident Press of London.

Natural Emirates: Wildlife and Environment of the UAE

Written by experts in their individual fields, this beautifully illustrated book provides a comprehensive treatment of the animals and plants that live in the UAE. Subjects covered include geology, fossils, habitats, beaches, plants, insects, other arthropods, land and marine reptiles, fish, birds, land and marine mammals, and traditional aspects of wildlife. It is published in English and Arabic by Trident Press of London.

Phoenix Rising

Containing excellent photographs by renowned photographer Werner Forman, this is essentially a pictorial essay on the UAE. Text has been written by Michael Asher and the book is published by the Harvill Press in UK.

Book on Sheikh Rashid bin Saeed Al Maktoum

Published on 9 September 1995, by the Rashid Paediatric Therapy Centre in Dubai, a new Arabic-language book on the late ruler of Dubai, Sheikh Rashid bin Saeed Al Maktoum, was released to mark the fifth anniversary of his death. The book highlights Sheikh Rashid's contribution to the growth and development of the UAE.

Setting-up in Dubai

A book containing information on setting up business in Dubai was published in late 1995 by Al Tamimi and Company, a law firm in the UAE. Written by Essam Al Tamimi, a lawyer, the book deals with legal implications and requirements for the establishment of business operations in the emirate. It also covers subjects relating to tourism and culture, serving as a practical guide to those moving to Dubai for business, employment or tourism.

The Relations Between Oman and France 1715-1905
& The Journals of David Seton in the Gulf 1800-1809

Both the above books, containing prefaces written by H.H. Dr Sheikh Sultan, were launched at the fourteenth Sharjah Book Fair, on 1 November 1995. Written by Arab authors the books help to place these periods in perspective for historians.

Islamic Encyclopaedia

The Islamic Encyclopaedia was published and distributed by the Intellectual Excellence Centre of Sharjah Department of Culture and Information.

From Rags to Riches

Abu Dhabi businessman, Mohammed Al Fahim, is author of a unique personal account of the UAE's development. This is a vivid eye-witness account of the total transformation of the UAE within the short space of 30 years.

Reflections of Dubai

The Dubai Commerce and Tourism Promotion Board, DCTPB, published Reflections of Dubai, a 168-page pictorial account of the emirate, in November 1995. The book is a visual record of the city and its hinterland. Pictures were sourced from over 15 leading photographers.

School in a Desert

A vividly illustrated book on the geography, religion and customs of the UAE was introduced during 1995 to primary schools in the United Kingdom. The book focuses on a girls' school in Al-Khawaneej, with the objective of familiarizing readers with the culture and traditions of the desert and to help British students know more about their UAE counterparts. It is part of the Longman Book Project and adheres to the UK National Curriculum syllabus, and is meant for seven to 12-year olds.

UAE Novelist

The Insane Window, a novel by UAE author Ali Abu Rish, is being translated to Swedish by Killy Ramsay, a teacher of Arabic at Stockholm University. Permission was also sought for translation of three other of Abu Rish's books.

Books in Newspapers

Scholars and newspaper editors-in-chief from 17 Arab countries took part in a two day conference held in Abu Dhabi during early 1996, designed to launch a project aimed at bringing the best of Arab literature and learning to readers throughout the world. The conference, organized with the support of UNESCO, reviewed a project whereby major literary works would be published simultaneously in newspapers throughout the Arab world. Conceived during discussions among Arab delegates at the fiftieth anniversary of the United Nations, the proposal was originally endorsed by a meeting of Arab newspaper editors in Granada, Spain, in October 1995. Its aim is to republish important works of Arab science and literature, making them available to the general public, by distributing them as supplements with major newspapers. The idea of Books in Newspapers was first conceived by the Peruvian poet Manuel Scorza and was adopted by UNESCO 23 years ago. Around the world, a total of 23 newspapers are already involved in the scheme, and a total of 40 books have been thus published.

ARCHAEOLOGY

THE UAE HAS A REMARKABLY RICH and varied heritage, encompassing a long history of human habitation, a significant variety of natural habitats with their accompanying plant and animal wildlife, and an evocative human tradition that is preserved in music, literature, poetry, crafts, and the unique character of its people. In the midst of all the progress and development over the past 25 years, the UAE's President, H.H. Sheikh Zayed, has been keen to nurture respect for these aspects of the Emirates, things that no amount of wealth can buy, but which form the very foundation stones upon which the country is built. He began with an interest to find out more about the people who inhabited the land of the UAE thousands of years ago, at the very beginning of civilization. Whilst there were economic priorities to exploration for oil and water, there were strong social and intellectual interests in archaeology and wildlife. The following review of archaeological research and discoveries in the UAE over the past 25 years, has been especially adapted for publication in this anniversary edition of the UAE Yearbook.

Ancient pottery vase recovered from tombs of Jebel Hafit on display at Al-Ain Museum.

THE UAE ARCHAEOLOGICAL RECORD

25 Years of Discovery

Few could have imagined, when the UAE was formed in 1971, that it possessed an archaeological heritage that would become the envy of many countries, or that so much of this heritage would be revealed in such a short period. From the early days of Sheikh Zayed's rule as President of this new nation, his own interest and enthusiasm for understanding all about the land and its people, nurtured a developing interest in exploration of the UAE's hidden past. Archaeological research has proceeded at a steadily accelerating pace, and there has been a veritable explosion of knowledge during the past decade. Reflecting the growth in knowledge and the ever expanding collection of artifacts from a growing list of excavations, archaeological museums have appeared all over the country.

A soft-stone vessel from Rumailah settlement, Al-Ain, dated to the period 1000-500 B.C. Al-Ain Museum.

Today's inhabitants of the UAE have an archaeological and historical past of which they can be justifiably proud, and which should dispel, once and for all, the notion that this region was peripheral in antiquity. Had it been peripheral, why would a series of Old Akkadian, Achaemenid, or Sasanian emperors have expended so much energy on campaigning in the area? The lack of a local written record comparable to the cuneiform archives of Mesopotamia or the hieroglyphs of Egypt must never blind us to the fact that, in antiquity, the region of the Emirates was a strategic, well-resourced, important part of the cultural mosaic of ancient Western Asia.

The Arabian bifacial tradition (c. 5000-3100 B.C.)

The last glaciation collapsed around 10,000 years ago, and the slightly moister conditions which ensued from c. 8000 to 3000 B.C. have often been described as a Climatic Optimum. It was during this period that the first securely dated human settlements in the region appeared. Finely pressure-flaked, bifacial stone tools belonging to what has been called the 'Arabian bifacial tradition' have been found on a large number of sites in a wide range of environmental zones throughout the Emirates. Tanged points, foliates, blades, knives, drills and other tools attest to the diversity of the tool-kit of the region's first inhabitants who may have been herders who supplemented their diet by hunting, rather than hunters who kept a few domestic animals.

Painted pottery of Ubaid-type, imported from Mesopotamia, has been found on many of the coastal sites in the Emirates, eastern Saudi Arabia, Qatar, Bahrain and the islands of Kuwait, revealing the existence of contacts between these regions and the peoples of southern Iraq in the fifth millennium B.C. It is important to underscore the fact that this introduction of pottery into the region did not lead immediately to the birth of a local ceramic industry, something which did not appear until the third millennium B.C.

As yet we know little about the people who inhabited the territory of the Emirates at this time. Burials in an Arabian bifacial site along the coast of the Umm al-Qaiwain lagoon have been excavated but not yet published. At Jebal Buhays, the Sharjah Dept. of Antiquities has begun the excavation of an important collective burial just beneath the surface at the base of the *Jebal*. This is certain to produce important results, particularly as the site is aceramic, shows evidence of tools attributable to the Arabian bifacial tradition, and contains exclusively cremated skeletal remains.

Large Iron Age steatite bowl with lid. Recovered from Al Buhays and displayed at Sharjah Museum.

The late fourth and early third millennium (c. 3100-2500 B.C.)
For the first time collective burials in the form of above-ground tombs built of unworked stone appear at two sites in the Emirates, Jebal Hafit (including Mazyad) and Jebal al-Emalah. Named after the site where they were first discovered, these 'Hafit'-type tombs are completely without precedent in the local archaeological sequence. They contain pottery of the Jamdat Nasr type, named after a site in Mesopotamia. In addition to their pottery, other imported finds of note include a class of roughly square, bone or ivory beads with two diagonal perforations. To date the settlements of the population buried in the Hafit tombs of southeastern Arabia (examples are also found further south in Oman) have yet to be discovered. Although there is no proof as yet, it has generally been assumed that the motivation behind the Jamdat Nasr-period contact between the Emirates and southern Mesopotamia was the incipient trade in copper.

The mid- to late third millennium (c. 2500-2000 B.C.)

The agricultural settlement of southeastern Arabia was predicated upon the domestication of the date palm (*Phoenix dactylifera*). Without the date palm, the shade necessary for the growth of other, less hardy cultivars, including cereals, vegetables and fruits, was lacking. Once the *bustan*-type of garden came into existence, watered by wells which tapped the relatively abundant and shallow lenses of sweet water found throughout much of the Emirates, the basis was laid for the development of the kind of oasis living which is so characteristic of the wadi settlements of the region. Herd animals, such as sheep, goat and cattle of course played a part in the development of a full oasis economy, but no single species was so critical in this process as the date palm.

The earliest agricultural villages of the Emirates were thus agriculturally based, and perhaps in order to safeguard their investment in land, water and natural resources, the inhabitants of those villages felt compelled to construct imposing fortifications. These buildings appear for the first time in the middle of the third millennium and are an architectural *leit-fossil* of the so-called 'Umm an-Nar' period (c. 2500-2000 B.C.). In the Emirates examples of such Umm an-Nar fortress-towers have been excavated at Hili 1, Hili 8, Bidya, Tell Abraq and Kalba. Whereas most of these range in size between 16 and 25 metres in diameter, the tower at Tell Abraq, at 40 metres in diameter, is by far the largest yet uncovered.

In general, the dead of the Umm an-Nar period were buried in circular, stone tombs faced with finely masoned ashlar blocks, although rectangular chambers, perhaps for secondary re-burial of bone from circular tombs which had become full, are also known. Examples of Umm an-Nar circular tombs were first encountered by a Danish expedition on the island of Umm an-Nar in Abu Dhabi in 1958. Thus it was that the island gave its name to the period of which these tombs are characteristic. By 1995 examples of Umm an-Nar tombs had been excavated in both coastal and inland Abu Dhabi (Umm an-Nar island, Hili area), Dubai (Al-Sufouh and Hatta), Ajman (Moweihat), Umm al-Qaiwain (Tell Abraq), and Ras al-Khaimah (Shimal, Wadi Munay'i). The better preserved examples show that literally hundreds of individuals were buried in these tombs along with a wide range of grave furniture, including soft-stone bowls; fine and domestic black-on-red ceramics of local manufacture; incised grey and painted black-on-grey pottery from southeastern Iran or Baluchistan; copper-bronze weaponry; personal items of jewellery such as bracelets and necklaces incorporating thousands of beads, a significant proportion of which are Harappan paste micro-beads from the Indus Valley; and other exotic items such as ivory combs, gypsum lamps, and linen. Most surprising in the tomb at Tell Abraq was the discovery of a female of around 20 years old who had suffered from polio: the first ever confirmed incidence of this disease in the archaeological record anywhere in the world.

Excavations at Asimah in the interior of Ras al-Khaimah have revealed the existence of stone alignments consisting of raised platforms and subterranean graves which, on the basis of their associated finds, also date to the Umm an-Nar period. These monuments, which have been compared with the triliths and alignments of southern and western Arabia, suggest that a degree of cultural diversity existed in late third millennium southeastern Arabia which has yet to be adequately investigated.

A religious book, transcribed by hand and dated to the end of the seventeenth century AD. Displayed at Al-Ain Museum.

The early and middle second millennium (c. 2000-1200 B.C.)

For many years it was thought that a major discontinuity occurred in the archaeological sequence of the UAE/Oman peninsula at the end of the third millennium. It remains true today that the absolute number of early second millennium settlements in the Emirates is not great, but on those which have been investigated, such as Tell Abraq, and from the surface indications at a site like Nud Ziba in Ras al-Khaimah, it is clear that some population centres continued to be inhabited on a full-time basis and show no signs of a cultural 'decline'. At Tell Abraq, for example, the large fortress-tower of the Umm an-Nar period continued in use down to the middle of the second millennium, with modifications to the outer walls and the construction of new buildings on the interior. Apart from these architectural modifications, there is a major change detectable in the diet of the site's inhabitants, with fish and shellfish becoming more important than they had been in the late third millennium and accounting for c. 50 per cent of all dietary requirements. A similar swing from the exploitation of terrestrial fauna (sheep, goat, cattle) to marine resources has also been observed at Shimal as one moves from the earlier to the later second millennium. The later Wadi Suq levels at Tell Abraq are paralleled by the occupation of the settlement at Shimal in Ras al-Khaimah, where an area of habitation at the base of the Al-Hajar mountains, and within sight of an ancient mangrove lagoon, was located. Shimal, and the nearby sites of Ghalilah and Dhayah

A mould for making coins recovered from excavations in Sharjah.

are, however, better known for the many collective tombs of the Wadi Suq period located there. Subterranean, horse-shoe-shaped tombs in the Wadi al-Qawr of southern Ras al-Khaimah and the Qidfa oasis of Fujairah must also be dated to the Wadi Suq period. Subterranean, T-shaped tombs, such as those excavated at Dhayah and Bithna also date to the Wadi Suq period. Finally, individual inhumation graves dug into the *sabkha* at Al-Qusais, a suburb to the east of Dubai, include many of Wadi Suq date.

The Wadi Suq period is notable for the explosion in metallurgy witnessed at this time. Although often robbed in antiquity, some Wadi Suq tombs, such as the horseshoe-shaped structure at Qidfa, have yielded literally hundreds of weapons and vessels. Where the Umm an-Nar period was characterized by daggers and spears, the Wadi Suq period witnessed the introduction of the long sword, the bow and arrow, and a new, light type of socketed spearhead. The appearance of these weapons, along with hundreds of cast bronze, lanceolate arrowheads with a raised, flattened midrib, suggest an evolution in the technology of warfare during the second millennium unprecedented in the earlier archaeological record of the region.

In the late third millennium an industry arose in the manufacture of soft-stone vessels - generally bowls, beakers and compartmented boxes - decorated with dotted-circles made using a bow drill. During the Wadi Suq period the numbers of soft-stone vessels deposited in tombs increased vastly, and new shapes along with the addition of incised diagonal and horizontal lines in clusters allow us to easily separate the later soft-stone vessels from their third millennium forerunners.

Studies of the teeth of people buried at Shimal have shown that the population there experienced low rates of teeth decay which may reflect a diet heavily dependent on fresh fish and shellfish and probable relatively few, if any, dates. Some indication of an accumulation of wealth during the Wadi Suq period is provided by an interesting class of gold and electrum plaques in the form of two animals, standing back to back, often with their tails curled up in a spiral. Examples are now known from Dhayah, Qattarah and Bidya. Some of that wealth may have been accumulated through long-distance trade in copper, a commodity for which Dilmun (modern Bahrain) became famous as a retailer to the southern Mesopotamian market city of Ur in the early second millennium. The discovery at Tell Abraq of over 600 sherds of Barbar red-ridged pottery, now shown to be compositionally identical to the pottery from the settlement at Saar on Bahrain, points to the clear existence of contacts in that direction. Moreover, both Tell Abraq and Shimal have Post-Harappan pottery in early second millennium contexts, providing evidence of continued contacts with the Indus Valley at this time.

From the late second to the late first millennium (c. 1200-300 B.C.)

Two innovations occurred in the late second millennium which were to revolutionize the economies of southeastern Arabia. The domestication of the camel, attested by the end of the second millennium at Tell Abraq, opened up new possibilities for land transport, while the discovery of the *falaj* system of transporting water from aquifers to gardens through water tunnels and channels made possible the extensive irrigation of gardens and agricultural plots which resulted in a veritable explosion of settlement across the UAE/Oman peninsula .

The period from c. 1200 to 300 B.C. has traditionally been referred to as the 'Iron Age'. No term could be less appropriate, however, for in southeastern Arabia iron was not used until the following period (see below). With the exception of a tomb at Asimah (As 100) which contains Iron I material, all of the evidence for early Iron Age occupation comes from the Gulf coast sites of Shimal, Tell Abraq, and a series of shell middens at Al-Hamriyah in Sharjah. Fish and shellfish continued to be important in the diet of the Iron I inhabitants, although domesticated sheep, goat and cattle were kept, and gazelle, oryx, dugong, turtle and cormorant were exploited as well. Domesticated wheat and barley were cultivated at this time and the date-palm remained as important as ever. The Iron II period is the 'classic' Iron Age in the Emirates and is attested at a number of extensively excavated sites with substantial

mudbrick architecture such as Rumeilah, Bint Saud, Hili 2, Hili 14 and Hili 17 in the Al-Ain area; Al-Thuqaibah and Umm Safah on the Al-Madam plain; and Muweilah in the sandy desertic area near the Sharjah International Airport. Many other sites, both graves and settlements, have been located and it is estimated that at least 150 sites of this period have been documented in the Emirates and neighbouring Oman. The explosion in settlement at this time is generally attributed to the invention of *falaj* irrigation technology, and cultivation using the hoe may be inferred from the recovery of a bronze hoe-blade at Rumeilah.

It is interesting to note that the Iron II period also witnessed the appearance of fortified strongholds, such as Hili 14 in Al-Ain, Husn Madhab in Fujairah, Jebal Buhays north of Al-Madam, and Rafaq in the Wadi al-Qawr. The purpose of these fortresses, it may be argued, was to safeguard the agricultural settlements associated with them, particularly their precious *aflaj*, and the concentration of power in such centres is an important social and political phenomenon.

Photographed at Sharjah Museum.

Political and economic control by central bodies may also be implied by the appearance at this time of a tradition of stamp seal manufacture evidenced at a number of sites, including Rumeilah, Muweilah, Tell Abraq and Bint Saud. Contacts with foreign regions are suggested by a soft-stone pendant from Tell Abraq which shows a figure reminiscent of the Neo-Assyrian and Neo-Babylonian depictions of the *lamashtu* demoness, an evil spirit who spread disease, and it is most probable that such pendants were worn to protect their owners from sickness. Some indication of how such foreign contacts were effected is given by another pendant from Tell Abraq which shows the only Iron Age depiction of a boat in the UAE/Oman peninsula. In this case the boat appears to be a square-sterned vessel with a sharp bow and triangular sail. The sail is obviously similar to the Arab lateen sail, otherwise unattested in the region until the Sasanian period and absent in the Mediterranean until c. 900 A.D. The Tell Abraq pendant is thus the earliest depiction of a lateen sail yet discovered.

The third and final sub-period of the Iron Age, Iron III, is not very well known, although occupation is attested at half a dozen settlements including Tell Abraq, Shimal, Rumeilah, Hili 17, Hili 2, Nud Ziba and Al-Thuqaibah, as well as graves in the Wadi al-Qawr and Dibba oasis.

The Mleiha (Late Pre-Islamic A-B) period (c. 300-0 B.C.)

The dissolution of the Persian Empire must have impacted on southeastern Arabia, for with the defeat and death of Darius III Maka (Magan) was no longer a Persian satrapy. On the other hand, Alexander the Great's conquests never touched the Arabian side of the Gulf and, while he inherited much of what had formerly been the Achaemenid empire, the famous 'last plans' of the Macedonian conqueror, which included an invasion of Arabia, never advanced beyond the stage of initial reconnaissance. Thus, by the third century B.C. southeastern Arabia was free of foreign political influence and it is in this context that the developments of the subsequent centuries must be viewed, for none of Alexander's Seleucid successors was able to establish any sort of Greek dominance in the region either.

With the exception of Mleiha, a sprawling settlement on the gravel plain south of Dhayd, which extends over an area several square kilometers in extent, we have no other settlements which can be attributed to this time horizon. The occupation of Mleiha represented the continuation of human occupation in an optimally watered and well-drained area which had begun in the late prehistoric era. The earliest, post-Iron Age settlement probably consisted of *barastis*, palm-frond houses eminently suited to the hot climate of the UAE/Oman peninsula. The dead, however, were buried in more substantial structures, mudbrick cists surmounted by a solid tower of brick, capped by crenellated stone ornaments. These structures, which have no antecedents in the region, recall the funerary towers of Palmyra, Qaryat al-Fau, and the early periods at Petra. Both settlement and graves have yielded quantities of ceramics, some of it of obviously local manufacture, carrying on and modifying the norms established during the Iron Age, and some of it foreign. This includes glazed pottery, perhaps produced in southwestern Iran or southern Iraq; red and black wares readily identifiable as coming from the northeast Arabian mainland or adjacent islands of Bahrain or Failaka; and even Greek pottery, imported from the Aegean or Mediterranean. Engraved bronze bowls and beehive-shaped, alabaster vessels from Mleiha II contexts recall examples from South Arabia, a fact which is important in connection with the recovery of several items (stone stelae, bronze bowls) inscribed in South Arabian characters. Several coins found on the surface of the site are unequivocally South Arabian.

One of the cultural innovations which characterizes the late pre-Islamic era is the appearance of iron for the first time in the archaeological record of southeastern Arabia. Alongside utilitarian items such as nails, long swords and arrowheads were used. Whether or not they were manufactured locally is another matter, but in addition to the existence of iron-bearing zones near Jebals Faiyah, Emalah and Buhays, south of Mleiha, the site itself has surface scatters of iron slag suggesting that secondary refining and casting were carried out there. Why iron was not adopted earlier is a mystery. Certainly the abundance of copper sources in the Al-Hajar mountains, and the ancient tradition of copper metallurgy may have been a factor contributing to a lack of interest in iron.

The ed-Dur (Late Pre-Islamic C) period (c. 0-200 A.D.)

By the first century A.D. we have reached a period for which considerably more literary documentation exists, albeit of a difficult nature to use. The Roman writer Pliny the Younger (23/24-79 A.D.) completed his *Natural History* in 77 A.D. and, to judge from his account of the peoples and places of southeastern Arabia (*Nat. Hist.* VI.32.149-152), combined with the second century A.D. testimony of Cl. Ptolemy's map of Arabia, the area of the Emirates was full of settlements, tribes, and physical features, the names of which he recorded for us. Fixing the locations of these, and linking them with archaeological sites, has proven difficult but it has been argued that the town of Omana, which previous writers have made out to be a famous port of Carmania, may be identified with the large, nearly 4 kilometres square settlement of ed-Dur in Umm al-Qaiwain. The same site is, moreover, mentioned at about the same time in the anonymous *Periplus of the Erythraean Sea*, an important text which documents the maritime trade between Alexandria in Egypt and Barygaza in India. Certainly the archaeological remains of ed-Dur leave us in no doubt that the site was the most important coastal settlement in the lower Gulf during the first centuries A.D.

Most of the architecture at the site is built of beach rock (Ar. *farush*), a calcareous concretion which forms offshore in shallow tidal areas and can be easily broken into slabs for use as building material. Large houses, some with numerous rooms and round corner towers, have been excavated as well as small, one-room dwellings. The use of alabaster for window panes is important and marks the earliest archaeological attestation of alabaster for this purpose in the Arabian peninsula. Graves may be either simple subterranean cists for individual burials, or large, semi-subterranean collective tombs consisting of a subterranean chamber reached via a stairway from the surface, surmounted by a barrel vault. The ceramics from the site are dominated by glazed wares, almost certainly of Parthian manufacture and imported either from southern Mesopotamia or southwestern Iran. Omana was the most important port in the lower Gulf, and was twinned with the port of Apologos at the head of the Gulf, a site perhaps located somewhere near modern Basra and one of the main maritime outlets for the kingdom of Characene.

While traffic down the Red Sea and across the Indian Ocean provided one means for the Roman acquisition of exotica from India and the east, overland caravan traffic

*Horse head showing remnants of gold
bridle, recovered from excavations at
Mlheia, on display at Sharjah Museum.*

HERITAGE

between Palmyra in Syria and the cities of Vologesias, Seleucia and Spasinou Charax in Iraq, followed by seaborne travel down the 'Characene corridor' to Omana and on to India provided an alternative route. The latter mechanism may well have been responsible for the diffusion of quantities of Roman glass to ed-Dur, most of which dates to the first century A.D.

The concentration of political power which one may presume to have existed in an emporium like ed-Dur was undoubtedly centred on the fort excavated in 1973 by the Iraqi expedition. Measuring roughly 20 metres on a side, and with four circular corner towers, each 4 metres in diameter, the fort is built of beach-rock and shows affinities to contemporary Parthian fortifications in Mesopotamia. South of the fort is an important temple, excavated by the Belgian expedition, which was a simple, one-room, square structure, roughly 8 metres on a side, of beach-rock faced

A small chlorite vase with four unpierced lugs, found at Shimal in 1978. It is typical of the Wadi Suq style and dates to the Early Wadi Suq Period (between 2000 and 1600 BC). Ras al-Khaimah Museum, reference 2222.

with finely worked gypsum plaster imitating ashlar masonry. An incense burner from the temple, inscribed in Aramaic with the name Shams, suggests that this was a shrine dedicated to the pan-Semitic solar deity.

While ed-Dur was the prime settlement of this period on the Gulf coast, Mleiha was certainly the leading centre in the interior. One of the most important discoveries made in recent excavations at the site was a square fort with square corner towers, the main outer wall of which was 55 metres long. Associated with the fort, moreover, was a stone mould for the production of coins, and as the right to strike coinage was generally a royal prerogative in the ancient world, it is likely that the Mleiha fort represents the power centre of the polity centred on the site. The coins minted at Mleiha - hundreds of which have been discovered at both ed-Dur and Mleiha - were modelled on the coinage of Alexander. They show a debased head of Heracles wearing the pelt of the Nemean lion on the obverse, and a seated figure, based on that of Zeus, on the reverse. Whereas the original Greek models had the name ALEXANDER clearly written in Greek on the reverse, the Mleiha/ed-Dur coins bear a legend which can be read as 'Abi'el, son/daughter of *bgln/tmyln/tlmyl/tym*.' We can safely conclude that Abi'el was an important ruler in this region during the late pre-Islamic era.

The end of the pre-Islamic era (c. 240-635 A.D.)

Although the extent of the political influence of the Parthians in southeastern Arabia has long been debated, there is little doubt that their Sasanian successors swiftly imposed their will on the inhabitants of the region shortly after coming to power. Archaeologically, however, there is little concrete evidence of Sasanian presence in the Emirates. The few coins recovered on the Gulf coast include a pair of badly preserved bronzes of Ardashir and Shapur II (309-379) from Ghallah, an island in the lagoon of Umm al-Qaiwain, as well as a silver coin of the latter king from Tell Abraq. In Fujairah, a small hoard of 18 silver coins was discovered which included issues of two late Sasanian monarchs, Hormizd IV (579-590) and Khusrau II (590-628).

In the interior, several intrusive burials with iron weaponry (spear, sword, pike) dug into the prehistoric tombs at Jebal al-Emalah can be attributed to the very end of the pre-Islamic period. A fragmentary individual buried with an iron sword in Tomb I has produced a corrected radiocarbon date of 455-583 A.D., while a fully articulated individual buried with an iron-tipped spear from Tomb III has been dated to 513-624 A.D. A third burial at Jebal al-Emalah with iron accoutrements was that of a camel in its own, oval grave ringed by stones. Yet it would be wrong to suggest that the religious climate of the era was dominated either by Arab paganism (viz. camel burial) or Zoroastrianism (viz. Sasanian influence). Nestorian Christianity was a decidedly important component of the religious milieu at this time as well.

In 424 Yohannon, bishop of Mazun attended an important synod at Markabta de Tayyae in Iraq, where the Nestorian church proclaimed its independence from Antioch. This is the first concrete evidence of Nestorian Christianity in south-eastern Arabia, although the *Vita Ionae*, an account of the life of a monk named Jonah who lived in the time of the *catholicus* Barb'ashmin (343-346), says that Jonah built a monastery 'on

Unusual fragment of Iron Age chlorite bowl with fish engraving, from Al-Buhays, displayed at Sharjah Museum.

Iron Age (1300-300 BC) chlorite (soft-stone) vessels found in collective (unpublished) tombs in the Wadi al-Qawr in southern Ras al-Khaimah, excavated by Carl Phillips, University of London, between 1986 and 1989. A common grave good, these vessels were very abundant in the Iron-Age tombs in the Wadi al-Qawr. Locally made, there are more than 900 chlorite vessels held at Ras al-Khaimah Museum. These four are of a typical Iron Age style, distinct from earlier Umm an-Nar and Wadi Suq styles.

the borders of the black island', a locale which some Nestorian scholars have sought amongst the islands between Qatar and Oman. In this connection it is obvious to consider the islands off the coast of Abu Dhabi as a likely site for Jonah's monastery. The recent discovery on the island of Sir Bani Yas of a monastery and/or church, complete with carved stucco ornamentation including a cross, is of enormous interest in this respect.

In 544 David, bishop of Mazun, attended the Nestorian synod of Mar Aba I, and in 576 Samuel attended the synod of Mar Ezechiel. Mazun is included in an important Armenian list of the provinces of the Sasanian empire compiled late in the Sasanian period, and it is certain that the region was under Sasanian control at the time of the Islamic conversion.

Two major towns of the period are mentioned in literary sources, Tuwwam and Dibba. Tuwwam, although identifiable with the region of present day Al-Ain and the Buraimi oasis, is invisible archaeologically, for no late pre-Islamic remains contemporary with the period of Sasanian governance have been unearthed there. Dibba, of course, is still the name of a major port and oasis settlement on the east coast of the Emirates which is today divided between Oman, Fujairah and Sharjah. Although the archaeology of Dibba in the late pre-Islamic era is yet to be investigated, the literary record is more ample.

In his *al-Muhabbar*, Ibn Habib called Dibba 'one of the two ports of the Arabs; merchants from Sind, India, China, people of the East and West came to it' . At this time Dibba paid a tithe to Al-Julanda b. al-Mustakbir on the occasion of a fair held each year for five nights beginning on the first day of Rajab. The commercial importance of Dibba at this time explains why Jaifar, one of the al-Julanda addressed by the Prophet in a letter carried by Abu Zaid and 'Amr b. al-'As in the year 630 (AH 8), sent a messenger to Dibba exhorting its inhabitants to convert to Islam. Just a few years later, however, Dibba became the base of Laqit b. Malik, the leader of the al-Riddah or apostasizing movement, and the crushing of that movement by the armies of Abu Bakr created one of the largest and most important historical sites in the Emirates, a vast cemetery said to contain upwards of 10,000 slain rebels on the outskirts of Dibba.

Christianity in Mazun certainly survived some decades after the Muslim conversion, for Stephen, bishop of Mazun, attended a synod in Mesopotamia in 676. The apostasy of the Christian community, however, was rife in this period, a fact amply documented by a series of letters sent by the Nestorian catholicos Isho'yahb III to Simeon of Rev-Ardashir in Iran, complaining about the conversions of 'your people in Mazun' . The subsequent absence of any more bishops from Mazun at the synods of the Nestorian church is an indication that Christianity probably did not survive in southeastern Arabia much beyond the seventh century.

The above account provides a brief overview of the rich archaeological evidence for the UAE's ancient heritage. Virtually all of the discoveries mentioned have taken place in the short space of 25 years, since the formation of the UAE. It is a great tribute to the interest in heritage and archaeology of the UAE's President, Sheikh Zayed, and of his fellow rulers of the other emirates forming the Federation, that so much has been accomplished. With the continued good will of the country's leaders, and active participation of an increasing body of UAE scientists, there is no doubt that archaeological research in the Emirates will continue to make important advances in the coming years.

The above article is a synopsis of a full length text on the same subject, written by Professor Dan Potts and published in *Perspectives on the United Arab Emirates*, Trident Press, 1996.

RECENT DEVELOPMENTS IN THE ARCHAEOLOGICAL RECORD

The following items concern matters of interest on UAE archaeology that have occurred during the last 12 months.

The site of an early Christian Monastery on Sir Bani Yas island was discovered by Abu Dhabi Islands Archaeological Survey team in April 1962. Test excavations carried out in 1993 revealed a large complex of finely constructed rooms with plaster floors and plastered walls, dating to the pre-/early Islamic Period. Large scale excavation of the site was begun in 1994 and has been continued during excavating seasons since then. The work has revealed a large, well-preserved Christian monastery with domestic buildings arranged in four wings grouped around a courtyard. In the middle of this courtyard is a large church, the first pre-Islamic Christian church to be found in the United Arab Emirates. The monastery is also the most easterly Christian site yet found on the Arabian Gulf coast. It was intricately decorated with crosses, flowers and grape designs impressed into white gypsum plaster, showing the high cultural level of these people at this time. The Christian monks who built and inhabited the monastery were probably Arabs who belonged to the Nestorian branch of the Eastern Church, effectively the native church of much of the Middle East in the time before the coming of the Prophet Mohammed.

Christian Monastery on Sir Bani Yas

Excavations being undertaken by the Abu Dhabi Islands Archaeological Survey continued at the Nestorian church which forms part of an early Christian monastic site on Sir Bani Yas island. The site occupies a commanding view across the plains of the island and there is little doubt that it must have stood out like a beacon to the sailors of the lower Gulf in the fifth and sixth centuries A.D. The dig unearthed remains of a grave situated close to the main entrance of the church and presumed to have been that of its founding Abbot. Walls of the church were plastered with lime which was decorated by crosses.

Early Christian Site on Abu Dhabi Mainland

An early Christian site was found on the Abu Dhabi coastline at Shaleala, about 40 kilometres northeast of Abu Dhabi. The first of its kind in Abu Dhabi, pottery discovered there establishes links to the site at ed-Dur in Umm al-Qaiwain which flourished in the first couple of centuries of the Christian era, in particular from between 25 B.C. and 75 A.D. Research from these sites yielded evidence of extensive trading in this period between the UAE, India and the Mediterranean region.

7000 Year Old Settlement in Heart of Sharjah City

Human settlements in the centre of Sharjah city, as long ago as 5000 B.C., were confirmed by archaeological excavations in the Abu Shaghara area. Excavations there yielded tools and pottery fragments associated with the 'Ubaid culture of southern Mesopotamia. The Abu Shaghara site is the second to have been found in the Emirate of Sharjah dating to this period. 'Ubaid sherds have also been found in previous seasons on small shell middens close to a former coastline in the Hamriyyah area, north of Ajman. The 'Ubaid civilization, one of the world's earliest settled civilizations, emerged in Mesopotamia around 7000 years ago, and was centred on the town of 'Ubaid. From archaeological discoveries in eastern Saudi Arabia, it is known to have had commercial links down the Arabian Gulf, but until recently, evidence of links with what now comprises the UAE was

Gold pendant from Qattarah in Al-Ain (1800-1500 BC). Al-Ain Museum.

Petroglyph discovered in 1996 in Fujairah.

confined to a few scattered pottery fragments found at Jazirat al-Hamra in Ras al-Khaimah and at Hamriyyah.

Rock Art Discovered in Fujairah

A major collection of petroglyphs (rock carvings) was discovered near the site of a long-abandoned village deep within Fujairah's Wadi Hail which runs into the mountains just southwest of Fujairah town. Among the drawings are animals, including two which may possibly represent the endangered Arabian leopard and another which shows similarities with human figures found on seals dating to the third millennium B.C.

Largest Tell in the UAE

Excavations in the village of Shimal, north of Ras al-Khaimah, identified the largest archaeological 'tell' (settlement mound), known anywhere in the Emirates. 'Tells' are made up of the collapse of successive layers of mud-brick buildings, and are common in Mesopotamia, but are rare in the UAE and the rest of southeastern Arabia. The only two other 'tells' identified in the UAE are at Tell Abraq, in Umm al-Qaiwain, and near Khatt, inland from Ras al-Khaimah.

The Shimal 'tell', known to local inhabitants as Qush, is made up of three connected mounds, covering an area of roughly 100 metres by 100 metres, and stands 6 metres high above the surrounding flood plain, with a further 2.5 metres of deposit now underground.

Wahalla Village Site

Studies at Wahalla, a village of less than a couple of dozen houses in the mountains of Fujairah, established links dating back over 4000 years. During surveys in the area, the team identified an extensive scatter of potsherds from the Iron Age (around 1000 B.C. to 500 B.C.) in and around the recent fort, which also extended to an area in the east around some abandoned buildings from the Islamic period. Besides the Iron Age site, the team discovered a number of massive rock tombs which are believed to date back to the third millennium B.C., judging by their surface similarity to tombs of a similar date found elsewhere in the Emirates.

Khor Fakkan Ancient Settlement

A new find in Khor Fakkan comprises a series of housing units with a large number of rooms of different shapes and sizes and with walls made of stone. The rooms are separated by wide corridors and halls, with large outside courtyards whose

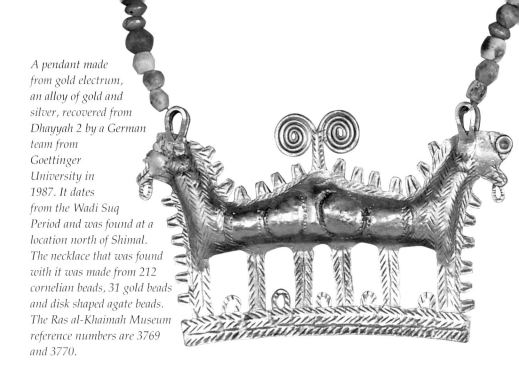

A pendant made from gold electrum, an alloy of gold and silver, recovered from Dhayyah 2 by a German team from Goettinger University in 1987. It dates from the Wadi Suq Period and was found at a location north of Shimal. The necklace that was found with it was made from 212 cornelian beads, 31 gold beads and disk shaped agate beads. The Ras al-Khaimah Museum reference numbers are 3769 and 3770.

brushwood roofs were once supported by strong wooden pillars. A considerable quantity of artifacts was also found, including shards of clay pottery which were beautifully painted and decorated, stone-made tools, hand mills, fishing implements and a multitude of other items that were obviously for daily use.

The 66 tombs found in the nearby mountains indicate that people remained settled at the foot of the Khor Fakkan mountains for a long period of time. Although the tombs had been rifled through by grave robbers, the finds still show how people were buried in groups with their jewellery and other items. This is the first time that such a large settlement from that period has been discovered, either in the UAE or anywhere else on the peninsula. The large number of houses and the graveyards will provide valuable evidence concerning life in the region over 4000 years ago.

Historic Buildings in Ras al-Khaimah

At least 75 castles, forts and fortified houses were identified in Ras al-Khaimah following a survey along the coast and in the mountains at the end of 1991 and the beginning of 1992, the results of which were published during 1995. Among them are substantial buildings like the former ruler's fort, now the National Museum of Ras al-Khaimah, 'pepper-pot' defensive towers like those to be seen just outside the village of Jazirat al-Hamra and fortified houses in villages like Al Falayyah and Dhayyah.

The publication, written by Derek Kennet, also covers more dilapidated structures like hill-top forts deep in the mountains, such as one at Wadi Dafta and the well-known Husn Shimal ('Sheba's Palace') near the village of Shimal, north of Ras al-Khaimah.

Old Mosque Preservation Project in Ras al-Khaimah

Gold pendant from Qattarah, Al-Ain Museum.

A team of French and Belgian archaeologists from the Sorbonne University in Paris began a study of the old mosques of Ras al-Khaimah, which date from the eighteenth and nineteenth centuries.

Al-Madam Excavation in Sharjah

A Spanish archaeology team, excavating in Al-Madam area, unearthed a large structure comprising several rooms, a wide courtyard and a staircase. The site dates back to the first millennium B.C. and the team has also discovered pottery fragments, as well as stone and metal artefacts.

Abu Dhabi Islands Archaeological Survey

Balghelam

Previous surveys on Balghelam, northeast of Abu Dhabi, during 1995 and 1994 yielded substantial evidence of historical occupation, including an old well, a number of fireplaces and raised circular mounds on an ancient shoreline. Excavations were undertaken during early 1996 with the intention of examining some of these features and to begin to build up a picture of the use of the island made by past inhabitants of Abu Dhabi. Close to the well, six more abandoned wells were discovered under surface sand cover. Digging through the sandy fill of one of the wells, the archaeologists reached water about 2 metres down. The wells themselves, the largest of which was up to 5 metres across, showed evidence of having been in use over a long period, with pottery fragments dating back to the sixteenth century A.D. Coupled with the evidence ADIAS has found of the presence of water on other islands such as Bu Khesheishah, Merawwah, Ghaghah, Yasat al Ulya and Kafai, this suggests a picture that is completely different from the commonly held, but erroneous, view that Abu Dhabi's islands were largely barren due to a supposed absence of water.

The second area to be examined yielded evidence of what could be described as some kind of industrial activity. Besides a number of small hearths, probably domestic fireplaces, the archaeological team also uncovered, beneath two small mounds, large pits, around 1.2 metres across and about 70 centimetres deep, lined with stone slabs and dug down to the bedrock. Within the pits were extensive deposits of burned material and it is likely that the pits may have been used to burn seashells to make lime for plaster.

Jebel Buhays: Fifth or Sixth Millennium B.C. Site

Jebel Buhays has yielded a number of significant sites in recent years. Skeletal material recently discovered there includes the remains of at least 108 individuals in an area of around 10.0 m X 6.0 m, with a further area yet to be investigated. Because of the discovery of the skeletons, which require specialized study, Supreme Council Member and Ruler of Sharjah H.H. Dr Sheikh Sultan bin Mohammed Al Qassimi authorized collaboration with Tubingen University whose Dr Hans Peter Uerpmann is a specialist in early skeletal material from southeastern Asia. A sample of the skeletons was taken to Germany for analysis and to be compared with other skeletons from other sites in the region in the prehistoric period. The Tubingen team will also undertake DNA analysis on some of the skeletal material. The skeletons were buried facing the direction of the rising sun, suggesting a religious connotation. Some were buried individually, others collectively. All the female skeletons appeared to have been buried with ornaments in their graves, including pearls. Pearling is known to have commenced in the UAE at this early period, with evidence of pearling having been found both in a cemetery from the 'Ubaid Period, in the fifth or sixth millennium B.C., and in a settlement on Abu Dhabi's Delma Island. As far as is known, though, the Jebel Buhays finds are the first evidence of the origins of the pearling trade to have been found well inland.

Excavations in Ras al-Khaimah

A five member German team carried out work in the Shimal area, excavating a number of 4000 year-old tombs. In that period, large communal tombs resembling small houses were built. Inside, all the members of the family or tribe, possibly up to 200 people, were buried. The tombs used to have a stone door that could be opened whenever needed and the dead were laid on the floor along with some items such as jewellery, weapons, pots and carved stone objects. The Shimal Tomb has already yielded four large copper dagger blades of a type so far unknown from Ras al-Khaimah. Two spearheads and a silver brooch in the shape of a bull were also found at the site.

Late Stone Age Site Discovered

Previously unidentified archaeological sites from the Late Stone Age, around 7000 years ago, were recently found in the desert about 40 kilometres southwest of Jebel Dhanna. A number of tools were discovered during the survey, including a bifacially-worked blade, a scraper or knife made of tabular flint and arrowhead fragments. The tools are comparable in technology to those found by ADIAS on the offshore islands of Merawwah and Ghaghah and can be ascribed to the Qatar-B period, around 7000 years ago.

Islamic coins from Wadi Al-Sharafe, north of Al-Ain. Three hundred silver coins from the Safawid era were found. The coins were struck during the reign of Shah Safi Al Thani, ruler of Iran (1077 - 1085). Hijira dates on the coins are 1085 to 1094. Al-Ain Museum.

Associated with the flint material at some of the sites identified during the survey was an extensive collection of ostrich shell fragments, suggesting that the Late Stone Age inhabitants of the region also hunted ostriches for food. Once common, the Arabian ostrich became extinct in the early decades of this century.

WILDLIFE and ENVIRONMENT

THE UAE IS FORTUNATE TO HAVE as its President a man who regards nature with a sense of deep wonder and admiration, and for whom conservation is a life's mission rather than a passing interest. Ever since Sheikh Zayed was a boy, he has lived close to the natural world, accepting the challenges of the desert, learning how to read the tracks of animals and to appreciate the special qualities of wild plants. With wealth has also come the ability to take a proactive role in conserving wild animals and their habitats. Sheikh Zayed long ago recognized that it is not sufficient to sit back and hope that a particular habitat will remain as it was, or that a particular animal will automatically recover from excessive hunting if left to its own devices. The web of nature is so complex, and man's intrusions are so encompassing, that we must now accept responsibility for ensuring the survival of nature. The UAE, under the guidance of its President and other members of the Supreme Council, has consistently worked towards saving its wildlife and encouraging a deeper appreciation of it among both UAE citizens and the people who visit the country.

This has been achieved in a variety of ways. Firstly, large tracts of privately owned land were set aside for wildlife protection and prevention of uncontrolled hunting. Secondly, breeding herds of endangered species were established, such as those for oryx and gazelle on *Rheem gazelle on Sir Bani Yas Island.*

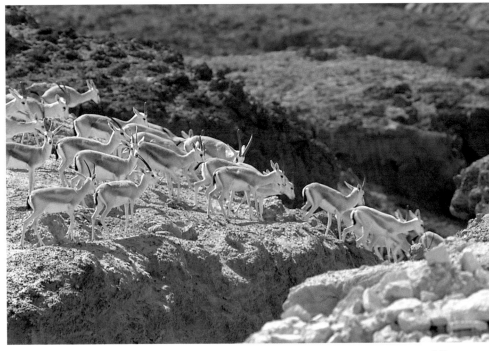

Oryx with young on Sir Bani Yas Island.

Sheikh Zayed's island, Sir Bani Yas. Thirdly, an active research programme on the UAE's wildlife was established, including studies on captive breeding of certain species, particularly the houbara bustard. Fourthly, falcon clinics were established which aimed at caring for, and improving husbandry of, falcons, especially with a view to enhancing their survival in the wild, following their release at the end of the hunting season. Fifthly, education was encouraged, aimed at teaching UAE nationals about their natural

environment. Sixthly, nature was adopted as a theme for special attractions in the form of zoos and museums. Throughout this process a growing natural history movement was supported in its efforts to discover more about the UAE's wildlife. Finally a federal body was established, the Federal Environment Agency, with a remit to coordinate efforts at environmental protection throughout the country.

The UAE's respect for wildlife and its efforts to promote conservation, nationally, regionally and on a global scale, have borne fruit both in real terms, for its wildlife, and also in terms of a wider recognition of its achievements in this sphere. The period 1995-1996 saw some important gains in the field of wildlife conservation and encouraging signs for the future. Among these, the international recognition for the work being carried out at Sir Bani Yas was especially encouraging; as was the massive public interest in the opening of the UAE's first Natural History Museum in Sharjah.

SIR BANI YAS: AN ARABIAN ARK

The island nature reserve and experimental agricultural base of Sir Bani Yas, which owes its present form to the vision and commitment of H.H. President Sheikh Zayed, has continued to impress all who visit it. A massive amount of land reclamation, planting, irrigation and wildlife husbandry has created a place that somehow defies all expectations in terms of what can grow and live in this southern Arabian Gulf region. Flourishing wildlife on the island probably reflects how the region once was, at a time of greater rainfall and greener pastures. Archaeological investigations on the island have continued to reveal a series of discoveries, including details of the early Christian church or monastery that has been under excavation for three seasons. Proposals were discussed with UNESCO during the year, concerning international recognition of this unique wildlife reserve with a view to enhancing its status as a wildlife conservation centre. The following account of the island is extracted from the book *Natural Emirates*, published in November 1996.

First impressions of the island of the Bani Yas depend upon one's method of approach. A boat-crossing of the narrow stretch of water between it and the mainland of Abu Dhabi at Jebel Dhanna, is dominated by sight of the island's cone-shaped central 'mountains', providing an easy navigational beacon. As one sails closer, these turn out to be formed from a strange mixture of red, green and brown rock formations. Circumnavigating the island, it soon becomes apparent that there is much more to Sir Bani Yas than this unusual structure, for it is surrounded by gently sloping plains which merge with a fairly level coastal shelf. The shoreline itself ranges from mangrove covered sand-banks and hidden inlets, to buttressed foreshore and, finally, a well constructed small harbour at which one lands.

Oryx at Sir Bani Yas Island.

The approach by air, on helicopter or indeed fixed wing aircraft, offers an entirely different view. Surrounded by a glittering blue sea the island stands out from all around like a green emerald placed on a jewellers display cloth. First impressions are of its serried ranks of trees, which cover almost half its land area, and secondly its obvious abundance of wildlife. Large herds of gazelle range across the mountain side whilst over a hundred white Arabian oryx graze contentedly within their large enclosure. Close to the helicopter pad are more exotic wildlife: giraffe, emu and a range of African mammals. The helicopter ride itself is a noisy experience and after being deposited on firm ground, the whirling blades once more lift the craft skywards. Immediately, a beautiful peace and tranquillity descends, calming jagged nerves. Finally, with the aircraft gone, a sense of urgency builds up to explore on land every-thing that has just caught the eye from above.

Sir Bani Yas has attracted man for a long time. The central salt-plug of Jebal Wahid, for that is what geologists tell us forms the strange crystalline mountain, was not always surrounded by water. Towards the end of the last ice-age, around 10,000 years ago, sea-level in the Gulf was considerably lower than it is today and much of the present day seabed was above high-water mark. At that time Sir Bani Yas was part of mainland Arabia and its craggy hills rose up above a green plateau on which a wide variety of wildlife flourished. This verdant countryside, watered by ancient rivers,

undoubtedly attracted fishermen, hunters and gatherers and we have firm evidence of people living here between 6000 and 7000 years ago. This Late Stone Age period was, in fact, quite a busy time for this region of Arabia, with its gradually emerging islands providing temporary or permanent homes for growing numbers of people.

The Abu Dhabi Islands Archaeological Survey owes its establishment to the personal enthusiasm for, and fascination with, the UAE's heritage by the Emirate's ruler and country's President, Sheikh Zayed bin Sultan Al Nahyan. Today's visitors to this unique island may well encounter the survey's team members at one of their growing list of excavations. Whether it is a Late Stone Age site at which a flint 'tile-knife' was discovered, a fisherman's midden containing the remains of dugong and turtle bones, or the pre-Islamic Nestorian church and monastery with its intricate plaster embellishments, Sir Bani Yas's past is gradually being revealed in all its varied facets.

Throughout history this fascinating island has offered challenges and opportunities for those who chose to make it their home. The Nestorian monks who lived in Arabia's most easterly monastery, undoubtedly traded with other communities further up the Gulf, but they would also have turned to the sea for their food, and probably also fed on wild birds that made the island their home during seasonal migrations. For the people of the Bani Yas tribal confederation, after whom the island is named, it offered a refuge and staging post, with a safe anchorage, good fishing and the prized Gulf pearling beds nearby.

Today the island is part of an unusual environmental and biological experiment. Initially Sheikh Zayed chose Sir Bani Yas as a place to spend time with his family, following an age old bedouin tradition that took advantage of the sea-breezes during otherwise hot summer weather. Away from the vast deserts, burgeoning conurbation's and affairs of state which constantly occupied Sheikh Zayed's time, Sir Bani Yas provided a place to think, and perhaps to dream of how Arabia once was. A love of wildlife and nature led Zayed to the idea of sharing his island with endangered Arabian species such as sand gazelle and oryx. Little by little, year by year, he developed the island into a special reserve where wildlife holds pride of place and where visitors are able to gain a taste of how it must have been thousands of years ago, when this landscape resembled the savannahs of Africa and shared many species with its neighbouring continent.

A brief trip around the island vividly demonstrates just how important wildlife is for the UAE's President, and what steps he is prepared to take to ensure its survival. There are basically three kinds of 'enclosure' on the island, i.e. ones to keep animals within a defined area, ones that provide living space for humans, and finally the rest of the island in which a large number of animals roam at will. Among the latter are the Arabian or mountain gazelle (*Gazella gazella cora*), known to the locals as *dhabi*. It was this animal that gave the emirate its name since the island on which the capital city now stands is known as 'possession of the gazelle' or Abu Dhabi. Other gazelles include the more numerous rheem or sand gazelle (*Gazella subgutterosa marica*), dorcas gazelle *(Gazella dorcas)* and grant's gazelle *(Gazella granti)*, an East African species.

Arabian oryx *(Oryx leucoryx)*, rescued only a few decades ago from the brink of extinction, are protected within their own compound which straddles a large section of the sloping plain beneath Jebal Wahid. Here they are free to wander over several square kilometres of natural landscape and their behaviour confirms that they feel quite at home. The herd is steadily increasing in size as a result of natural breeding within the enclosure. This quietly undertaken effort, little known internationally, is testimony to Sheikh Zayed's deep seated concern for protection of Arabia's unique wildlife, so elegantly personified by the white oryx.

Also to be found wandering the open countryside, or held within other large enclosures, on this exotic island reserve are blackbuck (*Antilope cervicapra*), common eland (*Taurotragus oryx*), beisa oryx (*Oryx gazella beisa*), scimitar-horned oryx (*Oryx dammah*), Arabian oryx (*Oryx leucoryx*), addax (*Addax nasomaculatus*), defassa

Houbara bustard at the National Avian Research Centre.

*Male houbara
bustard displaying
at NARC breeding
centre.*

waterbuck (*Kobus ellipsiprymnus defassa*), fallow deer (*Dama dama*), axis deer (*Axis axis*), hog deer (*Cervus porcinus*), barbary sheep (*Amnotragus lervia*), and wild sheep or Asiatic mouflon *(Ovis ammon)*.

One experiment of wildlife management that visitors are not encouraged to observe is a breeding pen for houbara *(Chlamydotis undulata)*, members of the bustard family. These birds need to be left strictly alone if they are to to have any chance to breed successfully under wild conditions, and a large area close to the coast has been set aside just for that purpose. This island bird sanctuary is only part of the many efforts by Sheikh Zayed and his family to revive the population of this bird in the wild. At the National Avian Research Centre (NARC) at Sweihan on the mainland, a highly scientific approach is taken to captive breeding, while NARC scientists are also studying the migration and breeding patterns of the houbara.

Sir Bani Yas's other birds are also impressive inhabitants of this Arabian Ark. Whilst Arabia's native sub-species of ostrich *(Struthio camelus syriacus)* is now sadly extinct, a captive population of closely related African ostrich is now breeding on the island. Meanwhile, successful breeding of two other flightless birds, the rhea *(Rhea americana)* and the emu *(Dromaius naavaehollandiae)* is raising the question of what to do with the rapidly increasing flocks. Another introduced bird, but one which now breeds in the wild on Sir Bani Yas, is the Egyptian goose (*Alopochen aegyptius*): adults, with goslings in tow, can be seen alongside the mangrove channel close to the main residential area. Other introductions include the ground nesting grey francolin (*Francolinus pondicerianus*), black francolin (*Francolinus francolinus*), see see (*Ammoperdix griseogularis*) and chukar partridge (*Alectoris chukar*). Some other free-flying species that have begun to breed include the African crowned crane (*Balearica regulorum*), helmeted guineafowl (*Numidia meleagris*), and possibly also the common pheasant (*Phasianus colchicus*).

The success of Sir Bani Yas as a nature reserve is further underlined by the number of wild bird species that made it a temporary or permanent home. Details of sightings of around 170 species are now kept in the files of the Emirates Bird Records Committee. Among these, a popular favourite is the greater flamingo *(Phoenocopterus ruber)*, also known as the pink flamingo, which can be seen in shallow intertidal lagoons protected by mangrove bushes, or at the artificial 'bird lake' where they can gather in dense flocks of over a hundred individuals.

Sheikh Zayed's success in creating a wildlife reserve has been matched by the results of field trials in which the island has been used as a testing ground for agriculture. One of the first plants that he encouraged to grow on the island was a species that has been much maligned elsewhere in the world, and which has suffered greatly at the hands of developers. Sheikh Zayed's fascination with, and respect for, the humble mangrove tree *(Avicennia marina)* is as strong today as it ever was. For someone who knows the true value of freshwater and the real dryness of the desert, a tree that grows in seawater creates a powerful impression. So powerful, in fact, that Sheikh Zayed has had agricultural teams planting new stands of these salt-tolerant bushes all along the coast of Abu Dhabi for the past 20 or so years, both in areas where they were previously present and in new areas, often along the edge of reclaimed land. Not only has this practice formed new stretches of coastal greenery, but it has also created important habitats for many birds, insects, fish and marine invertebrates. Such efforts are making new nursery grounds for commercial fish, as well as aesthetically pleasing coastal features.

But the most visible achievements at Sir Bani Yas are on dry land where hundreds of acres of old or reclaimed land have been planted with literally millions of trees and shrubs. Whilst some of these are grown to provide shade and comfort for wild animals, or simply to green the landscape, some are part of food growing experiments that aim to test new ideas and to find species that show the greatest tolerance for Abu Dhabi's hot arid climate. The fact that orchards of apples, oranges and pears are now flourishing on Sir Bani Yas, not too mention olive groves, is proof that where there is a will there is a way. The island of Sir Bani Yas, so loved by the UAE's President, is a testament to the age old adage, and a monument to his sustained efforts to make the Emirates a better place for his people to live.

SABKHAT MATTI: CROCODILES, HIPPOS AND MAN

Research undertaken by Dr Timothy Goodall, a petrochemical geologist, into the origins of the Sabkhat Matti, in western Abu Dhabi, has shown that it forms part of what was once a major wadi system draining much of today's Rub al-Khali, the 'Empty Quarter'. Now an area of sabkha salt flats, stretching deep inland from the coast, the area was biologically active during several periods, and particularly around 30,000 years ago.

migration flights, during March 1996, seven birds were caught in the east of Kazakhstan and two in the west. The tracking of these birds follows NARC's feat in 1995 when the UAE became the first country in the world to track a houbara bustard on its northerly migration flight from its wintering grounds in the UAE to its breeding ground in central Asia. Last year, a male houbara, caught in the UAE in February 1995, travelled a distance of 2765 kilometres to the border region of Turkmenistan, Kazakhstan and Uzbekistan carrying a satellite transmitter on its back. The tiny transmitter, weighing only 34 grams, was capable of sending signals 1000 kilometres to three orbiting satellites. This provided researchers at NARC with extremely valuable data on the bird's progress. The transmitter not only recorded the bird's location to within 5 kilometres of the true point but its highly sophisticated electronics also enabled researchers to record the temperatures of the houbara's surroundings.

Spring rains encouraged strong growth of all plant-life in early 1996.

WETLANDS AND BIRDS

The Directory of the Wetlands in the Middle East, a compilation of data on wetland sites in the region, covers 24 individual wetland sites in the UAE, ranging in size from the reed bed at the ADNOC Housing Complex at Ruwais to extensive mangrove stands on offshore islands. The 560-page Directory has been compiled by a group of organizations, including the World Conservation Union, the International Waterfowl and Wetlands Research Bureau, the World Wide Fund for Nature and Bird Life International.

UAE's Breeding Birds in Arabian Atlas

The importance of the UAE's birdlife is clearly demonstrated in *An Interim Atlas of the Breeding Birds of Arabia* which is based on data collected over a ten year period. The atlas underlines the importance of the UAE's offshore islands, particularly those in Abu Dhabi, for breeding populations of seabirds. It also draws attention to the increasing number of introduced 'exotic' birds, a number of which are now common residents of most of the UAE's population centres.

Status and Conservation of the Breeding Birds of the United Arab Emirates

A major new book on UAE birdlife was launched in February 1996, written by Simon Aspinall, Senior Ornithologist at the National Avian Research Centre, NARC, and supported by the Abu Dhabi National Oil Company, ADNOC. The book is an exhaustively-compiled collection of all available data about the more than 100 bird species which are known to breed, or to have bred, in the country. Aspinall shows that Abu Dhabi's offshore islands hold internationally-significant populations of breeding birds, including 95 per cent of the Gulf's osprey population. The red-billed tropicbird, the crab plover and the sooty gull are not known to breed anywhere else in the Arabian Gulf, while the population of some five tern species are also of major importance, as is the significant population of the Socotra cormorant. The island of Qarnein alone supports over 70,000 breeding birds a year.

NEW WILDLIFE BOOK ON THE UAE

The first comprehensive book covering all aspects of the UAE's wildlife was published in late 1996. The book, entitled Natural Emirates, has been written by a range of experts in their various fields, all of whom have conducted extensive field work in the Emirates.

NATURE WEB

Scientists throughout the world can now access data on the Miocene fossils to be found in Abu Dhabi's Western Region, thanks to initiatives by the British Natural History Museum in London. Details of the joint Museum/Yale University project studying Abu Dhabi's fossils have now been placed on the World-Wide Web computer network, part of the Internet system. The project is scheduled to run until the year 2000 and is sponsored by the Abu Dhabi Company for Onshore Oil Operations, ADCO.

SHEIKH MUBARAK BIN MOHAMMED NATURAL HISTORY PRIZE

The work of enthusiastic naturalists, both professionals and amateurs, who study the environment and wildlife of the UAE, is of benefit for all, Minister of Higher Education and Scientific Research Sheikh Nahyan bin Mubarak Al Nahyan stated in a ceremony marking the award of the annual Sheikh Mubarak bin Mohammed Natural History Prize to Dubai-based ornithologist Colin Richardson. Sheikh Nahyan described Richardson's work, and that of other naturalists, as of 'benefit not only for the environment and wildlife in the UAE, but also for the country's people.' Colin Richardson was given the award for his sustained efforts at watching, recording and promoting an interest in the UAE's birds.

UAE SIGNS MONTREAL PROTOCOL

On 1 January 1996 the UAE, along with Saudi Arabia, Bahrain and Kuwait, signed the Montreal Protocol which stipulates that industrialized countries cease production of ozone-damaging substances, whilst developing countries are required to freeze their production and consumption of ODS by the year 1999 and phase them out by the year 2000.

According to the UN, specific initiatives could be successfully pursued in the Middle East, including the use of abundant solar energy for refrigeration and air conditioning. Hydrocarbon reserves could be used for aerosol, foam and refrigeration conversion and waste heat from large chemical factories could also be used for refrigeration through the absorption process.

FEA DRAFT LAWS FOR ENVIRONMENTAL PROTECTION

In September 1995 the Federal Environment Agency, FEA, approved a draft federal law for the protection and promotion of the environment in the UAE. The FEA board also approved the agency's new action plan for environmental protection throughout the country which stresses the importance of coordinating its various activities with the United Nations Development Programme. The plan also calls for continuous liaison with all private and public groups concerned with environment protection in the country.

In March 1996 the FEA completed work on eight draft laws, all of them aimed at protecting the local environment, including water resources and marine and wildlife. The first stipulates a requirement for environmental impact studies for all projects. The second regulates the issuance of practice permits to pollution-causing facilities, whilst the other laws cover protection of coastal areas, liabilities of those who cause oil spills in the sea, protection of the marine environment, control of ozone-depleting substances, disposal of hazardous, medical and hard waste, and the protection of species threatened with extinction.

ACTION AGAINST POLLUTING OIL TANKERS

More than 30,000 oil tankers and merchant ships pass through the strategic Straits of Hormuz every year to transport crude and other commodities from regional states, which supply nearly a quarter of the world's total oil exports. Associated with this intense shipping activity there have been problems of marine pollution. The UAE resolved to take action against oil tankers and other vessels polluting its waters with sludge and industrial waste, following a surge in such incidents. The Federal Environment Agency draft law introduced a system of fines against ships dumping oil sludge, industrial waste, polluted water and other harmful materials into the UAE's territorial waters and onto its beaches.

The new law empowers local authorities to board any national or foreign vessel to check compliance with environment rules, which also stipulate carrying of anti-pollution equipment. Ships of all nationalities are banned from dumping oil and sludge into the UAE waters. In case of an accident, the ship's owner is to be held responsible for the cost of stopping the spillage and fighting pollution.

ARAB ENVIRONMENT DAY

Arab Environment Day, under the theme 'Green and Clean', was celebrated in October with a number of functions organized by the UAE Federal Environment Agency, FEA and the Abu Dhabi branch of the Environment Friends Society, EFS.

UNEP AWARD TO DUBAI

The Dubai Muncipality was awarded a certificate of merit by the United Nations Environment Programme, UNEP, for its valuable contribution to 'Clean Up the World Campaign '95.'

DUBAI DECLARATION

A Conference in preparation for the UN Conference on Human Settlements, Habitat II, was held from 19 November to 22 November 1995. The four-day meeting adopted an agenda of guiding principles, recommendations and follow-up actions called the

Dubai Declaration, in preparation for Habitat II conference which was held in Turkey in June 1996. Over 600 delegates from various countries, representing both the public and private sectors, reviewed a selection of 28 best practices from different cities, including Dubai, which have been documented for the Habitat II conference.

H.H. Sheikh Maktoum bin Rashid Al Maktoum, Prime Minister and Ruler of Dubai, donated a prize of US$150,000 to be awarded annually in connection with the Best Practices mission. Sheikh Maktoum observed that a culture was struggling to be born in the world on how to share problems. 'Best Practices is the best idea I have seen so far, the most concrete outcome of helping this new culture of sharing,' he said.

CLIMATE CHANGE CONFERENCE

A major international conference on deserts and climatic change opened in Al-Ain on 9 December 1995. Entitled 'Quarternary Deserts and Climatic Change', the conference was organized by the Desert and Marine Environment Research Centre of the Emirates University in collaboration with Britain's Aberdeen University, as part of the work of the International Geological Correlation Programme, an international scientific body.

Professor Ken Glennie of Scotland's University of Aberdeen, who is co-convener of the conference said that southeastern Arabia in general and the UAE in particular 'is a wonderful place for gaining understanding of deserts and climatic history.'

A study presented at the conference claimed that within the next 30 years, the percentage of methane in the atmosphere will be at its highest point at any time during the last half a million years.

DESALINATION

Water should be viewed as the ultimate natural resource and must be developed and used in a rational manner to sustain planned national, regional and international development, stated Minister for Higher Education and Scientific Research, Sheikh Nahyan bin Mubarak Al Nahyan, at the opening of a seven-day international conference on desalination. 'We live in an area in the world where our future development depends on our ability to utilize low-cost means of desalination, on the wise management of our water supply, and on our ability to articulate the vision that will help us deal with our water problems.'

HEAVY RAINFALL

The highest rainfall recorded on any one day in March, 84mm, fell on 12 March 1996. Dubai also experienced its wettest winter since records began there.

HIGH TIDAL WAVES

Rainfall was particularly heavy in early 1996, flooding wadis and certain roads.

The heavy rainfall wasn't the only meteorological phenomenon to hit the UAE in 1996. On 20 February 1996 high tidal waves broke over the concrete seawall at Dibba al-Fujairah and swept into the houses built alongside the Corniche. Power was immediately disconnected to avoid any catastrophe and the

Flooded inland wadi near Al-Ain, March 1996.

whole region went into darkness on the first day of Eid. It was the largest such wave that residents could recall over the last 40 years. Waves rose to a height of 15 metres and began to lash the high-voltage cable pylons along the road. Among the 25 houses affected by the flood, 11 were new houses recently distributed to nationals by the Government. Electric sparks could be seen flying from the high-voltage cables and the concrete barriers prevented an almost certain disaster from taking place.

DEPLETION OF GROUNDWATER RESOURCES

Contrary to popular belief the winter and spring '96 spell of heavy rains had relatively little impact on the groundwater reserve situation. While the heavier than usual winter and spring rainfall added a few inches to the water table level, the water table has dropped as much as 50 metres in some areas over recent years. Whereas indiscriminate use of groundwater could lead to total depletion in 20 to 50 years, proper management of the reserves, which have taken thousands of years to build, could bring sustainable usage for at least a hundred years. Whilst regulatory action by government may help, the long-term solution lies in educating the public on the careful use of water. In addition, artificial rechargers and cloud seeding could have some positive results.

TOXIC WASTE FACILITY

The Abu Dhabi National Oil Company, ADNOC, announced in May 1996 that it is developing an integrated hazardous and toxic waste disposal facility to handle and dispose of waste generated by the group companies. This facility, which will be located in Ruwais, will be the first of its kind in Abu Dhabi and will handle hazardous and toxic waste generated within all nineteen of the ADNOC group's operating companies.

UAE AT A GLANCE

National Day	2 December 1971
UAE	Is a federation comprising the emirates of Abu Dhabi, Dubai, Sharjah, Ajman, Umm al-Qaiwain, Ras al-Khaimah & Fujairah
Area	83600 km^2 (including approx. 200 islands)
Location	It lies between latitudes 22° - 26.5° North and longitudes 51° - 56.5° East. Bordered to the north by the Arabian Gulf, to the east by the Gulf of Oman and Sultanate of Oman, to the south by Sultanate of Oman and Saudi Arabia, and to the west by Qatar and Saudi Arabia.
Climate	Between November and March the UAE experiences warm sunny days with an average temperature of 26°C and cool nights with an average temperature of 15°C. High temperatures (up to 50°) and high levels of humidity are the norm between June and August.
Religion	Islam
Language	The official language is Arabic; English, Hindi and Farsi are also used.
Time	4 hours ahead of G.M.T.
Currency	Arab Emirates Dirham (= Dh or AED)
Exchange Rate	The Central Bank maintains a policy of achieving an average exchange rate of the dirham to the US dollar of Dh3.671 = $1.00

Distribution of Population in the U.A.E. by Emirate and Gender (Dec. 1995)

Emirate	Males	Females	Total
Abu Dhabi	638,526	289,834	928,360
Dubai	467,432	206,669	674,101
Sharjah	251,949	148,390	400,339
Ajman	70,656	48,156	118,812
Umm al-Qaiwain	20,832	14,325	35,157
Ras al-Khaimah	84,518	59,912	144,430
Al-Fujairah	54,830	59,912	144,430
Total U.A.E.	1,579,743	797,710	2,377,453

Source: Ministry of Planning.

Population (1995)	2,377,453
Live births (1994)	52,718
Registered deaths (1994)	4566
Labour Force (1995)	1,289,654
Population participation in labour force	54.2%
Percentage of female population participating in labour force	19.4%
Percentage of male population participating in labour force	71.9%
Unemployed as percentage of labour force	2.6%
Public revenues (1994)	Dh 38.7 billion
Public revenues (1995)	Dh 43.7 billion
Federal Government Revenues (1994)	Dh 29.17 billion
Federal Government Revenues (1995)	Dh 29.56 billion
Total oil revenues (1994)	Dh 29.9 billion
Total oil revenues (1995)	Dh 33.2 billion

Percentage of Development for Economic Variables in U.A.E. (1990-1995)

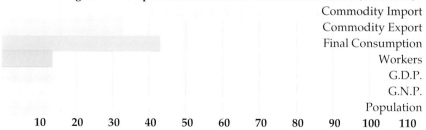

Commodity Import
Commodity Export
Final Consumption
Workers
G.D.P.
G.N.P.
Population

10   20   30   40   50   60   70   80   90   100   110

Economic Sectors in G.D.P. for 1994

Sector	Percentage
Crude Oil	33.4%
Trade, Restaurants & Hotels	12.4%
Government Services	11.3%
Construction	9.2%
Manufacturing	8.7%
Real Estate	8.1%
Transports, Storage & Communication	5.9%
Agriculture	2.5%
Other Sectors	8.5%

GDP (1995)*	Dh143.97 billion
GDP oil sector contribution (1995)*	Dh49.2 billion
GDP non-oil sector contribution (1995)*	Dh94.770 billion
Capital investment in industries (1995)*	Dh13.7 billion
Imports (1994)	Dh83.606billion
Exports (1994)	Dh97.924 billion
Trade balance (1994)	Dh14.318 billion
Production of desalinated water	300 million gallons/day
Electricity generated (1994)	23,402 million KWH
International airports	6
Commercial seaports	15
No. of housing units (1995)	37,534
No. of banks (1994)	47
No. of bank branches (1994)	349
No. of insurance est. (1994)	223
School enrolment ('95-'96)	c.500,000
Student-teacher ratio	12:1
No. of students at university ('95-'96)	c.12,000
No. of students at other third level inst. ('94-'95)	7,579
No of students at adult and illit. centres ('95-'96)	23,863
Area cultivated (1996)	250,000 hectares
No. of trees	130 million
No. of farms	20,000
Fish production (1994)	108,000 tons

Poultry and meat production (1995)	34,000 tons
Hospitals (govt.) (1996)	36
Hospital beds (1996)	4344
Primary health centres (1996)	98
Life expectancy	72
Infant mortality (per 1000)	<14
Crime rates (% of population)	1.5%
Radio stations (1996)	4
TV stations (1996)	4
Arabic daily newspapers (1996)	5
English daily newspapers (1996)	4
Internet subscribers (June 1996)	6000
Hotels (1994)	254
Cars	345,000+
Highways	6550 kms

*provisional figures

Sources: Central Bank Report 1995
Arab Organization of Investment Guarantees
Dept. of Statistics, Ministry of Planning
Emirates Industrial Bank Annual Report 1995

PHOTOGRAPHIC ACKNOWLEDGEMENTS

The majority of photographs in this book were taken during special photographic assignments involving four photographers: Adam Woolfitt, Charles Crowell, Hanne Eriksen and Jens Eriksen, during the first quarter of 1996. The publishers wish to express their sincere thanks for the enormous dedication they brought to the task of "photographing the UAE". In addition to these specially commissioned photographs we are grateful to a number of photographers and photographic libraries for permission to use their pictures. The following list is arranged in order of first appearance of each photographic source.

The British Petroleum Company plc. : 6, 7, 8, 9, 10, 11

Noor Ali Rashid: 12, 29

Mohammed Badr and Ministry of Information and Culture: 13, 14, 15, 17, 18, 19, 20, 21, 22, 24, 25, 26, 27, 30, 32, 33, 34, 36, 38, 40, 45, 49, 50, 53, 54, 55, 57, 60, 63, 64, 164, 189.

Christine Osborne: 31 (lower)

Adam Woolfitt (copyright: Mediatec LLC): 30, 65, 70, 72, 73, 78, 107, 112, 116, 117 (all except top left), 118, 119, 120 (centre left only), 121 (lower), 122, 123, 124 (centre), 129, 131, 151, 152, 159 (top), 166 (centre and lower), 169, 170, 171, 173, 174, 177, 180, 198 (centre and lower), 199, 200 (lower), 203 (top and lower left), 207 (top left), 209 (centre), 210, 211 (all except lower left), 214, 215, 217, 218, 219, 220, 221, 222, 223, 227, 228, 229, 231, 232, 237, 238, 239, 240, 243, 244, 245, 246, 248, 268, 272.

Charles Crowell (copyright: Mediatec LLC): 38, 39, 42, 43, 44, 68, 71, 74, 75, 76, 77, 79, 80, 90, 92, 95, 98, 99, 101, 103, 104, 105, 106, 108, 109, 110, 111, 114, 115, 117 (top left only), 120 (all except centre left), 124 (lower), 125, 126, 127, 128, 132, 133, 134, 135, 137, 138, 140, 141, 142, 144/145, 146/147, 150, 158, 159 (lower), 160, 161, 162, 165, 166 (top), 172, 175, 178 and 179, 184, 187, 196, 197, 207 (top right), 211 (lower left), 225, 226, 271.

ADMA-OPCO: 83, 84, 86/87, 88, 89.

Duncan Willets: 124 (top left).

Alex Tinson: 198 (top).

Gulf News: 200, 201, 202, 203, 205, 206, 207 (lower), 208, 209, 212, 213.

P. Vine: 242

Hanne and Jens Eriksen (copyright: Mediatec LLC): 249, 250, 252, 254, 255, 257, 258, 259, 260, 261, 263, 264, 265, 266, 267.

INDEX